MW00449676

ALSO BY ANDREA FREEMAN

*Skimmed: Breastfeeding, Race, and Injustice*

Ruin
Their Crops
on the Ground

# Ruin
# Their Crops
# on the Ground

The Politics of Food in
the United States, from the
Trail of Tears to School Lunch

## ANDREA FREEMAN

METROPOLITAN BOOKS

Henry Holt and Company    New York

Metropolitan Books
Henry Holt and Company
*Publishers since 1866*
120 Broadway
New York, New York 10271
www.henryholt.com

Metropolitan Books® and ⚏® are registered trademarks of
Macmillan Publishing Group, LLC.

Copyright © 2024 by Andrea Freeman
All rights reserved.
Distributed in Canada by Raincoast Book Distribution Limited

Library of Congress Cataloging-in-Publication Data

Names: Freeman, Andrea (Professor of Law), author.
Title: Ruin their crops on the ground : the politics of food in the United
    States, from the Trail of Tears to school lunch / Andrea Freeman.
Description: First edition. | New York : Metropolitan Books, 2024. |
    Includes bibliographical references and index.
Identifiers: LCCN 2023055948 | ISBN 9781250871046 (hardcover) |
    ISBN 9781250871053 (ebook)
Subjects: LCSH: Food supply—Social aspects—United States. | Food
    security—United States. | Food industry and trade—United States. |
    Agricultural industries—Government policy—United States. | United
    States—Territorial expansion. | Nutrition policy—United States. |
    Food law and legislation—United States.
Classification: LCC HD9005 .F734 2024 | DDC 338.1/973—dc23/
    eng/20240229
LC record available at https://lccn.loc.gov/2023055948

Our books may be purchased in bulk for promotional, educational, or business use. Please
contact your local bookseller or the Macmillan Corporate and Premium Sales Department at
(800) 221-7945, extension 5442, or by e-mail at MacmillanSpecialMarkets@macmillan.com.

First Edition 2024

Designed by Kelly S. Too

Printed in the United States of America

1  3  5  7  9  10  8  6  4  2

To Alia and Serafino

Our children cannot dream unless they live, they cannot live unless they are nourished, and who else will feed them the real food without which their dreams will be no different from ours?

—Audre Lorde,
"Poetry Is Not a Luxury," *Sister Outsider*

The idea of freedom is inspiring. But what does it mean? If you are free in a political sense but have no food, what's that? The freedom to starve?

—Angela Y. Davis (2008)

# CONTENTS

# Ruin
# Their Crops
# on the Ground

# The Palatable Is Political

Food is deeply personal. It is intimate, defining, and sustaining. Food reflects our history and expresses our cultural and racial identities. We live by the credo that we are what we eat or don't eat. Whether it is cheeseburgers, hush puppies, kugel, frybread, or dal, we guard the food of our ancestors and families fiercely. We want to believe that we choose what to put in our bodies. We want to own these choices, whether we view them as good or bad. But food choice is often little more than an illusion.

*Ruin Their Crops on the Ground* argues that food is, above all, political. Since its earliest days, the United States has used food as a tool of social and ideological control. From colonization, enslavement, and mass immigration to the corporate capture of government, food law and policy have furthered political and economic goals instead of meeting people's needs. This link between food and oppression is invisible to most people even though government officials and corporate representatives determine almost every aspect of food consumption. Their decisions shape the quality of our lives and reflect the racism and classism that stratify our society.

The statistics speak for themselves. In every food-related disease, Black, Indigenous, and Latine people suffer at higher rates than white people. Diabetes affects different groups at very different rates: Indigenous (14.5 percent), Black (12.1 percent), Latine (11.8 percent), Asian

(9.5 percent), white (7.4 percent).[1] The disparity in obesity data is similar: Black (43.9 percent), Indigenous (38.6 percent), Latine (36.7 percent), white (31.5 percent), Asian (13.2 percent).[2] Black people have the highest rate of death from heart disease (22 percent), five percent above the average.[3] Black men are 70 percent more likely to die from a stroke than white men and Black women are twice as likely to have a stroke as white women.[4] Black adults have higher rates of high blood pressure (56 percent) than white adults (48 percent).[5]

Food law, policy, and corporate influence are directly responsible for these disparities. Alliances between the government and agricultural interests began early in the nation's history, when the military destroyed Indigenous people's land and livestock and lawmakers supported enslavement for the purposes of white economic advancement. These close relationships continued as the government developed schemes to funnel undesirable surplus commodities to Indian reservations and public schools. Modern food policy represents a continuation of these practices, which target racialized and poor communities as vessels for unwanted and unhealthy foods that lead to illness and premature death.

IN OUR TIME, propaganda amplified by advertising and marketing for fast food and junk food peddles an explanation for why Indigenous, Black, and Latine people suffer food-related illnesses at such high rates. Marketing sells the lie that these consumers simply prefer unhealthy foods. Popular and pervasive stereotypes attribute these preferences to ignorance, weak will, or culture. Billion-dollar race-targeted campaigns disguise the reality that most people who eat too much fast food don't choose to eat it in excess. It chooses them.

Corporations spend millions on pitching fast food and junk food to Black and Latine consumers. Black youth saw 75 percent more fast-food ads than their white peers in 2019 while food companies promoted no healthy food on Spanish television.[6] Unrestricted race-targeted marketing exposes young people to McDonald's "Black and Positively Golden" website, Spanish game apps, celebrity TikTok challenges, and vending machines embedded in video games. This marketing creates the illusion of agency when we have none and pays off over consumers' lifetimes—the tastes we develop at an impressionable age are unshakeable.

Beyond marketing, fast food corporations rely on cheap, subsidized commodities to make their food the most affordable option in poor communities. This advantage allows them to dominate the food landscape of poor, Black, Indigenous, and Latine neighborhoods, in retail outlets and even in public schools, which have long been sites of forced cultural assimilation through food. This practice, which was central to federal Indian boarding schools and Americanization programs targeting Mexican girls, today takes the form of corporate infiltration of schools to prey on impressionable minds for profit.

In exchange for donating valuable educational resources to chronically underfunded schools, fast food gets prominent placement on school buses, signs, scoreboards, fundraisers, and rewards programs. School lunches are a smorgasbord of subsidized commodities—tater tots, chicken nuggets, and endless cartons of milk. More than half the meals served at public schools contain dairy, even though approximately 80 percent of Black and Indigenous people, 90 percent of Asians, 50 percent of Latines, but only 5 percent of Northern Europeans are lactose intolerant. The fact that white people seem to have a unique ability to digest milk, combined with its color, has made it a symbol of white superiority.

Corporations' overdue attempts to cover or atone for their aggressive race-based marketing campaigns have been paltry at best. After George Floyd's murder by police in May 2020, consumers demanded anti-racist action and accountability. Mars Food responded by retiring its racist Uncle Ben spokesperson for its now-named Ben's Original Rice. In hopes of keeping its share of the Black consumer market, it also created scholarships for aspiring Black chefs in Greenville, Mississippi. The $4 million it pledged was a mere drop in the bucket compared to the profits it reaped from over a century of racist branding. PepsiCo engaged in similar woke-washing when it fired its pancake mascot Aunt Jemima.

Debates about health and nutrition, with their blame-the-victim approach, have also taken aim at some comfort foods tied to cultural communities. Frybread is a deep-fried dough, invented by Indigenous cooks using rations intended to compensate them for the colonialist practices that deprived them of their land and foods. Their culinary creativity produced a delectable dish that is wildly popular across Indigenous nations. Yet Cheyenne and Hudulgee Muscogee activist Suzan Shown Harjo says, "If frybread were a movie, it would be hard-core porn. No redeeming qualities. Zero nutrition."[7]

Enslaved people similarly transformed rejected food into recipes that remain emblematic of celebrated Southern cuisine today. The pleasures of hush puppies, cornbread, and greens are more than sensory. Culinary historian Michael Twitty explains, "The Old South is a place where people use food to tell themselves who they are, to tell others who they are, and to tell stories about where they've been."[8] Food historian Jessica B. Harris describes soul food as "a combination of nostalgia for and pride in the food of those who came before."[9] But anthropologist Hannah Garth recounts being reprimanded during a visit to a high school in Los Angeles for claiming macaroni and cheese as her favorite dish. She pushes back against this dismissive attitude. "A refusal to acknowledge macaroni and cheese as a culturally Black food then renders the dish as merely an 'unhealthy' dose of fat and carbohydrates."[10] Instead of an important legacy, food associated with Black people becomes a symbol of poor choices that require correction from people who know better.

Mexican food suffers from similar misunderstandings. When the U.S. transformed this cuisine into something distant from its origins, introducing the world to "gloopy" tacos in hard shells and overstuffed burritos,[11] it became a symbol of bad choices and poor health. In contrast, 'high-end' Mexican food is often the product of white chefs, a phenomenon that Latine cultural studies professor Paloma Martinez-Cruz calls "culinary brownface."[12]

In the popular imagination, white foods represent sophistication, while Mexican food is for low-class people who lack education and intelligence. In an essay titled "How We Are Ruining America," *New York Times* columnist David Brooks laments his "insensitivity" at bringing a friend with "only a high school degree" to a gourmet sand-wich shop. "Suddenly I saw her face freeze up as she was confronted with sandwiches named 'Padrino' and 'Pomodoro' and ingredients like soppressata, capicollo and a striata baguette. I quickly asked her if she wanted to go somewhere else and she anxiously nodded yes and we ate Mexican."[13] Because Mexican Americans cling to poor eating hab-its, the reasoning goes, they deserve the bad health consequences they endure.

IT DIDN'T HAVE to be this way. Big Ag and Big Food's domination of food politics was not inevitable, but its roots run deep, with their ori-gins in Depression-era federal subsidies. During the Depression, the first Farm Bill, the 1933 Agricultural Adjustment Act, sought to relieve farmers' distress. Aiming to save them from destitution by limiting supply to keep prices up, the law put caps on the production of crops and livestock. After forcing farmers to destroy anything they harvested over those caps, the government compensated them for their lost prof-its. In short, it paid them not to produce food that people desperately needed. Even with much of the population on the verge of famine, farmers turned corn into fuel and piglets into fertilizer. Plows buried fertile farmland.

First Lady Eleanor Roosevelt led the charge of critics speaking out against this scheme's cruelty and waste. The administration reversed course by lifting the requirement for farmers to eliminate their excess supply and bought the surplus from them instead. The Federal Surplus Commodities Corporation gave this food away. Its charity didn't affect the price of the commodities because the poor people who received it couldn't afford to buy the food themselves. Without these government giveaways, they would have simply gone hungry.

After receiving a taste of federal financial support, agricultural companies did not want it to end. They became deeply invested in the Farm Bill, which renewed every five years (give or take). Over the following decades, the agricultural industry consolidated, grew, and gained power, managing to hold on to the subsidies for corn, soy, wheat, milk, and meat, even after the country's nutritional needs changed. What began as a program that provided cheap, filling foods to a hungry nation soon became one that caused, instead of fixed, nutritional problems. The surpluses that built up because of the Farm Bill's subsidies became the burden of the Department of Agriculture, which had conflicting mandates. On one hand, it needed to sell or give away these surplus goods to keep agricultural companies afloat. Otherwise, the flood of supply would drive prices too low. On the other, it was responsible for the population's nutritional well-being. The need to fulfill these twin duties led to an elegant if ultimately problematic solution.

The twentieth century saw the birth of the National School Lunch Program (1946), the Food Distribution Program on Indian Reservations (1973), and the Special Supplemental Nutrition Program for Women, Infants, and Children (1974). Billed as programs aimed at improving nutrition in underserved communities, their primary objective was in fact to offload commodity foods.

With diets dominated by dairy, meat, wheat, sugars, and oils (made from processed corn and soybeans) and devoid of fresh fruits and vegetables, poor people across the country began to experience a nutrition transition. Indigenous people, who had been receiving some form of government food since the eighteenth century, when President George Washington ordered his troops to "ruin their crops now in the ground," were the first to experience this change.[14] They went from being underweight and having high rates of communicable diseases to being overweight and suffering from diabetes and other nutrition-related diseases.

Had the government's focus been on health and nutrition, agricultural subsidies would have shifted to support different foods in the mid-twentieth century, when the nation's public health crisis moved from food insecurity to nutrition deficiency. In the twenty-first century, poor nutrition overtook smoking as the leading cause of preventable deaths. Still, the Farm Bill deems fruits, vegetables, and legumes (lentils, chickpeas, and beans) specialty items, unworthy of significant government funding. This is not a decision based in nutritional and medical knowledge. These crops' farmers simply lack the lobbying capacity of the prosperous corporations that the government initially singled out for subsidies. Without money or leverage, they lag behind soy, wheat, corn, milk, and meat producers, who continue to receive generous support.

The favored industries' influence grew over the century through generous campaign donations and a revolving door between their executive boards and the federal government. Monsanto, a corporation notorious for putting poisonous chemicals in U.S. soil and food, became a "virtual retirement home for members of the Clinton administration."[15] Within a few decades, a handful of corporations dominated the markets for corn milling, soybean processing, beef packing, and dairy manufacturing,[16] and they used their near monopolies to persuade Congress to make changes to the Farm Bill that would grow their gains even more.

Chicken giant Tyson and hog producer Smithfield successfully advocated for the 1996 Farm Bill to get rid of the requirement that farmers who grew animal feed keep some of their land idle. Freed from these restrictions, they planted and produced more crops, driving prices down and saving Tyson and Smithfield about $300 million on food for the animals they slaughtered. Over the next decade, this change saved the top four chicken producers $11 billion and saved hog producers $9 billion. Coca-Cola saved $100 million a year on high-fructose corn syrup when the Farm Bill eliminated production controls on corn.[17]

Ahead of the 2014 Farm Bill, Exxon Mobil, DuPont, Pharmaceutical Research and Manufacturers of America, Coca-Cola, Nestlé, Bayer, and the Grocery Manufacturers Association each spent at least $5 million on lobbying. Banks and insurance companies spent about $52.6 million to advocate—successfully—for switching the Farm Bill's primary form of support from direct payments to farmers to crop insurance. The American Bankers Association spent $14 million, and Wells Fargo, which owns the largest crop insurance provider in the country, Rural Community Insurance Services, spent $11.3 million.

Crop insurance, which the federal government subsidizes, does more than cover crop destruction. It guarantees agricultural corporations a specific price for their crops and then pays any difference between the actual and promised price, guaranteeing income even in unproductive years. Insurance providers pitched the idea of shifting subsidies away from direct payments to farmers and giving them to the insurance companies instead as an extra level of protection against corruption. This recommendation responded to concerns that payments were going to people who were not actually in the farming business. The insurance companies became gatekeepers that would vet Farm Bill claims for subsidies. The insurance framework evokes a portrait of a poor farmer in need of help during a bad harvest year, a convenient trope that misrepresents the scheme's corporate beneficiaries and the scale of the payouts.

Corporations easily made back the money that they spent on lobbying and then some. Commodity traders Cargill and Archer-Daniels-Midland gained control over the grain trading industry by advocating for the removal of agricultural production caps. With the caps gone, farmers began to amass surpluses that drove prices down. Commodities became available to processers at low prices while the USDA bought up the rest. Cargill and ADM resold the grains they bought cheaply at huge mark-ups. On top of their profits, Cargill and other commodity traders received $4.2 billion in federal subsidies between 1980 and 1990 for their agricultural outputs.

Between 1995 and 2014, fifty people on the *Forbes* 400 list of the richest Americans collected $6.3 million in farm payments. Thirty-six members of Congress or their family members got $9.5 million. Between 2007 and 2011, $3 million in subsidies went to people who owned land but grew nothing on it. Between 2008 and 2012, the government handed out $10.6 million in agricultural subsidies to people who had been dead for at least a year.[18] By 2011, the list of people who received federal agricultural subsidies included NBA superstar Scottie Pippen, media mogul Ted Turner, and David Rockefeller, who was the United States' first billionaire.[19] To prevent popular outcry, Congress made the list secret.[20] Industry advocates continued to promote subsidies as a way to keep small farmers afloat despite the fact that they were practically extinct. The farmers who did benefit were overwhelmingly white. Black, Indigenous, and Latine farmers were almost entirely left out of federal agricultural support and of popular conceptions of what farmers looked like.

*Ruin Their Crops on the Ground* traces the history of how food oppression in the United States has shaped cultural norms to make racial health disparities appear natural and impossible to fix through government intervention. The opposite is true. Legal and political acts, not cultural preferences, have baked these disparities into our society. This law and policy, which extends all the way back to Washington's order to starve Indigenous nations and enslavers' careful calibration of food portions to fuel labor but not revolt, is unconstitutional. It is not too late to change course.

Food inequality's roots as a tool that enslavers relied on to enforce their brutal regimes make it a vestige of enslavement, which the Thirteenth Amendment forbids. The Fourteenth Amendment goes even further, declaring unequal protection of the law unconstitutional wherever it appears, and whichever group it harms. Currently, the law not only fails to protect; it creates and exploits inequalities, with life and death results. The system is not broken because it acts as intended—to enrich corporations' coffers at the expense of the people with the least political power. While there are some fixes that can, and should, be applied to make incremental improvements, ultimately, we need a completely new approach to food production, distribution, marketing, and storytelling. First, we must recognize and repair what centuries of food oppression have wrought. Then we can build something completely new.

# 1

# Weapons of Health Destruction

Frybread, sometimes called "die bread" or a "weapon of health destruction,"[1] has multiple origin stories, and they all involve oppression and perseverance. In one rendition, the federal government's Indian agents in charge of providing rations stored flour carelessly, allowing weevil larvae to infest it. No other food was available, so Indigenous cooks fried the flour in hot lard to kill the larvae. With this stroke of genius, they salvaged the flour and created the first frybread.

Another tale locates frybread's birthplace on Fort Sumner's Pecos River, where U.S. soldiers incarcerated Navajos and Apaches after a military campaign. Army officers gave the captives sparse supplies of flour and salt and iron pots. Charged with creating something edible, Navajo women kneaded the flour into dough balls, flattened them, then deep-fried them in animal fat. The prisoners enjoyed the dish so much that even after leaving Fort Sumner and returning home, they continued to cook and eat it.[2]

Modern frybread is still made from simple ingredients: flour, baking powder, salt, and sometimes sugar, fried in shortening, lard, or oil. It is a versatile food that can be sweet or savory, perfect as the base of a taco, a filling breakfast, or a snack. When served sweet, it often has cinnamon and sugar sprinkled on top and comes with jam. A savory version might have pizza toppings.

T-shirts celebrating frybread abound: "Frybread Feels," "Got

Frybread?," "Frybread Power," "Frybread Is My Soulmate," "I Was Told There Would Be Frybread," "It's All About the Frybread." In "Commod Bods and Frybread Power," scholar Dana Vantrease explains that these popular T-shirts help Indigenous people find each other in environments where wearing traditional regalia is no longer common.[3] A'aninin anthropologist George P. Horse Capture called frybread "a divine gift in exchange for hardships such as racism and disease that native people have endured."[4] In 2005, South Dakota declared frybread its official state bread. A 2012 mockumentary, *More Than Frybread*, comically portrays the cutthroat competition among Indigenous nations in an Arizona frybread championship.

Ojibwe rock artist Keith Secola's song "Frybread" is a musical tribute to the beloved food. In one version of the song, he associates frybread with Indian resistance. "They couldn't keep the people down," Secola explains, "because born to the people was a Frybread Messiah, who said 'There's not much you can do with sugar, flour, lard and salt. You got to add something special, and that special ingredient is love.'"[5] Secola serenades the unifying power of frybread: "A mile long frybread line/ 'Cause we're all the same inside/We need frybread all the time/All I'm asking for . . . frybread." At the same time, Secola contends that "frybread has killed more Indians than the federal government."[6]

On the hit television show *Reservation Dogs*, the only series ever to feature all Indigenous writers, directors, and main cast members, the Indian Health Center invites rapper Punkin' Lusty, played by real-life Mvskoke rapper Sten Joddi, to perform his hit song "Greasy Frybread." The occasion is Diabetes Awareness Month. Lusty raps, "Baby girl looking deadly (Yeah!)/Why she acting all Rezzy (Yeah!)/Hotter than a pan of frybread grease!/Have a Native hittin' Powwow Beats!/ Gotcha Auntie in the kitchen/Like no he didn't/Got her Gramama's skillet/Like she 'bout to kill it!"

The song solidly locates frybread within Indigenous culture. "Sofkee [a corn drink or soup] on the burner/Hokte Hokte [woman] head turner/Water baking powder/Choppin' up that white stuff/All purpose flour/Gotta mix it right up/Hit the Rez with the Shits/They eats it right up! . . . Watch the grease pop/Watch her waist drop/She got that blue bird bag [Blue Bird flour comes in a twenty-pound cloth bag and claims to be "The Native American Frybread Secret"]/In her tank top/ She got that white powder/All over everything/She gettin' to bussin' man/But we ain't cousins man!/We from the same tribe/But a different clan/She my Rez Bunny/And I'm her Red Man/She love my Tattoos/ And my two braids/Frybread money at the Creek Fest get paid! On that!"

Foregrounding this song in the Health Center's battle against diabetes underscores the other side of frybread's legacy, also emblazoned on a T-shirt that announces "Frybread: Creating Obesity Since 1860." Cheyenne and Hudulgee Muscogee Indigenous rights activist Suzan Shown Harjo, who vowed to give up frybread as a New Year's resolution, explains, "Frybread is emblematic of the long trails from home and freedom to confinement and rations. It's the connecting dot between healthy children and obesity, hypertension, diabetes, dialysis, blindness, amputations and slow death."[7] Reflecting on stereotypes that dehumanized Indigenous people to justify colonization, such as the worn-out trope of Indians drinking "firewater," Harjo asserts that frybread love is another way to portray them as "simple-minded people who salute the little grease bread and get misty-eyed about it."

In *The Heartbeat of Wounded Knee*, scholar David Treuer introduces health educator Chelsey Luger, who is Ojibwe and Lakota. Chelsey talks to Indigenous communities about the perils of frybread as part of her efforts to steer their diets in new directions, even in the face of limited food options. "Sometimes people get defensive, but we are able to make the conversation positive. We say we grew up with it and like it and we say frybread is not power. We say frybread kills our people. It's that serious. It causes diabetes and heart disease. We have to look at those colonial foods as a kind of enemy."[8]

Frybread arouses passionate feelings in its fans and detractors. Some people celebrate it as culinary artistry, some consume it as a comfort food, some curse it as a colonial byproduct, and some hold it up as a sign of ignorance or self-destruction. But everyone agrees that it is a far cry from the pre-colonial foods that nourished Indigenous people for centuries.

Corn is the centerpiece of Indigenous agriculture. Because corn does not grow wild, its cultivation requires extensive knowledge and care. Indigenous gardeners produced five different types of corn—sweet, dent, flour, flint (for hominy), and popcorn—and dozens of varieties within these types. Processing corn is extremely labor intensive, requiring impressive strength. One Indigenous woman reports beating corn until "our arms felt like they would break."[9] Activist and environmentalist Winona LaDuke, a member of the Mississippi band Anishinaabeg, recounts her father's comment when she was a student at Harvard: "I don't want to hear your philosophy if you cannot grow corn."[10]

Before Columbus invaded the continent and began to export corn across the ocean, corn grew only in what we know today as the Americas. Beginning in 1500 B.C., the Huhugam people built canals that allowed them to grow the three sisters—corn, beans, and squash. Precolonization, many Indigenous nations relied on this trio for their primary sustenance. The corn stalks act as a ladder for the pole or climbing beans while the squash leaves guard against the intrusion of other plants while also providing shade, protection, and moisture for the corn's roots. Eaten together, corn, beans, and squash form a complete protein, rich in vitamins and minerals. The corn's sweetness perfectly balances the beans' heartiness and the squash's lightness.

Later, between 1450 and 900 B.C., the Huhugam built a complex irrigation system that allowed them to cultivate and then export surplus crops. They supplemented the three sisters with desert foods—cholla cacti (famous for their ability to jump on people or animals passing by, stinging them with their spiky spines), prickly pear, mesquite (tree pods that make a sweet, nutty flour when ground), and dense tepary beans.[11]

Some Indigenous cooks made bread out of persimmon seeds, while others combined poached and sifted corn, peanuts, and salt. Chestnuts, acorns, bamboo vine, and greenbrier vine, crushed and fried in bear grease, also made good bread. These breads were high in protein, dense, and flavorful. They also helped prevent disease. The Hopi technique of mixing ashes with cornmeal, common across Indigenous nations, protected against pellagra, a disease caused by a vitamin B3 (niacin) deficiency, which later tormented both Europeans and enslaved people whose primary food source was corn.[12]

Bison, or buffalo, were also essential to the diets and culture of Plains Indians—over thirty nations that include the Cheyenne, Arapaho, Sioux, Pawnee, Osage, Navajo, Comanche, and Apache. Being native to the northern and southern plains, bison traveled east with Indigenous people who used fire to transform forests into fallows that resembled the creatures' natural habitats. When settlers saw these paths, their untrained eyes registered only burned-out waste areas. They missed the carefully plotted trails that spread a vital food source across the land and later, they slaughtered the bison to near extinction as a military and political tactic.[13] In addition to bison, Indigenous people ate alligators, bears, beavers, caribou, deer, moose, elk, fish, geese, turtles, seals, shellfish, and whales.

Cherries, raspberries, strawberries, blackberries, potatoes, pecans, peanuts, peppers, black walnuts, acorns, hickory nuts, chestnuts, and cacao were staples of Indigenous diets. Black walnuts have more antioxidants than English walnuts, making them popular foods in the fight to reduce the risk of cancer, heart disease, and diabetes. Hickory nuts are hard-shelled, dense, and sweet. These traditional diets, consisting mainly of proteins, fruits, and vegetables, sustained health and strength.

Almost immediately upon arriving on the continent, settlers seized Indigenous trade networks, cutting off their access to food staples and sparking shortages. Lacking knowledge of how to survive in their new environment, colonizers claimed Indigenous farmland, stole corn and vegetables, and commandeered deer parks. Confronted with violence and intimidation, Indigenous people led the intruders to water and food sources like oyster beds.

In *An Indigenous Peoples' History of the United States*, Roxanne

Dunbar-Ortiz recounts the settlers' inability to fend for themselves after landing in Jamestown in 1607. Unequipped to hunt or grow their own food, the British demanded that the Powhatan Confederacy, comprised of thirty different polities, give up the food that they had cultivated and hunted for themselves. John Smith, part of the settlers' governing council, is famous for demanding self-sufficiency from his community: "He that will not work shall not eat." But Smith relied on theft and extortion to feed his followers.[14]

Smith threatened to kill all the Powhatan women and children if the confederacy failed to supply settlers with food, land, and labor. When the Powhatan refused, Smith waged war, following through on his promise to murder Powhatan children. The Powhatan protected their stores of grain and survived the assault, but in retaliation, Smith's men cut down the Powhatan corn ripening in the fields during harvest season.[15]

Food destruction was so central to settlers' treatment of Indigenous people that in 1779 George Washington ordered his troops to destroy their crops.[16] This command set the tone for U.S.–Indigenous relations. The change in political structure from British colony to independent country made little difference to the Indigenous nations, which continued to suffer the same ruinous approach established by the settlers. Attacks on Indigenous food sources and land continued unabated.

In the Cherokee nation, settlers allowed hogs to destroy the roots and plants the Cherokee grew to sustain themselves in years when their harvests were not fruitful. The hogs were an invasive species brought over by the English. This assault on Cherokee food sources laid the foundation for the 1830 Indian Removal Act enacted by President Andrew Jackson, who had built his reputation on the slaughter of Indigenous people. The law allowed for the exile of 70,000–80,000 people along the infamous Trail of Tears to land Jackson dubbed "Indian territory."

Ironically, Jackson justified this extreme mass deportation in part by the fact that the lands Indigenous people had always occupied could no longer support their way of life. Under Jackson's direction, soldiers seized the Cherokees' grain and cattle. Left with only the bark of the white oak tree to eat, Cherokee leaders agreed to move west in exchange for U.S. rations. But U.S. assurances proved hollow when government agents greeted the people who survived their dislocation with rotten beef and spoiled corn.

In 1833, a group of exiled Choctaw suffered long delays and cholera on their forced journey from southeastern Mississippi to land west of the Mississippi River. When they finally joined their fellow Choctaw, who had gotten there the year before, the food supply had just run out. The Choctaw had arrived too late in the season to plant, and the government had only allocated them one year's worth of provisions. The U.S. agent responsible for their rations responded to this desperate situation by offering the Choctaw food that they had previously rejected: condemned tins of six- and seven-year-old pork. The Choctaw had no choice but to eat the rancid meat and suffer bouts of food poisoning.[17] In DC, the office of the Commissary General of Subsistence washed its hands of the problem, calling it "much to be lamented."

While mourning the loss of beloved community members to hunger and disease, the Choctaw planted new cornfields to sustain themselves in the territory but still did not have enough to eat. Observing their plight, visiting U.S. officer F. W. Armstrong beseeched the War Department to send more provisions. But George Gibson, who served as the first commissary general of subsistence from 1818 to 1861, refused to budge on the one-year provisions limit. Unsympathetic, he blamed the situation on the Choctaws' "dependence on the bounty of the Government," refusing to acknowledge the government's responsibility for creating this reliance.

In 1838, half of the Cherokee, Creek, and Seminoles forced across the country died along the way, along with 15 percent of the Chickasaw and Choctaw. The paltry rations provided during the journey caused many deaths from starvation. The available food, including partially cooked bread made from unfamiliar English flour, led to more death from diseases like dysentery. Deprivation continued upon arrival.

After the government forced them to move from Iowa to Minnesota and South Dakota and then Nebraska, the Winnebagos relied mainly on rations to survive because their new land was "all dust." Dust covered everything they cooked, but the food they received from U.S. officers was rotten to begin with. Chief Little Hill recounts, "The superintendent . . . had a cottonwood trough made and put beef in it, and sometimes a whole barrel of flour and a piece of pork, and let it stand a whole night, and the next morning after cooking it, would give us some of it to eat. We tried to use it, but many of us got sick on it and died. . . . They also put in the unwashed intestines of the beeves and the liver and lights, and after dipping out the soup, the bottom would be very nasty and offensive."[18]

Some Indigenous nations encountered a bounty of fruits, vegetables, and game in the land carved out as Indian Territory, which encompassed Oklahoma, Kansas, Nebraska, and part of Iowa. Some better-off families brought livestock with them. With this advantage, they were able to produce corn, wheat, and cotton after they arrived and could afford to sell their surplus and build wealth. An abundance of trees supplied wood for shelter in addition to nuts and fruits. Some households had also brought apple, pear, and peach tree seeds with them that flourished on their new land and grew into large orchards—one with more than two thousand trees.

The Creek harvests were so plentiful that Creek farmers sold beans, pumpkins, melons, potatoes, squash, and corn to officials at Oklahoma's Fort Gibson, named after the stingy subsistence commissary general. The soil was as fertile as the land that the Creek left behind, if not more so. But not everyone was able to take advantage of its potential. Families who started out with some means became richer while those without lived hand to mouth.

Food inequality became even more pronounced as white people moved into Indian Territory and set up stores where prosperous Indigenous families could shop for a variety of foods. Their poorer counterparts relied solely on what they could grow, gather, or hunt. Wealthier families could also travel to neighboring Arkansas or Texas to shop for a range of goods. Still, they did not escape the harm of new, nontraditional foods. White-run stores brought drastic dietary changes that Wilburn Hill, who grew up in Indian Territory, called "the greatest enemy to the Indians."[19]

Government officials had initially envisioned Indian reservations as European-style farming communities that would gently assimilate their populations into Western culture. But the forced relocation of Indigenous peoples to unfamiliar land and the failure to give them assistance or training in the settlers' agricultural practices doomed the project from the start. Chief Delgadito, who lived on the Bosque Redondo Reservation assigned to the Navajo, described his struggle to re-create his traditional diet on new land.

> He had made up his mind to live at the Bosque and do right. He planted seeds but could raise no crops. Three more times he tried to grow corn and failed. Now he did not believe that crops could be raised at the Bosque. The ground on the Pecos was not the best land for the Navajos. In the old country, abundant crops and numerous herds were commonplace. He was deeply saddened by not owning sheep or cattle, and he regretted that he would never again see the large flocks of the old days.[20]

The Civil War brought new destruction to food sources. Just prior to the war, in 1860, severe drought hit much of Indian Territory. Then the war brought soldiers who destroyed crops, slaughtered livestock, and stole Indigenous tools and food reserves. Soldiers coerced Indigenous women to submit to sexual assault by offering them rations.[21] The 1862 Dakota War, sparked by the government's withholding of rations, ended in President Lincoln ordering thirty-eight Dakota men to the gallows, the largest mass execution in U.S. history. When it was over, the state of Minnesota put a bounty on the head of every member of the Dakota nation. One-quarter of the Dakota died the following year from exile, imprisonment, famine, or illness.

The assault on buffalo intensified as well. On May 10, 1868, General Sherman told General Sheridan that "as long as Buffalo are up on the Republican [River] the Indians will go there. I think it would be wise to invite all the sportsmen . . . there this fall for a Grand Buffalo hunt, and make one grand sweep of them all. Until the Buffalo and consequent Indians are out [from between] the Roads we will have collisions and trouble."[22] Responding to this dictate, in 1871 and 1872, the U.S. Army killed five thousand buffalo a day. By the 1880s, when only a few hundred buffalo were left, commercial hunters simply skinned them, leaving the rest of their corpses to rot, while others gathered their bones and shipped them east, where factories turned them into fertilizer or bone china. When a hunter tasked with exterminating the Plains Nations' bison expressed remorse at killing thirty buffalo at once, General Dodge chided him: "Kill every buffalo you can! Every buffalo dead is an Indian gone."[23]

The Sioux nation regards buffalo as spiritual ancestors and sacred beings that help mark important moments. Threatened with impending starvation from the buffalo's near disappearance, Sioux nation leaders signed an 1868 treaty that compelled them to sell their land to the government at $1.50 an acre in return for the promise of rations. Although the Sioux eventually turned to cattle ranching for survival, this new enterprise did not make up for the economic, cultural, and spiritual absence created by the massacre of the buffalo. Over sixty years later, in 1997, the Montana Department of Livestock repeated history by killing 1,100 bison, claiming that the animals were a nuisance and there was not enough food to sustain them on public land. Winona LaDuke responded to this state massacre by explaining that, "We believe that the way they treat the buffalo is the way they treat the Indians."

BEYOND DESTROYING FOOD sources to achieve land theft, successive U.S. governments used rations as part of their ongoing "civilizing" efforts.[24] In 1883, the Code of Indian Offenses restricted and outlawed many Indigenous cultural and religious practices, leveraging rations to punish traditions that interfered with the U.S. Indian assimilation project. Designed to change Indigenous relationships into Western-style, patriarchal marriages, the code deemed a male head of household's failure to provide for his wife and children an offense punishable by ration reductions. The code also decreed plural marriage an offense, stating that "so long as the Indian shall continue in this awful relation he shall forfeit all right to receive rations from the government."[25] Missionaries achieved similar goals by offering food to converts. The Indian Offenses code remained in place for almost a century, until the 1978 American Indian Religious Freedom Act rendered it unenforceable.

Indian agents also withheld rations to staunch Indigenous resistance to the shift from communal land to private property. The 1887 Dawes Severalty Act divided previously shared reservation land into allotments that agents distributed to men with families, single men, and boys. This division allowed the government to acquire coveted land by reversing the longstanding policy of allowing Indigenous nations to retain their control over it. After severing the land into parcels, instead of allocating the most desirable sections back to the reservation, the United States sold it to white settlers. Over the course of forty-seven years, this allotment process reduced Indigenous land by two-thirds, from 138 million acres to 48 million acres.[26]

In Oklahoma, the influx of white people depleted Indigenous resources to such an extent that fishing, hunting, and foraging could no longer sustain many families. To survive, they turned to canned, salted, sugared, and pickled products, sometimes making do with food that their white neighbors rejected. A white man living near an Indigenous community claimed in 1901, "If a cow got sick or died, all you had to do was notify some of the Indians and they would drag it off, even though it had been dead three days."[27]

At the same time, medicine previously prepared with acorn and corn flour became less potent when there was no access to those ingredients. This led to weakened immune systems that left people more vulnerable to a host of new dietary ailments. Although corn was still a staple in many households, without the traditionally added ash, it lacked essential nutrients. The white man in Oklahoma elaborated, "The Indians are literally starving . . . they used to have plenty of hogs, cattle and ponies and could kill game, but they now have nothing to live on and are absolutely destitute. . . . A little Tom Fuller, which is nothing but cracked corn, and corn pone (cornmeal mixed with water, salt, and fat), is all the majority of them have to eat."[28]

A NEW SITE of food coercion emerged toward the end of the century: Indian boarding schools. The schools were the brainchild of Captain Richard Henry Pratt, who insisted that children's immersion in English language and culture was the way to achieve assimilation. His proposal offered a solution to seemingly endless and expensive wars against Indigenous nations. Pratt served in the U.S. military, where he spent eight years fighting in the Plains Wars and Red River War of the 1870s. Charged with escorting captured combatants to Florida's Fort Marion at war's end, he mused that "if wild turkeys could be domesticated then surely Indians could be civilized."[29] To prove his point, Pratt experimented on the prisoners, replacing their traditional clothing with army uniforms and cutting off their hair, a practice that traditionally signaled an expression of grief over the loss of a loved one or another traumatic event.

Pratt was pleased with the academic performance of his captives at both Fort Marion and the Hampton Normal and Agricultural Institute, a school initially founded to teach free Black men. His next step was to lobby Congress for funds to establish Pennsylvania's Carlisle Indian Industrial School, the first federal Indian boarding school. He famously explained his philosophy: "A great general has said that the only good Indian is a dead one. . . . In a sense, I agree with the sentiment, but only in this: that all the Indian there is in the race should be dead. Kill the Indian in him, and save the man."

In 1875, Carlisle's first class contained eighty-two students, most of them children of the Plains Indian leaders. Sun Elk of the Taos Pueblo describes how integral food and cooking practices were to Carlisle's mission. "We all wore white man's clothes and ate white man's food and went to white man's churches and spoke white man's talk. And so after a while we also began to say Indians were bad. We laughed at our own people and their blankets and cooking pots and sacred societies and dances."[30] Considered a success by Pratt and his supporters, Carlisle became the prototype for federal Indian boarding schools across the country. Some of the money raised from the sale of reservation land to white outsiders during allotment went to fund the schools.

Exploiting hunger, U.S. agents threatened to withhold rations from parents who refused to turn their children over to the boarding schools. Faced with the prospect of their children's starvation, many parents unwillingly let them go. In some instances, parents begged the schools to take them so they would survive. In Louise Erdrich's Pulitzer Prize–winning novel, *The Night Watchman*, she describes the dilemma parents faced. "Thomas was always hungry. They were down to desperation food then—a bit of bannock smeared with deer fat. The day schools on the reservation gave out just one meal. The government boarding school would feed three meals."[31]

Withholding food rations to coerce children into boarding schools was a low tactic that even some Indian agents found distasteful. John Williamson of the Dakota Agency considered the practice "hardly humane or just. If taking ration tickets only meted out merited punishment to the heads of families, who are alone guilty, it would be a wise provision, but the children have to go hungry and suffer the disobedience of the parents. It is better, in my opinion, to compel attendance through police than taking up ration tickets for non-attendance."[32]

Once in the boarding schools, students performed grueling labor to produce the meals they ate. Girls were responsible for preparing the food in institutional kitchens—debilitating work that many were too young, small, or weak to perform. Initially, sourcing food on site was a common boarding school practice. J. Norman Leard, who was one-sixteenth Choctaw, went to two Presbyterian Indian academies in Oklahoma in the 1880s, Spencer and Wheelock. He remembers raising the food he ate, except for the rice, sugar, coffee, and prunes. He liked the prunes until he found out that the school fed the children the moldy ones, keeping the best ones for the staff. Then he stopped eating them.[33]

The Phoenix Indian School, which opened in 1891, produced fresh vegetables at first. Students raised chickens, turkeys, and dairy cows that yielded nutritious and plentiful food. But their diet still reflected the schools' mission to indoctrinate students into a white, English way of life. Pratt's pedagogy centered on the teaching of English food rites, from cutlery use to table settings. Boarding schools also used food as part of harsh disciplinary measures. Students who resisted cultural erasure and rigid military conditions found themselves locked in a guardhouse for long periods with only bread and water to sustain them.

Boarding school diets had a dramatic impact on the students' well-being. At the Cherokee Female and Male Seminary schools, "students felt the effects of the unfamiliar bread and pancakes; gravy made with white flour and lard; pies, syrup, and candy made with sugar; coffee with every meal; and butter, cheese, and cream. . . . The vast array of seminary food items also included meats, eggs, butter, oil, sugar, salt, buttermilk, and twice-a-day desserts, in addition to foods obtained on Tahlequah field trips, such as bread, candy, sugar cookies, salted nuts, suckers, chewing gum, and tamales. Flour was a major ingredient in dishes three times a day."[34]

The seminary doctor worried about students' weight gain and various other ailments, including constipation, "bowel complaint," hemorrhoids, headaches, diarrhea, rheumatism, jaundice, ulcers, and "skin eruptions." The sickness caused by boarding school diets compounded the trauma of forced separation and abuse that many students endured in the schools. Still, many students became fond of boarding school food and brought this diet home to their communities.

By 1978, Phoenix Indian School had abandoned its fresh foods. Patty Talahongva, a Hopi woman, faced an onslaught of unfamiliar and unappealing meals when she began her junior year of high school. "P.I. stacked a crate of small milk cartons at the front of the serving line. It was like starting the day with a cup of poison because most American Indians are lactose intolerant." As part of required student labor, Patty toasted and buttered "hundreds and thousands of bread slices." The bread was new to her. "Bread for my Hopi people . . . contains just three ingredients: blue cornmeal, water, and ashes from the saltbrush. It is not heavy, it is light. It is not loaded with empty calories, it is packed with nutrition."[35] Patty's school breakfast consisted of dehydrated scrambled eggs floating in murky yellow water. Lunch was bologna and processed cheese on white bread. Beautiful orange trees dotted the campus, but their fruit was inedible.

FOR SOME INDIGENOUS people, white people's food, despite its physical harms, represented luxury, status, and wealth, prompting them to make candy, cake, and tinned fruits a regular part of their diets. Households that grew fresh produce often preferred trading it for processed foods to eating it themselves. After receiving beef instead of bison so frequently in U.S. rations, many Navajo developed a taste for it. The 2023 film *Killers of the Flower Moon* was based on the Reign of Terror endured by members of the Osage nation targeted by white men seeking to take over their mineral headrights. In it, a doctor conspiring to poison Molly Burkhart (played by Lily Gladstone) through insulin shots for her diabetes warns, "You'll lose your feet or worse if you eat like a white." Consuming whiteness through beef, milk, bread, butter, coffee, and sugar offered a way to achieve a semblance of equality in practice, even though the United States denied citizenship to Indigenous people until 1924.

This placebo for disenfranchisement took its toll. By the turn of the century, local newspapers featured dozens of articles and advertisements offering cures for obesity, stomach ailments, and kidney problems. They also mentioned tooth decay, hemorrhoids, "bowel problems," "liver complaint," appendicitis, sour stomach, indigestion, bloating, colic, and diarrhea. In 1901, the *Indian Chieftain* ran a story declaring obesity to be the product of "racial and individual predispositions." It claimed that this affected the "well-to-do" more often than "laborers" because rich people eat more, exercise less, and live in apartments with elevators instead of stairs. The *Chickasha Daily Express* reported on the 1903 opening of a sanitorium designed to treat obesity. In 1907, a *Cherokee Republican* news item claimed that glycerin was the best cure for stomach "affections."[36]

Despite this new awareness, government schemes to convert Indigenous agriculture to English farming methods persisted. In 1901, the U.S. gave land to members of the Comanche, Kiowa, Apache, and

Wichita nations to grow corn, wheat, millet, oats, and fruit trees. Then it cut off rations to their families and required other households to meet work requirements before receiving food. In time, dust, drought, and the Depression eliminated any gains made by Indigenous farmers. Then, after President Roosevelt's 1930s New Deal legislation sought to prop up U.S. agriculture by distributing surplus food to state-run institutions, Indian reservations and boarding schools became dumping grounds for surplus commodities, a new form of rations.

By 1926, 83 percent of Indigenous children attended boarding schools. The 800-page Meriam Report of 1928, *The Problem of Indian Administration*, shared the results of a survey of their living conditions. The report revealed that many students were too malnourished to play during their rare recreation sessions because they received few or no fresh fruits or vegetables. It also noted that students' onerous work schedules left almost no time for leisure or exercise.[37]

Horrified by the Meriam Report's revelations, John Collier, who became commissioner of the Bureau of Indian Affairs in 1933, immediately shepherded in the Indian Reorganization Act (IRA), or Indian New Deal. Collier, a white man from Atlanta, became an orphan at the age of sixteen after his mother died of pneumonia and his father accidentally shot himself while chasing a burglar. After graduating from Columbia University in 1906, Collier went to work at New York's People's Institute, a community educational center for workers and immigrants. During a 1920 trip to visit an artist friend in Taos, Collier became fascinated by Pueblo cultural expression. His new obsession set the stage for a crusade to alter U.S. policy toward Indigenous people.

In the 1920s, Collier began advocating for Indigenous rights and against Indian assimilation as the editor of *American Indian Life* magazine and executive secretary of the American Indian Defense Association. Although Collier ardently advocated for Navajo land rights and oil and gas royalties in the 1920s, some of his acts as commissioner undermined his earlier efforts. His patriarchal attitude, commitment to an agrarian ideal, and support of white agricultural interests belied his professed support of Indigenous sovereignty.[38] His betrayal began with his insertion of land management training for Indigenous farmers into the IRA, revealing his preference for the white, Western farming model over traditional practices. Next, he sided with white landowners in a scheme that deprived the Navajo of their sheep.

The dispute originated in 1864, when the U.S. government forced the Navajo onto the Bosque Redondo Reservation and then tried to compensate for the loss of three hundred lives with 14,000 sheep. By 1933, the Navajo had grown this herd into a million sheep. Following Navajo tradition, they divided the sheep among men, women, children, and grandchildren, giving each person in a household an independent right over their allotted sheep. John Collier disrupted this system by implementing rules in 1934 that allowed only men to own sheep. Women and children instantly lost their share of the family wealth.

Collier then wrongly blamed Navajo herding practices for soil erosion, even though giant swaths of the country, including those without sheep herds, were experiencing similar problems. From Texas to Nebraska, high winds and choking dust were relentlessly besieging land and livestock. Inexperienced white farmers who had moved west failed to plant prairie grasses with strong roots to ground their fields. Their unmoored soil blew away under the pressure of the storms' intense winds. Severe drought and dust combined to render 35 million acres of U.S. land useless and another 125 million without topsoil.

Under economic duress, agricultural companies based in New Mexico and Arizona set out to eliminate competition from the Navajo herds. In 1934, they persuaded Collier to meet with the all-male Navajo Tribal Council to propose the slaughter of Navajo sheep and goat herds, under the pretense of forestalling further land deterioration. Navajo medicine man Eli Gorman laments, "Collier was referring to this bad condition, telling people that it was the over-grazing that caused the situation. He was lying because it was evident that the lack of rainfall had caused the bad condition, but he kept on telling us that we had caused the grasses to disappear."

Although the Navajo Tribal Council agreed to the extermination of 150,000 goats and 50,000 sheep at the meeting, its members did not believe Collier would get the federal funds to go through with the plan, based on their past experience. Historian Marsha Weisiger describes the tactics that let Collier succeed, even though his proposal depended on a lie about Navajo bad practices. "In many instances, when bureaucrats in Washington asked for facts, agents *simply made them up*, based on previous reports and their impressions as to whether the number of animals had gone up or down, given the weather."[39] Collier's deal with the Navajo cut their herds in half in just ten years. Meanwhile, neighboring agricultural companies kept all their animals.

The loss of their livestock had a lasting cultural and social impact on the Navajo. "Long ago, when we had more sheep, we were always generous and thoughtful. When we had relatives or a good friend visit us we usually butchered a fat lamb so that we could feast and tell stories. . . . Today, all this is gone." After seeing the senseless slaying of his goats, the husband of a Navajo woman named the Blind Man's Daughter told the Bureau of Indian Affairs, "You people are heartless. You have now killed me. You have cut off my arms. You have cut off my legs. You have taken my head off. There is nothing left for me." Collier's treachery hit Navajo women, who were traditionally responsible for their nation's goats and sheep, particularly hard.

Compounding this loss, devastating blizzards compelled Congress to airlift food into the Navajo and Hopi reservations in the winter of 1947–48. Frustrated with this drain on federal funds, Congress enacted the 1953 Indian Termination Act to disband reservations, stripping Indigenous nations of their rights, resources, and communities. Virulent opposition led the government to stop enforcing the act in 1961 and Congress to repeal it in 1988. But the damage had already been done to the one hundred tribes terminated under the act, many of which later sought restitution from the government.

A sister to the Termination Act, the 1956 Indian Relocation Act, allowed the Bureau of Indian Affairs to offer Indigenous families one-way fares from their reservations to cities along with a one-month subsistence allowance. The BIA also pledged job training and placement after relocation that rarely materialized. Despite these broken promises, the relocation program led to mass migration from rural to urban areas over a relatively short period.

By 1960, 30 percent of Indigenous people lived in cities. Ten years later, that figure was 45 percent. In 2020 it was 60 percent. The first cities to receive an influx of migrants through the program were San Francisco, Oakland, Chicago, Denver, Los Angeles, Cleveland, Cincinnati, Dallas, St. Louis, and Seattle. Relocation was bad for Indigenous diets and overall health. Urban Indigenous communities had life expectancies of fifty to sixty-five years compared to over seventy years in urban white communities.[40] Indigenous infant mortality was one and a half times white infant mortality. Liver disease rates were six times higher and deaths from diabetes four times higher. By 2000, reverse relocation had begun, with many Indigenous people returning to rural areas crossing paths with the white people leaving them.

Relocated people often found themselves in low-income food swamps rampant with fast and junk food. In these neighborhoods, convenience stores and liquor stores that charge more than supermarkets are the only places to buy groceries. These stores mirror the convenience stores on reservations that evolved from trading posts. Being the sole source of food other than rations in some communities, these posts were "an opportunity for super-exploitation."[41] By the 1950s, the Navajo relied heavily on trading posts' processed offerings.

A movement seeking to shift the ownership of trading posts from white hands led many of them to close, opening the door for convenience stores to fill the gap by selling soda, peanut butter, canned milk, lard, sugar, and wheat flour. But even exploitative local vendors attract the loyalty of their reservation customers. The Choctaw prefer shopping at local stores over driving to retail outlets farther away.[42] Taking advantage of their customers' frequent lack of cash, store owners with captive customers tack on penalties for credit purchases.

The lack of reasonable food options at local stores makes it virtually impossible for people living on or near reservations to access the most common form of USDA food assistance, the Supplemental Nutrition Assistance Program. SNAP gives out debit cards (originally food stamps) to spend at grocery stores, which most reservations lack, forcing them to rely on "commods" boxes instead.

THE 1997 FOOD Stamp Reform Act launched both SNAP and the Food Distribution Program on Indian Reservations. The FDPIR sends commodity foods to reservations and households that include one member of a federally recognized tribe living on or near a reservation or in Oklahoma. Approximately 276 out of 573 federally recognized tribes get FDPIR. One hundred and two Indian Tribal Organizations and three state agencies administer the program.[43] These agencies store food, determine program eligibility, and offer nutrition education. People who receive Supplemental Security Income, or social security, are not eligible for commods, even though their SSI income goes to their rent and bills. This restriction means that Indigenous elders often suffer from severe food insecurity.

FDPIR boxes are supposed to reflect the nutrition standards set by the federal dietary guidelines, published by the USDA and the Department of Health and Human Services every five years since 1980. Congress requires the guidelines to follow medical and scientific research on nutrition. Instead, as with the Farm Bill, they bow to the desires of the agricultural and food industries. According to Dr. Neal Barnard, president of the Physicians Committee for Responsible Medicine, these guidelines' "meaty, cheesy diet amounts to, perhaps inadvertently, the nutritional equivalent of smallpox-infected blankets."[44]

In 1990, activist Charles "Red" Gates started advocating for better and more culturally appropriate food in FDPIR boxes. In 2016, he recounted an exchange with representatives from the Congressional Hunger Committee at the Standing Rock Sioux Reservation about the boxes' contents. "'Did you ever see what's in these cans?' This guy said, 'No. Show us. We want to see,' so I grabbed a can of pork and I told him, 'You're going to get a bad smell. It doesn't smell good and it doesn't look good when I open it.' . . . I got a can of chicken, a can of beef, and a can of pork. The first one I opened everybody crowded around. . . . As soon as I opened it up a couple of them backed away and grabbed their noses and their mouths. When I began to dump it out they both ran outside and threw up. That's what they were giving us . . . and I showed them all the connective tissue, the blood vessels. It was some pretty terrible stuff."[45] Gates' and others' efforts eventually led to the inclusion of culturally appropriate items, like bison meat, in some boxes beginning in 2008.

Still, because the protein and produce in FDPIR boxes are usually undesirable or inedible, many recipients eat only the sugars and carbs. A typical box contains processed, shelf-stable foods—canned meats, canned beans, canned vegetables, canned soups, canned fruits (often prunes), bottled juices, cereals, rice, dried pasta, flours, processed cheese, powdered egg mix, shelf-stable milk, buttery spread, corn syrup, and vegetable oil. Boxes sometimes have lettuce and other vegetables, but they are often rotten by the time they reach the reservation. White rice is a subsidized commodity, but grains traditionally eaten by Indigenous peoples—wild rice, barley, quinoa, blue sorghum, and rye—are not, so they don't show up in the boxes. The addition of bison was a step in the right direction, but not all Indigenous people eat it.

Relying on commods has grave consequences, and people who cannot afford to supplement the boxes suffer the most. While staunching hunger, commods can cause malnutrition, obesity, and diabetes. Indigenous people have the highest rates of type 2 diabetes, a condition that often leads to paralysis, amputation, and blindness. The Indigenous rate of death from diabetes is 177 percent higher than for any other group, and Indigenous adults are diagnosed with obesity 60 percent more often than white adults.[46] Life expectancy on the Sioux reservation is forty-eight years old for males and fifty-two years old for females. Half of everyone over forty years old living on the reservation has diabetes.[47] Indigenous people had higher infection rates and twice the number of deaths from Covid-19 than white people, in part because of high rates of the underlying high-risk factors of obesity and diabetes.[48]

Karuk ceremonial leader Leaf Hillman describes the FDPIR program as nutritional colonialism and considers it "a modern extension of tribal termination and genocide."[49] The USDA defends the poor nutritional quality of commods by claiming that they are only sup-plemental. This claim is false. Sixty percent of FDPIR participants rely on the boxes for all their nutritional needs. This makes USDA control over their diet virtually complete. The result is the "commod bod," a body shaped by the low nutrition of FDPIR boxes. The commod bod is embedded in popular culture through Commod Bod Clothing and Red Fever's song "Commod Bods," which laments, "although there was, was a time, USDA tasted fine . . . commodity cheese has taken its toll, I'm a little obese."

In cities, a burger is often cheaper than an apple. Along with pro-viding more calories for less cash, fast food can help Indigenous youth get along with their peers. A mother explains, "I can buy them each a breakfast bun at Mickey's for a buck and some change. Then they can go to school with the bag. It helps them fit in. They don't want to stand out because they eat stuff that the other kids think is gross!" A young woman adds, "I'm not embarrassed to be Indian. I just don't like to call attention to it. I just want to be myself. Sometimes, if wearing the right clothes or carrying around fast food stuff makes it easier, okay."

Fast food also helps people distance themselves from past pov-erty. Historian Devon Mihesuah of the Choctaw Nation explains, "McDonald's food, hamburgers, chips, and soda are foods of the white mainstream. . . . Mainstream white society is what they want to iden-tify with. . . . If you grew up with only access to your small garden, squirrels, deer, and fish because you couldn't afford to buy much food from stores, you might indeed equate hunting and gathering with being impoverished."[50]

OUTSIDERS OFTEN BLAME Indigenous people for their health prob-lems, ignoring the history of colonialism and attempts at genocide and assimilation that created structural barriers to good health. In the 1890s, white observers listed "unhygienic cooking" by the Sioux as a cause of their high rates of tuberculosis.[51] Over a century later, a 2000 National Institutes of Health study of obesity in Indigenous elemen-tary school students concluded that their caregivers and communities were responsible. Narrowly examining only the nutritional content of their food, researchers neglected to question if these were the only foods available and why. Understanding Indigenous diets requires a close reading of the past that acknowledges displacement, broken treaties, and destruction of traditional food sources. It demands a deeper analysis of the effects of poverty, racism, and government actions that led to inadequate medical services on and off reservations and lack of access to nutritious food.

Frybread embodies the contradictions of trying to hold on to familiar foods while staying healthy. Terrol Dew Johnson, co-director of Tohono O'odham Community Action, an organization that promotes traditional food, shares "I'm six feet, three hundred pounds, you know, and that didn't happen overnight. You know, that was because of the foods that I grew up eating, and one of them was fry bread." Johnson does not consider frybread a traditional food. "Is there traditional songs about fry bread? You know, is there a ceremony you should perform when you do fry bread? So you're looking back into your culture in your own tribes and see, 'What kind of prayers do I pray to our creator about fry bread?'"

But an Indigenous woman who moved away from her reservation feels the opposite. "I don't want to lose all of who I am, you know? I want my kids to at least have some kinda sense that they are special and not like everyone else here. So, I cook up fry bread instead of donuts on the weekends." Another woman describes how frybread connects her to her family: "Fry bread is important for me.... The smell of it keeps us happy.... It makes me think about my moms and how she'd cook that up every morning. [My boyfriend] used to dance in the powwow circuit, so it also reminds us of being young and kicking our heels up."[52]

Because frybread emerged from persecution and a broken connection to pre-colonization food, activists have compared it to soul food. Scholar Dana Vantrease explains, "Just as commodities are an artifact of the reservation system, African American soul food is an artifact of enslavement. Like commodities, 'soul foods' are used as ethnic signifiers and considered traditional. And like commodities, items like chitterlings, fried chicken, and cobblers are linked to numerous health problems." Soul food and frybread also share the role of scapegoat for poor choices.

But frybread does less damage than the food provided under the guise of nutrition assistance. The boxes of commodity food that the USDA distributes to reservations are at least as bad, without providing frybread's redeeming cultural comforts. Ultimately, the demonization of frybread only serves to distract from government policies that have dictated Indigenous food and health since colonization.

## 2

# Survival Pending Revolution

As an enslaved child, Booker T. Washington found creative ways to feed himself when his mother was not with him. He "used to go to the places where the cows and pigs were fed and make my breakfast off the boiled corn. . . . If I was not there at the exact moment of feeding, I could still find enough corn scattered around the fence or the trough to satisfy me."[1]

Frederick Douglass escaped enslavement at age twenty. He scavenged for food as a child. "Many times have I followed, with eager step, the waiting-girl when she went out to shake the table cloth, to get the crumbs and small bones flung out for the cats."[2] Enslavers called Douglass and others to the trough, "like so many pigs . . . some with oyster-shells, others with pieces of shingle, some with naked hands, and none with spoons. He that ate fastest got most; he that was strongest secured the best place; and few left the trough satisfied." He battled his beloved dog, Old Nep, "for the smallest crumbs that fell from the kitchen table, and have been glad when I won a single crumb in the combat."

Louisa Everett, known by her enslaver McClain in Florida as Norfolk or Nor, became married to Sam Everett after McClain forced them to have sex with each other. They had several children but no time to care for them. McClain demanded that they work the fields from sunrise until after sundown every day. An elderly woman fed their children twice a day by pouring "pot likker" (vegetable broth) and skimmed milk into a wooden trough. The children used wooden spoons to scoop it out, the older ones making sure that the younger ones got a share.[3]

Harriet Jacobs, in her autobiography *Incidents in the Life of a Slave Girl*, laments how enslaved children in the Flint household, which bought her as a companion for their young daughter, got half the food allowance that the women received. She was horrified when an elderly man, enslaved by the family through three generations, "hobbled up to get his bit of meat, the mistress said he was too old to have any allowance" and that he "ought to be fed on grass."[4]

Throughout the centuries of chattel slavery, first in the colonies and then in the United States, food scarcity and uncertainty led to malnutrition, anxiety, sickness, and death. Enslavers calculated precise portions that would keep workers laboring but not rebelling. Physicians supported this deprivation by attributing their illnesses and deaths to biological or genetic weaknesses. Beholden to enslavers for their livelihood, these doctors supplied rationalizations for decisions to deny enslaved people proper nutrition and healing.

In *Medical Apartheid*, Harriet A. Washington explains how ill health caused by abusive conditions served as a justification for continued enslavement. Physicians claimed that Africans' weak constitutions made them dependent on enslavers' food and care for survival.[5]

Of all enslaved people, children fared the worst. Half of those who survived birth died in their first year.[6] Malnutrition was the leading cause of death. Those who lived subsisted on the barest minimum of food. Mothers were forced to wean their infants, usually by the time they turned three months old. After that, children received a monotonous diet of gruel or cornmeal porridge until they turned three. At that age, they began to consume vegetable soups, potatoes, molasses, grits, hominy, and cornbread. Their white fathers were indifferent to the near starvation they imposed on their children.[7]

One enslavers' pamphlet advised giving enslaved workers one peck of corn and a pint of salt each week and a piece of meat each month.[8] Children and elders were to get less. Sometimes, they got nothing.

At Monticello, Thomas Jefferson's plantation, a typical week's worth of rations was "a peck of cornmeal, half a pound of meat, usually pork, occasionally half a dozen salted fish."[9] These portions are similar to the amounts recommended by *DeBow's Review*, a magazine for enslavers that began publishing in 1846. The *Review* advises its readers to feed enslaved people mostly bacon and cornmeal. The quantity depends on whether they are field hands or indoor hands, and whether they are men, women, or children. It also suggests adding milk, buttermilk, or molasses to the cornmeal.[10]

One book on plantation management recommends that enslaved people eat a diet of unlimited vegetables—potatoes, cabbage, turnips, peas, and yams.[11] In 1937, when Mary Reynolds turned one hundred years old, she reminisced about eating the potatoes, or "taters," that grew in the patch her family tended while enslaved in Texas. "Taters roasted in the ashes was the best-tastin' eatin' I ever had. I could die better satisfied to have just one more tater roasted in hot ashes."[12] On some properties,[13] particularly in South Carolina and Georgia, enslaved workers had hens that supplied them with eggs to eat or trade.

But more often, enslavers dispensed only cornmeal and salt along with meats that they wouldn't eat themselves.[14] This included chickens' innards, gizzards, and feet and the heads, intestines, hearts, kidneys, and ribs of other animals. Rose Williams compared the rations her family received on two enslavers' properties. They endured constant whippings and survived on meager, monotonous diets of cornmeal, milk, molasses, a bit of beans and peas, and a small portion of meat once a week. After moving to Hawkins's land, Rose tasted white flour in biscuits for the first time, tried coffee (which she didn't care for), and ate plenty of meat.[15]

Harriet Jacobs recounts how New Year's Day—known as hiring day—exposed which enslavers provided the best food. "At the appointed hour the grounds are thronged with men, women, and children, waiting, like criminals, to hear their doom pronounced. The slave is sure to know who is the most humane, or cruel master, within forty miles of him. It is easy to find out, on that day, who clothes and feeds his slaves well; for he is surrounded by a crowd, begging, 'please massa hire me this year. I will work *very* hard, massa.'"[16] Enslavers who wanted to make more money from their sales tried to give a false impression of generosity by smearing grease around their enslaved workers' mouths to make it look as if they had eaten meat.[17]

Enslavers also pitted people against each other by dispensing all the available food at one time—the quickest got the most. Ethel Daugherty remembered how they "were lined up to wooden troughs, which were filled by pouring all the food in at once in the manner of slopping pigs."[18] Haphazard feeding denied people the simple act of eating a meal at their own pace. Booker T. Washington's family got their meals like "dumb animals get theirs. It was a piece of bread here and a scrap of meat there . . . a cup of milk at one time and some potatoes at another. Sometimes a portion of our family would eat out of the skillet or pot, while someone else would eat from a tin plate held on the knees using nothing but hands . . . to hold the food."[19]

Being in the wrong place at the wrong time could mean missing a meal. Betty Cofer describes how, "on one plantation, the field hands had to hustle to get to the end of the row at eleven o'clock dinner time, because when the cooks brought their dinner they had to stop just where they [were] and eat, [and] the sun was mighty hot in those fields." Betty felt fortunate that she got enough to eat because she cared for her enslaver's daughter, Miss Ella, who slipped her extra food while she worked. She remembers the stark difference between meals served on the fields and in the house. "They only had ashcakes without salt and molasses for their dinner, but we had beans [and] grits [and] salt [and] sometimes meat." Hiding food was one way to keep it safe. Lula Jackson recalls, "They never could find my grandfather's meat. That was Grandfather William Down. They couldn't find his meat because he kept it hidden in a hole in the ground. It was under the floor of the cabin."[20]

Frederick Douglass also reflects on the ways that enslavers enforced a hierarchy through food. He describes "a sort of Black aristocracy" of attractive, loyal servants chosen to serve in the house. This group of enslaved people shared in the food and drink that enslavers chose for themselves—asparagus, celery, cauliflower, cheese, butter, cream, wine, and brandy. Their culinary privilege created an "immense" divide "between these favored few, and the sorrow and hunger-smitten multitudes of the quarter and the field."[21] But Black cooks often created sumptuous meals that they never got to taste, for fear of retribution.[22]

Mrs. Flint, the wife of Harriet Jacobs's enslaver, punished people by depriving them of extra food, even when it would have otherwise gone to waste. "If dinner was not served at the exact time on that particular Sunday, she would station herself in the kitchen, and wait till it was dished, and then spit in all the kettles and pans that had been used for cooking. She did this to prevent the cook and her children from eking out their meager fare with the remains of the gravy and other scrapings. The slaves would get nothing to eat except what she chose to give them. Provisions were weighed out by the pound and ounce, three times a day. I can assure you she gave them no chance to eat wheat bread from her barrel. She knew how many biscuits a quart of flour would make, and exactly what size they ought to be."[23]

Her husband, Dr. Flint, "was an epicure. The cook never sent a dinner to his table without fear and trembling; for if there happened to be a dish not to his liking, he would either order her to be whipped, or compel her to eat every mouthful of it in his presence. The poor, hungry creature might not have objected to eating it; but she did object to having her master cram it down her throat until she choked."

Enslavers also used food to coerce women who resisted rape to comply or face starvation. Raping enslaved women was legal. To facilitate enslavers increasing their number of workers through forced pregnancies, Southern kinship laws departed from the more common patrilineal system. They assigned the mother's status to her children, enslaving infants at birth.

Inadequate food led to high rates of pellagra, beriberi, rickets, kwashiorkor, tetany, scurvy, anemia, and pica. Pellagra, a condition that causes skin lesions, diarrhea, dementia, and death, is a severe deficiency of the complex B vitamin niacin. There is almost no niacin in a diet consisting of meat, cornmeal, and molasses. Beriberi, the result of diets dominated by white rice, can lead to extreme swelling and cardiac arrest. Lack of vitamin D causes rickets, a softening of the bones that manifests in bow-leggedness. Enslaved children had rickets fourteen times more often than white children.[24] In pregnant women, rickets can distort the pelvic canal, trapping a fetus inside. The high number of rickets cases contributed to countless stillbirths and maternal deaths.

Kwashiorkor, related to protein deficiency, causes distended stomachs and thin limbs. Tetany, the product of calcium deficiency, leads to muscle spasms. Scurvy, a lack of vitamin C, was common among enslaved people who ate either no vegetables or vegetables stripped of their nutrients due to overcooking. Many enslaved people also suffered from anemia. Their children often ate dirt, a practice called pica, and then suffered from intestinal worms. Lack of vitamin A caused sore eyes and blindness.[25]

Some state laws prohibited providing insufficient food, but prosecution under these laws was very rare. In two extreme cases, the state convicted an enslaver for practices that their peers regularly engaged in without consequences. The primary purpose of South Carolina's 1740 "Bill for the better ordering and governing of Negroes and other slaves in this province" was to deny enslaved people the rights to grow food, learn to read, move around freely, assemble, or make money. It read: "That no slave who shall dwell, reside, inhabit or be usually employed in Charlestown, shall presume to buy, sell, deal, traffic, barter, exchange or use commerce for any goods, wares, provisions, grain, victuals, or commodities, of any sort or kind whatsoever."[26] It also held enslavers liable for some forms of deprivation.

South Carolina charged Bowen with refusing or neglecting to provide "sufficient" food and clothing to his enslaved worker Eliza for a period of five months.[27] Bowen challenged his conviction in *State v. Bowen*,[28] arguing his innocence based on the fact that the law did not define the term "sufficient." The court allowed evidence of local custom to determine what the standard for sufficiency should be. It found that Bowen went against local custom by providing only cornmeal when common wisdom held that "animal food is necessary." But Bowen's transgressions went even further.

Bowen's overseer, Jackson, testified that, on many days, enslaved workers received no cornmeal at all. "The defendant did not give his negroes enough even of meal, the only provision he did give. Five bushels of meal weekly, the largest quantity stated by any witness, even if not reduced in the ratio of three-eighths of a bushel, in two bushels, to the standard of the defendant's measure, was plainly insufficient for a family of eight whites and twenty-one slaves. But it appears from the testimony of Jackson, the defendant's overseer, that this supply was not regular. The grown negroes had only a quart of meal a day. Many days, he says, they had no meal. Sometimes it gave out Thursday and sometimes Friday. They would then have a quart to last them till Monday evening."

The court observed that withholding the daily food allowance like this "must have reduced the wretched slaves to famine. For seventeen months." On top of that, "Jackson did not know that shoes had been given either. Their feet were frostbitten and sore. No clothes were given to them during that period also."

Bowen responded by proposing that the court find him innocent based on his oath that Jackson's testimony was not true. The court refused Bowen's offer while acknowledging that its decision to do so, or even to entertain the charges, was highly unusual. It defended its departure from normal practice by explaining that "instances do sometimes, though rarely, occur, in which it is necessary to interfere on behalf of the slave against the avarice of his master." Although Bowen died during the appeal, the higher court upheld his conviction based on Jackson's word.

The court explained that the South Carolina law, which was the first of its kind, was a response to "public sentiment" that found it necessary "to protect property from the depredation of famishing slaves." South Carolina legislators were not trying to protect enslaved people from starvation. They wanted to shield enslavers from theft.

Other states followed South Carolina's lead.[29] A Tennessee law required enslavers "to provide wholesome food for his slaves and white servants."[30] A Texas constitutional provision allowed its legislature to enact laws requiring "necessary food and clothing."[31] Georgia's Act of 1817 created the offense of withholding "proper food and sustenance."[32] Some of these laws provided no relief for enslaved people. They simply required enslavers to pay damages to compensate for stolen food.

In the only other recorded case of a prosecution under this type of law, a grand jury in Lowndes County, Alabama, indicted Randall Cheek under the 1852 Code of Alabama.[33] The code promised that "Any master, or other person standing towards the slave in that relation, who inflicts, or allows another to inflict on him, any cruel punishment, or fails to provide him with a sufficiency of healthy food or necessary clothing, or to provide for him properly in sickness or old age, or treats him in any other way with inhumanity, on conviction thereof, must be fined not less than twenty-five, or more than one thousand dollars."[34] The law's wording suggests some concern for enslaved workers' well-being.

When Cheek challenged the indictment in 1861's *Cheek v. State*, his overseer, Snelgrove, testified against him, over Cheek's objections. Snelgrove swore that meat had run out on Cheek's property by the summer of 1858. The Alabama Supreme Court declined to decide the case based solely on Snelgrove's word, giving Cheek a chance to prove his claim that he had slaughtered thirty-two hogs to feed his enslaved workers in December 1858. There is no record of what happened after that.

*Bowen* and *Cheek* were not enough to deter deprivation. Hunger inevitably provoked resistance. To survive, people took hogs, sheep, chickens, turkeys, and geese. They milked cows in the middle of the night. They secreted away vegetables that grew at the ends of rows or in other inconspicuous places.[35] In the narrative of his "life and adventures," Charles Ball describes how people disposed of the evidence of these necessary acts. "They burned chicken feathers and dumped the bones and guts of shad far out in rivers to escape detection."[36]

On the Georgia plantation that enslaved George Womble, "If their food gave out before the time for another issue they waited until night and then one or two of them would go the mill-house where the flour and meal was kept . . . they would take an auger and bore a hole in the barrel containing the meal. One held the sack while the other took a stick and worked it around the opening made by the auger so as to make the meal flow freely.

"After their bag were filled the hole was stopped up and a hasty departure was made. Sometimes when they wanted meat they either went to the smoke house and stole a ham or else they would go to the pen where the pigs were kept and take a small pig out. When they get to the woods with this animal they proceeded to skin and clean it. All the parts that they did not want were either buried or thrown in the nearby river. After going home all of this meat was cooked and hidden. As there was danger in being caught none of this stolen meat was ever fried because there was more danger of the odor of frying meat going farther away than that odor made by meat being boiled."[37]

One of Booker T. Washington's "earliest recollections is that of my mother cooking a chicken late at night, and awakening her children for the purpose of feeding them. How or where she got it I do not know. I presume, however, it was procured from our owner's farm."[38] He explains why, from a moral standpoint, his mother's actions were not theft. "Taking place at the time it did, and for the reason it did, no one could ever make me believe that my mother was guilty of thieving. She was simply a victim of the system of slavery." Psyche A. Williams-Forson elaborates that "taking and removing foods—whether surplus or not—was a rightful entitlement to the goods that slaves helped produce."[39] Tales of "trickster heroism," where people outwitted their enslavers to feed themselves and their families, were popular folklore.

Frederick Douglass Opie describes the harsh retribution meted out to people discovered with unauthorized food. "If caught, say, eating an orange from the owner's abundant fruit garden, the punishment was flogging. When even this proved futile a tar fence was erected around the forbidden fruit. Anyone whose body bore the merest trace of tar was brutally whipped by the chief gardener."[40] Yet, some enslavers directed enslaved people to steal others' property.

Where Henry Johnson lived, "The master would make us slaves steal from each of the slave owners. Our master would make us surround a herd of his neighbor's cattle, round them up at night, and make us slaves stay up all night long and kill and skin every one of them critters, salt the skins down in layers in the master's cellar, and put the cattle piled ceiling high in the smokehouse so nobody could identify skinned cattle."[41]

When neighbors took revenge, the law was not always on their side. Courts weighed the value of the items stolen against the value of the labor of the people who stole them. In an 1859 Louisiana case, *Gardiner v. Thibodeau*, the court ruled that the defendant did not have the right to kill an enslaved person who was fleeing his property with a stolen chicken because the worker was worth more money than the chicken.[42] The Louisiana court came to a similar conclusion in *McCutcheon v. Angelo*, where the defendant had blinded but not killed the enslaved person who took his chicken.[43]

Growing, making, and selling food was a way for people to get better food and clothing than their enslavers provided. Harriet Jacobs's grandmother was an exceptional woman, beloved in her community for her kind heart and delicious crackers. She became free as a child but was later captured by the owner of a large hotel during the Revolutionary War. Harriet remembers how word of her baking skills spread. "She was much praised for her cooking; and her nice crackers became so famous in the neighborhood that many people were desirous of obtaining them."[44]

Instead of sleeping, Harriet's grandmother started baking at midnight every night. Her plan was to make enough money to buy her children's freedom. The hotel owner allowed her to sell her baking on the condition that she use some of the money she made to pay for her children's clothing. Her talent and hard work allowed her to put aside $300. Then, the hotel owner's wife "borrowed" her savings, never to return them. In the end, her children were not freed. Still, her after-hours baking brought some joy to her grandchildren, Harriet and Willie, who "often received portions of the crackers, cakes, and preserves, she made to sell."

Sometimes, when people grew their own food, they stopped receiving provisions. Enslavers raided their gardens whenever they felt like it or destroyed them as punishment for infractions, real or imagined. Some believed that cultivating soil or livestock would tie people to the land, making escape or revolt less likely. Others feared that the ability to make money would facilitate independence, allowing some people to save enough to buy their freedom. And they resented the competition in the marketplace. The law stepped in to limit enslaved people's ability to prosper from their efforts. South Carolina's 1740 bill ensured enforcement by allocating half the value of goods sold illegally to the person who turned in the suspect. The other half would go to charity, "the commissioners of the poor of the parish of St. Philips, Charlestown."

Virginia passed similar laws in 1792 and 1798, prohibiting enslaved people from buying or selling from or to anyone but their enslavers.[45] These laws also penalized allowing enslaved people to "go at large"— hire themselves out or participate in markets. The laws permitted "any person," not just law enforcement, to arrest and bring before a justice of the peace a person who they suspected of going at large.[46]

Some people continued to participate in markets despite these laws, making covert arrangements when necessary. But they were still vulnerable to exploitation by the people who did business with them. They might renege on or change agreements, offer below-market rates, or make the type of borrowing arrangements that robbed Harriet Jacobs's grandmother of her hard-earned savings.

EMANCIPATION BROUGHT NEW sources of food insecurity. Martha Allen's family, enslaved in Craven County, North Carolina, always got by on very little food. When Martha was a baby, her mother would drop her off in the kitchen in the early morning on her way to work in the fields, then "go by the slops bucket and drink de slops from a long handled gourd." Martha herself was not even "half fed."[47] But still, she says she "was never hungry til we was free and the Yankees fed us. We didn't have nothing to eat except hard tack and middlin' meat. I never seen such meat. It was thin and tough with a thick skin. You could boil it all day and all night and it wouldn't cook, I wouldn't eat it. I thought it was mule meat; mules that done been shot on the battle field then dried. I still believe it was mule meat. . . . Dem was bad days. I was hungry most the time and had to keep fighting off them Yankee mens."[48] Martha was one of the many freed people who sought refuge in Union Army camps. Officers at these camps were woefully unprepared for the arrival of dislocated, freed people on their doorsteps.

The military's destruction of agricultural land, the disruption of major transportation routes, and bad weather made food scarce for everyone during the Civil War. But freed people suffered the most. In *Sick from Freedom*, Jim Downs explains that "disease and sickness had a more devastating and fatal effect on emancipated slaves than on soldiers since ex-slaves often lacked the basic necessities to survive. Emancipation liberated bondspeople from slavery, but they often lacked clean clothing, adequate shelter, proper food, and access to medicine in their escape toward Union lines. Many freed slaves died once they secured refuge behind Union camps."[49] Without food, freedom simply meant death.

Lack of nutrition also lowered freed peoples' immune systems, increasing their vulnerability to sickness. Freed men who joined the ranks of Union soldiers received food and compensation but the women, children, and elders who accompanied them did not. Neither the North nor the South anticipated a long, drawn-out war. Before their victory, when Union leaders discussed the future, they talked about political and civil liberties, but they failed to plan for the poverty, displacement, and hunger facing freed people.

On most days, enslaved people received some amount of food, even if it was small. After emancipation, without gardens, hunting or fishing tools, family, friends, or provisions, freed people went hungry. Sometimes the Union Army gave them scraps similar to or worse than the food they had eaten before. Freed people who did not go to army camps lived on deserted plantations or in barns, often forced to choose between eating diseased animals or eating nothing.

The pro-slavery *Richmond Dispatch* blamed freed people for the crisis. "We shudder to think of the scores of hundreds, of black men, women and children whose miserable deaths are attributable solely to the change in their condition produced by the war—to their own helplessness, and to the neglect and indifference of those whom they in their ignorant and strange faith looked upon as their benefactors and friends."[50] Many white Southerners believed that freed Black people would become "extinct."

The Union Army held some freed people in makeshift camps until they could figure out what to do with them. It sent others to work under military surveillance at confiscated plantations. These were unsustainable, short-term solutions. Southern states refused to offer any relief. Benevolent societies in the North were generous with charitable donations but could not keep up with the limitless need. The federal government had to step in. In 1865, it created the Bureau of Refugees, Freedmen, and Abandoned Lands, shortened to the Freedmen's Bureau.

Freedmen's Bureau hospitals established the United States' first federally funded health care system. As an official arm of the bureau's Medical Affairs division (the other divisions managed Government Controlled Lands, Records, and Financial Affairs), the hospitals took charge of distributing food rations. A single ration was enough cornmeal, flour, and sugar to last one person a week. In the first fifteen months after the Civil War ended in April 1865, bureau hospitals gave out over thirteen million rations. Over two-thirds of those rations went to Black households. By the end of the program's run in 1866, bureau hospitals had given out over eighteen million rations.

Some states added pork, syrup, rice, or seeds to the basic rations. But still they failed to use all the money they got for food. The War Department allotted $350,000 for the Freedmen's Bureau to give states for rations but they only used $35,000.[51] Florida was allocated $1.91 per person but only spent 87 cents. North Carolina had 80 cents per person but only spent 45.[52] Some hospitals used the rations they received to pay the local white people who worked for them instead of giving the food to the freed people who needed it.

A Louisiana medical officer lamented, "Great difficulty has been experienced in the hospital from inability to furnish a proper diet for the sick, and a fair proportion of the deaths reported can be readily traced to a lack of proper nourishment."[53] Bureau officials and doctors blamed strikingly high death rates on freed people's diets. They zealously committed themselves to weaning Black people off unhealthy food, which they assumed they preferred.

But finding fresh food for patients did not prove easy or cheap. Costs fluctuated with the market, sometimes rising beyond the reach of hospital budgets. Jim Downs reports how doctors approached this problem: "Instead of waiting for shipments of rations to arrive or worrying if they had enough money to buy supplies . . . they converted plots of land at the outer perimeters of their hospitals into vegetable gardens. Growing corn, squash, and beans provided doctors in Arkansas, Georgia, and Louisiana with nourishment for the sick. Creating their own vegetable gardens also enabled Bureau doctors to lower the expenses of the hospital by assigning patients to sell and barter the vegetables to members of the surrounding community."[54]

The plan's success backfired. After hearing of it, General Oliver Otis Howard, the Freedmen Bureau's commissioner, decided that every bureau hospital should start a garden. He ordered overworked doctors to tend the gardens even when physicians lacked the time, skills, or proper conditions. Frustrated by the increasing numbers of freed people applying for food aid, Howard cut the rations program in half instead of expanding it. Believing that aid created dependency, Howard declared that freed people would be better off without it. But he did not explain how they would acquire the resources to become self-sufficient in its absence.

Howard's concerns about charity dovetailed nicely with white Southern landowners' desire for food aid to end so that they could get their labor back—cheaply if not for free. Without enslaved people's work, the Southern economy was on the verge of collapse. History delivered the landowners a stroke of good luck. After Lincoln's assassination in 1865, Andrew Johnson became president and withdrew Lincoln's promise of forty acres and a mule to each freed Black person.

Johnson leveraged hunger to force Black people back to working other people's land, instructing the Freedmen's Bureau to supervise contracts between free Black people and their former enslavers. The terms of these contracts were often indistinguishable from enslavement. Bureau hospitals now healed Black people with the purpose of strengthening them for work. Finally, in the fall of 1866, Howard canceled the rations program altogether.[55]

With the retreat of Freedmen's Bureau aid, Black people faced an untenable choice between starving or agreeing to their former enslavers' exploitative contracts.[56] Thomas Hall, who was enslaved by Jim Woods in North Carolina before emancipation, explains the complex relationship between food and freedom: "Lincoln got the praise for freeing us, but did he do it? He [gave] us freedom without giving us any chance to live with ourselves and we still had to depend on the southern white man for work, food, and clothing, and he held us out of necessity and want in a state of servitude but little better than slavery."[57]

When they returned to plantations, freed Black people were less likely to receive adequate, palatable food. White landowners no longer viewed their relationship to their workers as lifelong. Instead, they assessed them in terms of their daily production capacity, treating them as expendable. Under this new regime, single Black women faced particularly difficult challenges. Government aid organizations were reluctant to condone their "immoral and licentious" (meaning unmarried) situations by providing them with basic necessities. At the same time, the criminal legal system was snatching up able Black men who could have offered them support through marriage.

SOME WHITE SOUTHERN landowners turned to the legal system to find Black people to perform grueling labor for no or low pay. As powerfully demonstrated in Ava Duvernay's documentary *13th* and detailed in Douglas Blackmon's book *Slavery by Another Name*, after Reconstruction, white people could easily arrange for the prosecution of Black men for trivial crimes that they did or did not commit. After conviction, incarcerated Black men could be legally re-enslaved because the Thirteenth Amendment abolishes slavery except "as a punishment for crime."

The Missouri Black Code, first enacted in 1804 to control free Black people, allowed for the imprisonment of "all rogues and vagabonds, idle and dissipated persons, beggars, jugglers, or persons practicing unlawful games or plays, runaways, common drunkards, common night-walkers, pilferers, lewd, wanton, or lascivious persons, in speech or behavior, common railers and brawlers, persons who neglect their calling or employment, misspend what they earn, or do not provide for the support of themselves or their families, or dependents, and all other idle and disorderly persons, including all who neglect all lawful business, habitually misspend their time by frequenting houses of ill-fame, gaming-houses, or tippling shops."[58] Men who committed any of these transgressions were "deemed and considered vagrants."

These vagrancy laws, which also criminalized walking without purpose and walking at night, were so expansive as to include all human behavior. Post-emancipation, they served the economic interests of white Southerners by taking advantage of the Thirteenth Amendment's loophole. Prisons leased out Black men convicted of the crimes codified in vagrancy laws to former enslavers and to coal mines, steelworks, railroads, and other industrial enterprises. These employers had no vested interest in the well-being of their workers. In the face of this profound indifference to their humanity, convicts often suffered mistreatment that was worse than enslavement. They received scant food and died at alarmingly high rates from malnutrition, brutality, and often avoidable accidents.

Ninety-five percent of men in criminal custody in the South were Black.[59] In the first two years of this new system, 20 percent of Alabama's leased convicts died. In its third year, 30 percent of leased convicts died, and, in the fourth year, 45 percent of leased convicts died.[60] Once the sheriffs in charge of arresting and leasing Black men were paid, they lost interest in the convicts. But even before leasing out prisoners, sheriffs stood to gain from starving them. The federal government provided a fixed sum for each prisoner's food provisions, and the sheriffs pocketed whatever they didn't spend. Jail inspector Dr. C. F. Bush confides, "I have had several sheriffs admit to me that, without profit from the feed bill, they would not have the office, as it was one of their greatest sources of revenue."[61]

Parallel to Black Codes, Pig Laws, enacted in 1866, targeted agricultural laborers and households on the verge of starvation. A Mississippi Pig Law deemed the theft of property worth more than $10 ($168 in 2023), including cattle and swine, to be grand larceny, punishable by up to five years of hard labor.[62] Georgia made stealing hogs a felony. North Carolina did not distinguish between petty and grand larceny, so a person could receive a sentence of between three to ten years for stealing two chickens.

Landowners often cooked up false charges against Black men they wanted to re-enslave. After the sheriff charged an innocent man, a landowner would offer to pay his fines in exchange for a commitment to work for a set amount of time. Faced with bogus charges that would likely end in incarceration, death, disfigurement, or permanent separation from their families, many Black men agreed to unconscionable contracts to avoid conviction. The terms of these contracts were often no different from the conditions that conviction would have imposed. Usually, the men agreed to work for no wages and very little food.

Sometimes, a landowner would sell these coerced contracts to copper, turpentine, or iron operations. These industries began leasing enslaved people before the Civil War and continued acquiring cheap labor after it ended through convict leasing and by purchasing indebted people. Industrial work had no room for families. It required only strong laborers to do repetitive tasks.

Many Black men caught up in this system ended up at sites run by the Milner Coal and Railway Company. A *New York Times* feature on Milner's Newcastle mine reported that "'Revoltingly filthy' food was served cold from unwashed coal buckets."[63] Milner's Coalburg prison "had no floor or toilets; prisoners were fed only meat and bread." In the Pratt mines fueling Milner's Alabama railroad, observers saw "men eating out of coal shovels." The article inspired new rules requiring railway companies to provide their workers with adequate food, but no one enforced the rules.

On Texas farms, "prisoners were chained at the neck and held in boxcars at night. Working from sunup to sundown, they survived on food 'buzzards would not eat.'" In 1887, the *Chicago Daily Tribune* reported that Mississippi prison hospitals held men so "emaciated that their bones almost came through their skin."[64] Excessive deaths at prisons, prison mines, and other convict leasing sites did not seem to alarm the white medical community. Dr. Judson Davie claimed in 1895 that "it is a fact that the negro race is inferior to the white race physically as well as mentally and morally—their powers of resistance, so far as a great many diseases are concerned . . . does not compare at all favorably with the white race."[65]

MANY SHARECROPPERS ALSO endured subsistence-level conditions. After contracting to receive a share of the income from the crops they grew on a landowner's property, they worked all year without pay. They were supposed to collect their share of the profits at the end of the season. But in practice, after landowners calculated the share, deducting costs as they saw fit, sharecroppers rarely received any payment. They survived mostly on what they could grow themselves and on rations that their landlords dispensed throughout the year.

Black sharecroppers who worked for white landowners largely returned to the restricted diets they ate during enslavement. On the Carolina Sea Islands, the white property owner whose land Annette Coleman's family worked "handed out a food allowance each week— molasses, meat, cornmeal, and flour. Much of the food was scraps from his table, scraps that had to be shared with his dogs."[66]

Mason Crum's life as a sharecropper on the Carolina Sea islands was one with "flies all around; no lawn, no bath, no toilet, a hand to mouth existence, a diet of grits, fatback, collards, cabbage, sweet potatoes, molasses, butt meat."[67] But even though "we was raised up just like cattle is, and we experienced hard times . . . I rather get on with eating once a week on bread and water than be a slave with plenty."[68]

Loretta Davis Khan and her sister lived with their grandparents, Manison and Mozelle Revell, in Rocky Hock, North Carolina. "We lived in an unpainted, tin roof house with no indoor plumbing and no electricity while the 'patron family' lived in relative luxury. . . . The land had no trees and, therefore, no shade. In the summer we played under the house, which was propped up on stones. Our grandmother planted a garden and raised chickens and our uncles and grandfather raised pigs. So we ate well and never went hungry. Vegetables were canned and hams smoked for winter eating."[69] After "squaring up" with the landlord, Loretta's grandfather made "only 92 cents for that year of hard work. He was charged for rent on the house, all supplies, seeds and more. We have learned that nobody, no matter how hardworking, can lift himself to independence by sharecropping."

In many cases, sharecroppers ended the season owing money to their landlords for seeds, tools, food rations, and shelter. This left sharecropping families with little or no money to feed themselves. Lin-fred Moore, who was born on the George White cotton farm in York County, South Carolina, in 1934, lived with his parents, grandparents, and five siblings in two shacks on the landlord's property. "Half of everything we made went to the boss. He took it, and he gave us what he called half . . . the boss on the farm would provide us with fertilizer, seeds and cane. At the end of the year, we'd owe him. So to get our half of the profits, we'd have to pay him what we owed. The money would just go right back to him."

Many sharecropping contracts also forced farmers to buy food at the plantation store, either for cash, scrips, or on credit. But they could not always get credit when they needed it. "Back in our days, some white folks say we can have a garden just no chickens. . . . Come Christmas time in hole, couldn't get no food. Eight people on a farm made good cotton that year, went to the store and was told [they were] in debt, couldn't get nothing."[70] When they couldn't purchase groceries, some families relied on rations. "Mama would start to wash and iron so we could eat, so she could feed us, because they'd cut your groceries out, because every two weeks Mama would go to the commissary, they called it, and get our weekly ration, they said, and sometimes it would last and sometimes it didn't."[71]

Women took on the brunt of landowners' willingness to starve their workers. "We had problems, sometimes we didn't have enough food on the table. I would fix it . . . put it on the table and walk out until my husband and the children eat. If there was anything left then I eat. If not, I did without until maybe I could scrap together something for the next meal."[72] The sharecropping contracts usually required wives to do field work. This left the women with little time to make meals or watch their children and exposed them to diseases like typhoid.[73]

Sharecroppers faced a host of dangers, harms, and indignities: sexual assault; poisonous snakes, flies, and relentless mosquitoes; homes with no water, electricity, indoor plumbing, air-conditioning, or heat; lung damage from inhaling pesticides and cotton fibers; asthma, migraines, diabetes, and arthritis; oppressive heat, and freezing cold. Annie Williams-Madojemu's family were sharecroppers on a farm in Roxboro, North Carolina. "Our drinking water came from a well, which we kept in buckets in the kitchen. It was common for the water to freeze in winter. Sometimes we would find drowned rats in the frozen water."[74] After working from sunup to sundown all week from the age of three, Annie spent her Saturdays helping with "cutting down trees for wood, which was used for cooking and heating. All winter, my parents would keep the fire burning throughout the night and we would sleep in the same room to stay warm. In summer, fans could do little to stop us from sweating as we slept. To use the bathroom, we had to go to an outhouse during the day and use a chamber pot at night."

Sharecroppers who earned enough to get ahead had to deal with white resentment and violence. Kathy Dews tells the story of her grandfather John Wilkes, who "was a sharecropper during the Jim Crow era [roughly 1877–1950]. He lived in Oak Park, Georgia, with his wife and children. He was allowed to build a shanty for his family on the property of the landowner. The land was rich and he was successful at yielding crops such as tobacco, cotton, and vegetables. The family story is that white neighbors were envious of his success and burned the house several times during the time he lived there. He always rebuilt it. The last time the house was burned he was run off and his life was threatened."

Some sharecroppers got ahead by running their own food businesses. Hughsey Childs survived by baking and trading bread. "You see the bread I made, you had to eat it while it was hot, because if it got cold, you couldn't taste it because I made it with water. So what I would do, I would save it till I get a bag. And I never was ashamed, I'm still that way to today. I saved this big bag of stale bread and take it up on the farm and holler before I get to the house because most all the farmers had dogs. And I'd get their attention whether they was white or colored. I said: Do you all have pigs? They said Yes. I say Well I have a big bag of stale bread here. I'll exchange it for you or some milk.

And I had—and I would take a pail with me and they would give me sometime a nice big pail of milk. Well I'd have good biscuits that night because the milk made better biscuits than water."[75]

Hughsey recalls the plight of his mother's friend, whose hunger changed the course of her life. "This white man that they sharecropped with . . . he found out the condition she was in. She was hungry. The kids was hungry. And he told her: if you have a relationship with me, I'll give you enough food to last you for the month. And unfortunately she was hungry. . . . But unfortunately she got pregnant by him. And the baby was born. And she was kind of light too because she was half-white herself. She said, I was so hungry. . . . If it hadn't been for that, I don't know what me and my children would have do. We would have starved."

The law supported landowners' desire to exploit, cheat, and starve sharecroppers. When landowners feared that hunting and fishing would increase Black people's independence, some states enacted game laws that limited hunting and fishing in counties with large Black populations. They banned specific techniques preferred by Black fishers, such as nets, and banned hunting and fishing on the days and times that Black sharecroppers weren't working. In 1866, Georgia banned hunting with guns and dogs on Sundays, in seventy-two counties that had plantations. In 1876, Georgia banned shad fishing on Saturday and Sunday.

Other state laws restricted who sharecroppers could sell their goods to, prohibiting sales to Black merchants and authorizing sales only to "legitimate" (white) merchants.[76] Some laws criminalized moving if a person had outstanding debts, which all sharecroppers did.[77] Others prohibited selling cotton after sunset, which is when Black sharecroppers would finish their day's work. In some cases, there was a very thin line between sharecropping and convict leasing. Sometimes white landowners accused Black laborers of injuring a borrowed farm animal through overwork or abuse then manufactured a charge and conviction to convert the relationship into convict leasing.

Sixty years after emancipation, a USDA survey of 750 Black rural households found that eight out of ten families subsisted on diets that did not meet minimum nutritional recommendations.[78] Black share-croppers suffered from the same nutritional deficiencies that had plagued their enslaved parents and grandparents. Pellagra continued to afflict poor Black people in the South. From 1906 to 1940, it affected three million people, killing 100,000.[79] This scourge represented one of the largest public health crises of the early twentieth century.

Even Black Southerners who did not become sharecroppers strug-gled to improve their diets. Many did not have the time, space, or skill to garden or prepare nutritious meals. Households lacked refrigeration systems. Others had a taste for and cultural connection to the foods that they and their ancestors had always eaten. In New Orleans, food was so scarce in the city that people said politicians were trading it for votes. Idelle Elsey recalls, "Back in the turn of the century, the early years of the century, that in the colored districts—that they could buy votes with fish 'cause they weren't too far out of slavery, you know? Any-thing to eat, they . . . would do anything to get a meal."[80]

LIFE UP NORTH during these years was not much better than it was in the South. Isabel Wilkerson, author of *The Warmth of Other Suns*, dis-pels myths idealizing the North. "Even in the places where they were permitted, blacks were relegated to the lowest-paying, most dangerous jobs, barred from many unions and, at some companies, hired only as strike breakers, which served to further divide black workers from white. They were confined to the most dilapidated housing in the least desirable sections of the cities to which they fled. In densely populated destinations like Pittsburgh and Harlem, housing was so scarce that some black workers had to share the same single bed in shifts."[81]

Diets reflected these harsh circumstances. Many Black women who migrated to northern cities did domestic work that provided food as part of their payment. Minnie S. Whitney, who worked for a Jewish family, "didn't know how to eat the Jewish food, but I found out. Like the time I was hired, I didn't eat nothin' but their food. And I become accustomed of it. So many things that I had to get adjusted to."[82]

Beulah Collins paid another woman to watch her son but felt bad that, with Beulah's salary of $13 a week, she could not pay her employee enough for her to eat well. "She had cheap food. She had cabbage, she had a lot of cabbage and sweet potatoes and put a little piece of ham in it and cooked it and they all went to the table and set down and eat it." Meanwhile, Beulah "had different from that because I lived with a rich family. I eat what they had because they bought enough for me. . . . And I, the only one in the family, I mean help. I never was a big eater and I always got a plate. I had a lot, my relatives and people, I used to feel sorry for them. During the depression when they didn't have this and that or the other. I felt I was blessed because I lived with rich people and always had enough to eat."[83]

Not all domestic workers were as lucky as Beulah. To get work in Philadelphia during the Depression, Fannie Hutchinson would go to "Montgomery Avenue, and wait on the corner, and then people would tell us to come. They would give you 25 cents an hour or give you 25 cent to come scrub their kitchen. And then some of them would tell you, I'll give you your lunch if you come and scrub my kitchen. No pay, just lunch."[84] Even barely making enough to get by, she offered food to her neighbors. "There was a bond of welfare that went beyond need. I mean, if I knew the family next door was hungry, I shared what I had. Even when we were living among those Italians down there, I saw my grandmother hanging pots of food over the fence to her Italian neighbors, and they would do the same."

In the cities, it was common to work hard every day and still not be able to feed a family. Charles Vance went from the South to Philadelphia, where he "couldn't make enough money to feed myself because the wages were so low. I used to go to work in the morning, I'd go to work in the morning and early. And you know you used to have milk on the porches, and bread? Used to take the milk and the bread off the porches there and go on and eat it. Take it home and eat it, because you didn't make enough money to take care of yourself."[85]

Black migrants who longed for a taste of home often faced challenges trying to re-create it. Ingredients that were cheap and plentiful in the South were either seasonal or simply unavailable up north. Supermarket chains Winn-Dixie[86] and Piggly Wiggly[87] led the way in stocking popular Southern food, such as pork fat, salt pork, ham hocks, and pigs' feet. Other chains eventually found a market for these products along with other Southern-branded salty, fatty, and over-sweetened foods.

Migrants with agricultural skills dreamed of planting home gardens to feed themselves and soothe their homesickness. But when they tried to keep chickens or goats like they did back home, they bumped up against city nuisance ordinances prohibiting the animals. This was no coincidence. City governments believed that Black migrants and the immigrants who often lived alongside them should adopt white American diets and customs. When white neighbors complained that keeping animals was loud and unsanitary, city councils enacted laws that made it impossible for newcomers to source their eggs and milk at home.[88] These laws steered migrants toward prepackaged, bland convenience foods produced by the relatively new industrial food system. But Black migrants, who shared space with immigrants from China, Italy, and Mexico, resisted white food. Instead, they became early adopters of dishes like chop suey, pizza, and chili.[89]

When food was scarce in the North, Black relief organizations, restaurants, street vendors, and stores often stepped in to feed hungry people.[90] Black churches gave food, clothing, and fuel to community members. In Ypsilanti, Michigan, Reverend Harvey E. Leggett and other church leaders would "pick up a whole lot of kids all over the city of Ypsilanti and in the township and we bring them to this church every day and there is a concern that furnish the lunch in here."[91]

Louise Bass was a leading member of the State and National Association of Colored Women's Clubs, the Brown Chapel AME, the NAACP, the Palm Leaf Club,[92] the Girl Scouts, and other community organizations. She raised three children, including Mick Bass, a star NFL cornerback. Louise joined forces with other women at the Ypsilanti Association of Women's Clubs' nursery school to run a kitchen where "kids could come and stay all day . . . if they were in kindergarten, come in the morning, eat lunch, and go to school in the afternoon. Or they could just come for lunch and then come back after school. And the big price was $3 per week . . . we had a rather standard menu. We either had tomato soup and sandwich, or vegetable soup and sandwich." Some community members came to Louise's nursery school kitchen "to get some water because the water at the nursery school was better than the water at home."[93]

When the Great Depression hit in the 1930s, the federal government developed its first emergency food program, the Federal Surplus Relief Corporation. Designed to help farmers and hungry people, it bought surplus harvests from farms and distributed those commodities across the country. It also set up soup kitchens and breadlines, primarily in white neighborhoods. But when hungry Black people came seeking government food, the people in charge of distributing the rations often refused to give them a share, preferring to save scarce resources for white people.

Ben Neely,[94] who moved to Ypsilanti from North Carolina as a teenager in 1914, was outraged that "During the Depression, they wasn't feeding the people. They'd give the whites what they, anything they wanted, and give the blacks practically nothing. . . . The federal government had this extra supply of foodstuffs . . . you could go there and they'd have meat, ham, and everything else that you'd want and give it to you." Ben recalled that "Thomas, who was in charge of government handouts in Ben's neighborhood, would say there was nothing left whenever a Black person showed up.

"The blacks would go down there to get something, they didn't have nothing, so they had to go away. So I, I got a group of people together and I said, "Now we're going to get some food today. I'm going to tell you what's liable to happen. The police department is liable to come down here and want to drive us away. If they tell you to go, don't tell them no you're not going, move! We run away. But soon as the cop goes away, come back to the same spot. And he will tell you to move again, go ahead, but as soon as he moves, you move."

Ben's plan worked. While some protesters ran from the police, "the rest of them was begging Thomas for food. Pretty soon it pretty near drove Thomas mad—he, he rushed out and he said, 'Give these goddamn people anything they want! Give them the whole damn thing, 'cause I don't want no part of it no more!' Negroes walking out of there with whole hams, sacks of flour, five-pound bags of sugar. They couldn't get a two-pound bag of sugar before!"[95]

The struggles of the Depression forced some people to leave their homes looking for a better life. Charles Vance moved from Philadelphia to New York to scrape by doing restaurant work. "You go down to Sixth Avenue and get a job down there, they'll pay you a dollar a day for washing dishes. And, of course, they'll give you something to eat and a dollar a day, washing dishes, to get something to eat."[96]

SEGREGATION MADE IT difficult for Black people to access or enjoy food outside the home. Very few restaurants served Black people, although some offered take out from a back window or separate entrance. On rare occasions, white diners could vouch for a Black companion. Ben Neely regularly ate at the White Tower with his coworkers, fellow members of the Amalgamated Clothing Workers. "Now they wouldn't serve no blacks, but I'd go along with the union brothers over there and eat my breakfast along with them. I don't realize that they had made an agreement with them to allow me to come in because the union wouldn't allow no discrimination. They would allow me to eat over there as long as they were with me." Everything went smoothly until Ben went to White Tower alone. "I went over there by myself one day to get something to eat. I know this woman looking at me, never said nothing. Pretty soon she told me no, she wasn't going to serve me. I said, 'Why?' 'You know you ain't supposed to come in here.' So I called the police to get my order [and they] come down here and arrested me. Yeah. Y'know? They put me in jail. The union had to come get me out of there."

In 1936, New York postal worker Victor Hugo Green published *The Green Book*, a guide for Black travelers in the United States that listed restaurants that would serve them—which were few and far between. Sometimes people tried their luck in restaurants that did not officially declare themselves as white, but made their preferences clear. In Harrisburg, Pennsylvania, Arthur H. Fauset, Esther Winters, and

Helen Morales lost their patience at the Penn-Harris hotel. Milo Manly describes how "they waited, and waited, and waited. No service. Finally, they demanded service. And the manager or whoever he was came on out to them and called them in, said serve this, so they ordered, and brought their food, set it down in front of them. The manager came up in back and poured a box of salt in each plate. They sued. And the case went on into Commonwealth Court." The Pennsylvania District and County Court issued a preliminary opinion in the resulting 1937 case, *Commonwealth v. Moore*,[97] ruling that "in as much as they had been served, that met the purposes of the civil right law. . . . It was before the city had its equal opportunity, equal rights law."[98]

In Ypsilanti in the 1940s, Marguerite Eaglin and her friend Yvonne Williams "would go downtown for lunch and we'd go into a place and sit and sit and sit. Nobody actively insulted us, but they just didn't wait on us. They just ignored us like we weren't there. Finally in one place, I said, 'Look, I have to go back to school. Do you know when we could get served, please?' They finally served us, but they burned the bread. They burned my bread or made me wait a long time, but none of them really put me out. I was never refused."[99] YWCA secretary Mamie Davis faced the same treatment in Philadelphia's Stouffer's restaurant, where they "dosed her food up with a whole bunch of salt and pepper."[100]

Philadelphia resident Edgar Campbell found a way to fight back against the discrimination. "They were painted a beautiful picture of the North, everything wide open. But then there were places they couldn't even go in and eat in the North, right here in Philadelphia. Horn & Hardart, 1508 Market Street. We used to go in there after dinner dance, and whatever we ordered, they didn't have. So we'd order coffee. And after—you ordered a cup of coffee, I ordered a cup of coffee, and we drank it. We said, 'Give us another.' They'd break that cup up. We made them break up all the dishes in the place one night."[101]

But Arthur Dingle had no time for places that wouldn't serve him. "I came to Philadelphia, and Linton's Restaurant was on Market Street, near Fifteenth. And I went to Linton's Restaurant and I sit down. I said, 'Hey, could I get a sandwich?' He said, 'I'm sorry, we out of sandwiches. Sorry.' So I knew what he meant, so I got up and went on out."[102]

Although many Black migrants settled in Philadelphia's German-town neighborhood, John Jones struggled to get service there. "So some stores would ignore you when you came in. . . . And you'd have to suffer many times because you'd be the next person to be waited on, but if white people came in, they would wait on them first. So some stores were worse at this sort of thing than others. So you—by elimination, you went to the stores that treated you in a way that you wanted to be treated. The full length of Germantown Avenue, there wasn't a restaurant that a black could go in and sit down and eat. The first to be opened, it wasn't a restaurant per se but a hot dog place, Coney Island . . . which was opened in 1921." John had a better experience at Horn & Hardart, which opened its first automat in 1906,[103] than Edgar Campbell had. John believed that the owners "opened it to serve everyone—everybody."[104]

The South was even worse that the North. Luriese Moore made occasional trips back to her hometown of Boligee, Alabama. "Everything was mixed in South Omaha," where she had moved, but traveling south, "There were certain places they wouldn't even sell us gas. . . . We couldn't even get any food to eat, we had to pack up our own food to take south and to come back until we hit the St. Louis line."[105]

Even dressed in uniform, Ken Mashatt had trouble getting a sandwich in the South. "I was nineteen years old, had just joined the United States Army. I come home on leave. On my way back I stopped in Memphis, Tennessee, two o'clock in the morning, okay; nothing was open but a white grill, and I was hungry. I was sure enough hungry. I went to this grill and I said, 'Listen, lady,' big old redhead lady, white lady. I went in. I said, 'Can I get a sandwich?' She said, 'No, you can't get a sandwich.' She said, 'Get your black ass out of here.' I said, 'What's so wrong?' She said, 'Well, we don't serve niggers here.' Well, that didn't bother me too much. I said, 'Well, look, all I want is something to eat. If you give me a sandwich, I'll leave.' So she called the manager. He come out there and he said, 'We don't serve blacks here; you got to go.' And I said, 'Well, I'm in a United States Army uniform.' He said, 'We going to give you a sandwich, but you have to go outdoors to eat it.'"[106]

Things began to turn around in the 1950s. The year before 1953's *Brown v. Board of Education* ordered the integration of public schools, *District of Columbia v. John R. Thompson, Co.* declared segregated restaurants in the capital illegal.[107] The holding relied on two laws enacted during Reconstruction that barred restaurants, hotels, barbershops, bathing houses, and soda fountains from refusing to sell or serve any "well-behaved" customer, regardless of race or color. The penalty for violating these laws was a $100 fine or a one-year license suspension.[108] These "lost laws" fell into disuse but were never repealed. Mary Church Terrell, founder of the National Association of Colored Women, revived them to convince the court that DC lunch counters' refusal to serve her and her friends was illegal.

Her victory was the culmination of years of activism. In a 1906 speech, Terrell spoke out against the injustice of the fact that "as a colored woman I may walk from the Capitol to the White House, ravenously hungry and abundantly supplied with money with which to purchase a meal, without finding a single restaurant in which I would be permitted to take a morsel of food, if it was patronized by white people, unless I were willing to sit behind a screen."

ALTHOUGH THE 1964 Civil Rights Act eventually outlawed racially segregated restaurants, it did not address the perpetual poverty that made political participation challenging in the face of persistent hunger. In *Food Power Politics*, Bobby J. Smith II documents how Mississippi's Leflore county board of supervisors cut off access to the food assistance provided by the Federal Surplus Commodities Program in 1963 to try to suppress Black votes.[109] This food blockade was not unprecedented—the same thing had happened in Tennessee in 1960 when Black people tried to register to vote and in the Mississippi Delta's Sunflower county in 1962. But the winter of 1963 was one of the coldest the Delta had ever seen. People were freezing to death and near starvation without the commodities that white plantation owners relied on to feed workers through the lean months. Resistance took the form of a national Food for Freedom campaign, promoted by Martin Luther King Jr. and comedian Dick Gregory, that gathered provisions from around the country to send to the Delta. After a report on the blockade reached the USDA, prompting the agency to threaten to take over the program, the board of supervisors gave in. A shipment of surplus food arrived in Leflore county for the first time in over a year in late March 1963.

Still, as Reverend Charles Koen, a minister and civil rights activist in Cairo, Illinois, preached, "voting rights could not be eaten or made into clothing or shelter."[110] Koen was a leader in the United Front of Cairo, a Christian group that worked to realize racial justice and community uplift through strength and religion. As part of this mission, the United Front partnered with Chicago's Urban League to create a food distribution network. Together, they sent canned goods and other basics from Chicago to Cairo in trucks donated by retail giants Sears, Roebuck and Company and Montgomery Ward.

The United Front also constructed prefab housing and ran a day care center, a pig farm, a women's clothing store, and a collectively owned grocery store that shared profits with the community. The United Front paired the support of Black-owned businesses with the boycott of white-owned ones, causing some white stores to close. Reverend Koen explained that "protecting Black Cairo meant not only keeping a rifle in the home and meeting people's basic needs for food, clothing, and shelter, but also marshaling collective power to boycott and picket racist businesses."

In the 1960s, California faced similar issues. "There were a lot of people who were eating out of garbage cans . . . indecent conditions that they were living in."[111] The Black Panther Party, founded by Bobby Seale and Huey Newton in Oakland in 1966, made food justice a central pillar of its struggle. The party's survival programs included the Free Breakfast Program, the Free Food Program, and nutrition classes. Newton explained, "All these programs satisfy the deep needs of the community but they are not solutions to our problems. That is why we call them survival programs, meaning survival pending revolution.

We say that the survival program of the Black Panther Party is like the survival kit of a sailor stranded on a raft. It helps him to sustain himself until he can get completely out of that situation."[112]

The Panthers strove for structural reform while recognizing that this goal would be difficult to achieve with so many community members hungry, weak, or sick because they did not have enough food, or the right kind of food. Many Black children did not receive government food at school in the 1960s. USDA breakfasts were only available in a few rural communities, and school lunches were subsidized but not free. Recognizing that hungry children could not learn, the Panthers kicked off the Free Breakfast Program at Oakland's St. Augustine's Church in January 1969 under the leadership of Father Earl Neil and parishioner Ruth Beckford-Smith. Through donations from churches, activists, businesses, and white philanthropists, the program fed children hot breakfasts in communal spaces that were safe, loving, and joyful. Oakland's sample menu laid out daily recommendations for Free Breakfast Programs across the nation. Wednesday's meal was eggs, home fries, ham, toast with jam, and milk or juice.

"The children, many of whom had never eaten breakfast before the Panthers started their program think the Panthers are 'groovy' and 'very nice' for doing this for them."[113] School officials were grateful, too. Ruth Beckford-Smith recalled, "The school principal came down and told us how different the children were. They weren't falling asleep in class, they weren't crying with stomach cramps." In its first year, the Panthers fed more poor children in California than the state's school meals programs, which were sponsored by the USDA National School Lunch Program established in 1946. The Party's Free Breakfasts spread to twenty-three cities in the first year and operated in at least forty-five cities at its peak. Black businesses that contributed to the program got free advertising in exchange, helping them stay afloat in a white capitalist economy.

The program's success eventually attracted the attention of J. Edgar Hoover's Federal Bureau of Investigation. Labeling free breakfast "the greatest threat to the internal security of the country," Hoover set out to destroy the program.[114] In San Francisco, detractors told parents that the Black Panthers had infected the food with venereal disease.[115] Chicago police broke into the church housing the city's program and urinated on the food. The FBI sent forged letters to local businesses warning them against donating food or supplies. It raided breakfast sites where children were eating, taking their pictures and intimidating them. These actions, along with the arrest and murder of party leaders, scared families away. Hoover's sabotage succeeded, shutting down most cities' Free Breakfast Programs by 1973. The Seattle program lasted the longest, until 1977.[116]

The Free Breakfast Program threatened the FBI because it transformed public perception of the Black Panthers. Suddenly, liberal white and moderate Black people saw the Party as a legitimate organization worthy of their support. Historians credit the Free Breakfast Program with motivating Congress to increase funding for the National School Lunch Program in 1973. But Analena Hope Hassberg argues that the victory of expanded government-sanctioned food programs was hollow because they co-opted and usurped the Panthers' much broader, liberatory agenda. Hassberg explains, "By providing free meals and groceries to people whose wage-based labor was not sufficient to keep food on the table . . . the Black Panther party reframed food and wellness as rights instead of commodities. . . . The food handouts themselves were not, in themselves, the revolution. Rather, meeting the basic needs of oppressed people was a precursor to the organization . . . that the revolution required."[117] The party designed the Free Food Program to supplement "the groceries of Black and poor people until economic conditions allow them to purchase good food at reasonable prices,"[118] not to keep people reliant on food assistance.

With the end of the Panthers' programs, food insecurity remained high. A 1974 *Time* magazine article reported that poor people were spending at least 60 percent of their income on food and still not getting enough to eat.[119] Rising prices of staple foods, including rice, flour, and dried beans, which increased by 256 percent over four years, left families hungry. With only 37 percent of people eligible for food stamps actually getting them and inadequate amounts doled out to those who did, some people turned to pet food for protein. The *Time* article blamed poor administration of USDA food assistance programs for the problem and the Senate Select Committee on Nutrition and Human Needs recommended replacing them with a basic income.

Faced with increased hunger in the population, Reagan cut instead of expanded food assistance. Under his watch, a million people lost access to food stamps, twenty million got less money to spend, and 2.6 million children became ineligible for school lunches.[120] Students who still ate them became increasingly prey to obesity and diabetes. A 2002 *Time* magazine article, "Flunking Lunch," reported "an almost threefold jump in the number of overweight teens since the 1990s," with school cafeterias looking "little different than the food court at the mall." Kelly Brownell, who went on to head the World Food Policy Center, called the school lunchroom "a toxic food environment."

But food eaten at home often isn't much better. Subsidies make the unhealthiest food the cheapest. And prices for basic goods are higher in poor neighborhoods. Items sold in bigger packages cost less per ounce but stores in poor areas generally stock only small quantities. People who shop at chain supermarkets, which are mostly located in suburbs, pay 10–40 percent less for staples like oatmeal and flour. Even when Black income levels are equal to white ones, Black areas have the fewest stores—predominantly white neighborhoods have four times the number of supermarkets as predominantly Black neighborhoods.[121] In many areas, dollar stores have moved in to capture the market for cheap foods.

USDA nutrition programs also take a toll on health. People who rely on federally subsidized foods are 40 percent more likely to be obese and suffer metabolic disease and to have higher levels of belly fat, blood sugar, cholesterol, and inflammation.[122] Compared to white Americans, Black Americans have higher rates of diabetes (12.1 percent vs. 7.4 percent), obesity (43.9 percent vs. 31.5 percent), high blood pressure (56 percent vs. 48 percent), strokes (52.3 percent vs. 35.9 percent), cancer deaths (17 percent vs. 1 percent), and food insecurity (21.7 percent vs. 7.1 percent). These statistics mirror the health disparities between enslaved people and enslavers that reflected their use of food as a tool of subordination. Health authorities continue to explain these disparities as biologically based or rooted in personal taste and poor choices. These myths mask corporations' and government's economic and political incentives to dump unwanted, unhealthy food in Black communities, underfund social assistance programs, and doom history to repeat itself.

# 3

# Americanization Through Homemaking

"The noon lunch of the Mexican child quite often consists of a folded tortilla with no filling. There is no milk or fruit to whet the appetite. Such a lunch is not conducive to learning. The child becomes lazy. His hunger unappeased, he watches for an opportunity to take food from the lunch boxes of more fortunate children. Thus the initial step in a life of thieving is taken."[1] This passage from Pearl Idelia Ellis's 1929 instruction manual, *Americanization Through Homemaking*, illustrates how nativists linked Mexican food to criminality. They saw American food as a pathway to the political and social assimilation that would eliminate this danger.

Indigenous peoples living south of what is now the United States ate beans and tortillas along with a stunning collection of fruits, vegetables, and herbs. These included avocado, corn, tomatoes, chiles, pumpkins, squashes, berries, pineapples, mangos, chocolate, vanilla, and wild greens (quelites and verdolagas—pigweed and purslane). Aztec tastes ran to roast turkey, quail, duck, fish, lobster, frogs, green plums, and peas. Through colonization, Spanish staples like cinnamon, garlic, onions, rice, wheat, sugarcane, and pork entered Mexican cuisine. Goat meat, poultry, and beef became popular, but cheese did not.

Settlers in what are now Mexico, South America, and Central America used food as a tool of oppression in many of the same ways that settlers in the United States did.[2] Colonialism, violence, assimilation, corporate domination, and cultural appropriation had a ruinous effect on Indigenous diets. As food jumped across moving borders, a new version of Mexican food emerged that eventually spread across the globe.[3] People came to revere it as decadent and fun but not nutritious. In the late 1800s, Americans viewed Mexican staples with suspicion.

In 1894, a medical missionary journal warned that Mexicans' passion for beans would lure them into theft. "Frijoles, or black beans, are a very common article of diet; they are, in fact, the principal food of the lower class and are largely used by all classes. These are made hot with pepper and cooked with any kind of grease the cook can get hold of. If it is so strong as to be patent to the nostrils a long way off, it doesn't hurt the flavor for the low-class consumer. In one locality the railway employees had to guard the grease they used for their car wheels so strong was the temptation to the predatory leperos"—low-class Mexicans—"who coveted it as a seasoning for their bean stews."[4] This perception reflected the missionaries' beliefs that Mexicans did not understand either nutrition or food safety and were unable to control their desires.

In 1908, an advertisement for the Post cereal company disguised as a *New York Times* letter to the editor sought to capitalize on nativist fears about Mexican food to promote its products. The anonymous writer reveals, "After about thirteen years in Mexico, where I was on a Mexican diet into which coffee and greasy food enter largely, I found that everything I ate distressed me. Nervous breakdown with pain in the heart caused me to give up mental work. After trying various stomach remedies without benefit, I found relief, at last, by eating Grape Nuts and cream."[5] The cereal corporation's tactic helped lay the foundation for future Americanizing projects that relied on food as a proxy for nationalism.[6]

Like the founders of Indian boarding schools that came before them, leaders of the Americanization movement, which emerged in the 1910s as a national effort to assimilate recent immigrants, recognized the power of food as a tool for homogenizing cultural identity and compelling conformity. Teacher Alfred White explains why Americanizers set their sights on young immigrants instead of their parents.

"The children of these foreigners are the advantage to America, not the foreigners. They are not 100 percent American but their children may be."[7] Americanizers put their faith in the power of "reverse socialization," where children influence their parents, teaching them new skills and attitudes, an approach that turns the traditional understanding of the parent-child relationship on its head.

California Americanizers zeroed in on Mexican newcomers after immigration laws severely restricted Asian immigrants.[8] In the early twentieth century, millions of peasants in Mexico lost their land rights. The violence of the 1910–20 Mexican Revolution inspired many workers to look for opportunities in the more politically stable United States,[9] and World War I created new industries to support the war effort and led to shifts in the labor market. Open immigration policies sought to fill gaps in the agricultural and domestic labor force. Mexican immigration to the U.S. increased by 300 percent between 1910 and 1930, with 10 percent of the Mexican population heading north. Many of these newcomers were poor. After arriving in the U.S., they moved into overcrowded neighborhoods with scarce and overburdened resources.

Seeing these newcomers as a monolithic group that they feared would reject American values and habits,[10] nativists deemed this turn of events "the Mexican problem." Mexicans' racial status was, and still is, unclear. White people saw them as somewhere between Spanish and Indian, not Black or white. Organized labor feared competition from the new workforce. Stereotypes labeling Mexicans as uneducated, unsanitary, docile, lazy, sinister, unpatriotic, and overly fertile supported Americanization programs. American Studies scholar George J. Sanchez provides an example of a typical nativist perspective, published in the 1928 *Saturday Evening Post*, describing Los Angeles's "endless streets crowded with the shacks of illiterate, diseased, pauperized Mexicans, taking no interest whatever in the community, living constantly on the ragged edge of starvation."[11]

To tackle the issue, California funded two major Americanization programs, one aimed at Mexican girls and one at their mothers. The primary instructional materials, Amanda Matthews Chase's 1918 *Primer for Foreign-Speaking Women* and Ellis's later *Americanization*

*Through Homemaking*, offer excruciatingly detailed directions on how to create lessons in English, democracy, and proper domesticity for Mexican women. Nativists positioned these programs as a lifeline for Mexican children. "Shall the children of Mexican immigrants—children who will grow up to be American citizens—be reared in shacks, without adequate home care, without play facilities, without protection from habitations which are infected with tubercle bacilli, without proper nutrition, without being safe-guarded from the vices lurking in dark alleys and streets?"

The California 1915 Home Teacher Act brought a cadre of mostly white, well-off women into Mexican homes in a crusade to create and control a new class of patriotic service workers. "John and Mary might come to school breakfastless, dirty, half blind, and troubled with adenoids, and we did not feel that we could do anything about it,"[12] complains Commission of Immigration and Housing representative Chase at a joint session of the National Congress of Mothers and Oakland's Parent Teacher Association in 1915. "It was not that sympathetic teachers did not view these conditions with sorrow, and with the realization that John and Mary's minds were hampered thereby. It was only that dealing with such matters was not considered a legitimate part of school activity."[13]

Chase's choice of the names John and Mary to represent the Mexican children she describes is an interesting one. Perhaps she surmised that these names would evoke more empathy from her audience.[14] "Little by little we have made John and Mary's bodies our concern—their recreation, their home life, everything about them. We will probably find still more to do for them in the future—nor can we do too much."[15]

Chase advocated greater intrusion into Mexican homes, departing from the Americanizers' credo of children influencing their parents. "Heretofore the cry has been 'Americanize the children and they will Americanize the home!'" But Chase had lost faith in this approach's potential, pointing to its reversal of the parent-child role. "This topsy-turvy method flies in the face of natural social evolution. What it has brought into the home is confusion and often disaster, since un-Americanized parents lose control over their Americanized children who consequently are liable to fall into lawless ways and frequently bring up as delinquents before the Juvenile Court."

Chase's answer to this problem was to reach even further into Mexican immigrants' homes and families. "The fault does not lie in giving the children too much education, but in dividing the family against itself by bestowing too little on its other members. . . . The immigrant mother . . . has been left almost entirely out of account. We have ignored the natural home-maker and yet tried to Americanize the home." It was not too late to make up for that oversight. "We now see our error and are undertaking here in California to educate the entire family instead of discriminating against that important member, the mother."

Acknowledging that the Home Teacher Act does not specify instructors' gender, Chase still insists that "it seems natural to speak of the home teacher as feminine since most of the activity outlined is such as would naturally be assigned to women." But male teachers also have a role to play in this assimilation project. They are "naturally" suited to "finding out where the men and boys spend their evenings and their money—whether or not and why the saloon is the pleasantest spot in the district—dealing with men's lodging houses and rendering other valuable service along lines not practicable to women—connecting every abiding place with the school."

It takes special skills to be a home teacher. "The home teacher, like the family doctor and the family pastor, is to be a real and intimate possession of the family." This requires a calling. "May she be endowed with wisdom and grace to be worthy of this high phase of her profession and may she emulate doctor and pastor in her sense of the sacredness of confidence." The home teacher must also be discreet and hold herself back from the racist remarks that she would otherwise make to her colleagues. "She must refrain from making the morning's experiences the theme of racy, gossiping narratives to entertain her friends or fellow workers." She must police her language at all times. "She will, surely, never use the word 'slum' and will be chary of the word 'case.'" Here, Chase puts herself in the shoes of one of the mothers she intends to subject to the program. "We would not like to be 'cases,' not even to the angels of Heaven, nor would we appreciate hearing those same angels refer to their earthward flights as 'slumming expeditions.'"

In addition to making home visits, Chase's protegees set up "school cottages" to show Mexican mothers how they should run and furnish their homes. If constructing a cottage was not possible, "its equivalent in housekeeping rooms within the school building" was acceptable. "This must be a model American home, small but complete, attractive, but simple and inexpensive." Although it was not advisable for the home teacher to live there full time because of the need to "keep in human touch with the outside world . . . she should be distinctly a hostess, welcoming the mothers as into her own home."

Cooking in the school cottage is a specialized skill that sometimes requires an expert to help the regular home teacher. "The cooking taught in the 'real kitchen' of the cottage should be confined to simple wholesome dishes. About once a month each cooking class should jointly prepare a complete dinner, set it forth on a white table cloth with flowers in the center of the table and partake of the feast. Yet nothing must be too fine and elaborate for home copying." Chase's insistence on making lessons simple to follow reflects her belief that many adult foreigners "are illiterate in their own tongue."

The cottage also doubles as a "miniature grocery store where brisk trading is carried on." Mexican mothers in the cottage must do their cooking, sewing, singing, and weaving in English. Stooping to her audience's level, "the Home Teacher must recognize and appeal to the dramatic spirit of a play folk." She will also attempt to arouse feelings of nostalgia, allowing the mothers to "feel almost as if they had enjoyed an afternoon back in the far lands from which they came." Chase seems unaware of the fact that Mexico borders California and is really not that far at all.

The course curriculum, laid out in Chase's *Primer*, consists of four progressive series of ten lessons. The first lesson concentrates on "household objects and actions" and culminates in "the purchase of staples at a grocery store." By acclimatizing Mexican mothers to American grocery stores and the canon of American foods, home teachers aimed to fashion them into good consumers. The series culminates in a play store where "each pupil of the group must be able to make purchases in English." This unit requires the teacher to have specialized knowledge. "The teacher should know the market prices of groceries and compare with what pupils are paying to see if they are being cheated. In presenting the lessons the real prices should be used to familiarize the mothers with actual values." In the second series, participants graduate to a simulated dry goods store.

Each lesson comes with English vocabulary. Mothers learn the phrases, "I cook. I wash, I sweep. I mop." They learn the words for staples such as "water, milk, bread, meat, beans" and utensils—plate, knife, fork, spoon—and some basic exchanges: "Can you cook? Yes, I can cook;" "I want a pound of butter. I want half a pound of tea. . . . How much are eggs today?" The lessons also celebrate the joys of consumerism. "I am happy. I have money. I go to the store."

Fruits and vegetables appear late in the program, along with some recommendations and prohibitions: "Fruit is good for us. It helps us to keep well. I will buy fruit to eat. I will give it to my children. Beer and wine are very bad for children. Tea and coffee are bad for children. Milk is good for children. Cocoa is good for children."

Beyond naming foods, the lessons tackle preparation. "The lessons can show new and better ways of cooking staples already in the [mother]s' possession. For instance, there are families who always fry their potatoes and know nothing of boiling and baking them.

"Another important aim is to enlarge the diet by the addition of common fruits and vegetables prepared in simple, wholesome ways. How many families in a foreign district ever bake apples? Investigation will show many surprising lacks."[16]

Families must eat the right foods at the right time in the right way. "I cook eggs and coffee on the stove for our breakfast. We eat oranges for breakfast. We do not cook oranges. We eat our food from our plates and cut our food with a knife. We drink coffee from a cup. I put sugar in my coffee. . . . Children drink milk for breakfast. . . . We eat our food at meal times. We eat three meals a day. We call our meals breakfast, dinner and supper. We buy our food at the grocery store and the market."[17]

By the fourth series of the lessons, families are ready for the heart of the matter: patriotism. "I love the American flag. It is my flag now. I love its stars and stripes. This flag gives us protection and liberty. My husband honors it. We teach our children to love the flag. *Salute.* This is my flag. It stands for my country; I will love my flag and be true to my country as long as I live."[18] Finally, the lessons progress to hygiene: "We must bathe often. We must sleep with our windows open. We must not stay in the house all the time."

Dietitian Bertha M. Wood, author of the 1922 cookbook *Foods of the Foreign-Born in Relation to Health*, has a more open-minded, if lukewarm, assessment of Mexican cuisine. "Mexicans eat beans, rice, potatoes, peas, and all sorts of vegetables. The chili, or pepper, is often considered a sacred plant which furnishes health to those who eat it. Therefore it is found in many of their dishes. They still prepare their food largely as they did in Mexico. . . . they eat less meat than Americans eat, and generally it is mixed with vegetables and well cooked. When not too highly seasoned, Mexican dishes are very tasty."[19] Wood encourages institutions to incorporate foreign dishes into their menus to help ease immigrants into an American diet without alienating them.

Nonetheless, Wood identifies problems with the Mexican diet. "During the winter, when vegetables are scarce, their food is limited almost entirely to beans, rice and potatoes, using a little meat when they can afford it. Such a diet abounds in starch and has too little protein and mineral matters, thereby causing stomach troubles of all kinds." Also, "The diabetic must be furnished with dishes that have no rice in them. This is difficult, as rice is used in many combinations with other foods." And "clean milk . . . is not always easy to procure. Rice and oatmeal are the cereals most commonly used. These are boiled in water, with milk added when nearly done. They are eaten as a thick gruel instead of with cold milk poured over them as we have them." Even so, Wood believes that Mexican mothers are receptive to change. "Any nurse or dietician can persuade them to use cereals or baked or boiled fish and meats or vegetables, if they gradually reduce the amount of tomato or pepper for flavor until it becomes a bland dish, easier to digest and not harmful to the kidneys."

Wood even concedes that "In some ways . . . their foods are superior to ours, and by making adjustments, if they do not acquire some of our bad habits, there ought to come from their dietary a sensible, economical, and nourishing group of foods. Only lack of variety and the use of hot flavors keep their food from being superior to that of most Americans."

Taking a different tack in *Americanization Through Homemaking*, Ellis warns of the far-reaching dangers of Mexican diets. "Efficient brain power is not found in an undernourished people. Nowhere is this better illustrated than in a Mexican community in a year when the supply of cheap labor exceeds the demand. Men congregate in idle groups. The severe strain falls on the housewife, who deals out sustenance to each member of her family from her meager and disappearing supply of food stuffs. The crisis comes. The pangs of hunger are accelerators of criminal tendencies. Forgery or stealing follows. The head of the family lands in jail. The rest of the family are helpless, and soon become county charges. Property owners pay the taxes for their maintenance."[20]

Ellis tries to protect these property owners from the peril of higher taxes by diluting Mexican diets, thereby making Mexican people look and act more like white people. Failing this, Mexican women could become good nannies, cooks, cleaners, and food service workers. Americanizers considered them easier to mold than Mexican men, "more easily educated." In "'Go After the Women,'" George J. Sanchez explains why Americanizers had no compunction about targeting women, since they perceived them as victims of Mexican machismo. They believed that Americanization would give Mexican mothers "the best end of the bargain by the changing of relationships between men and women . . . under the new American order."[21]

If Mexican women refused to adapt, programs aimed at schoolgirls could transform their households even faster. Ellis implores, "The efforts of Neighborhood Houses and charitable organizations furnish relief for the time being and deal with adults, who for the most part are unchangeable. Our main hope lies in the rising generation, and the public school is the greatest factor in its development. Since the girls are potential mothers and homemakers, they will control, in a large measure, the destinies of their future families."[22]

Ellis generously sees Mexican girls as capable of absorbing her lessons, despite her low estimation of their intellects. "It is not expected that the average Mexican girl in our elementary school can comprehend chemical terms as applied to household science but we can teach her a general knowledge of foods for regulating, building, and furnishing energy to the body, also the methods of preparing, cooking, and serving them." Wood also adheres to cultural stereotypes. "They are not a people who love academic work, but they enjoy any educational training which develops the use of their hands. Their interest lies largely in music, flowers, and the arts."[23]

Ellis views nutrition education as fundamental to Americanization because "Mexican families are malnourished, not so much from a lack of food but from lacking the right varieties of foods containing constituents favorable to growth and development."[24] Wood agrees. "Undernourished and malnourished children are frequently found in Mexican families. They are served with the same foods as the adults, foods highly spiced, with a large amount of fat added, or corn meal fried in fat. Bland foods are quite unknown in their dietary."[25]

Wood blames high rates of infant mortality in the Mexican community on nutritional ignorance, overlooking factors like limited access to medical care and language barriers. "Infant mortality is always high among the Mexicans in both city and rural districts and this is no doubt entirely a matter of feeding and bathing. Most babies are breast fed, especially during the first few months, but in addition to the milk Mexican mothers generally insist on feeding the children heavier foods as soon as they will begin to take them."

"Very small infants are taught to eat frijoles or beans, and when the melons begin to ripen, the babies are stuffed with cantaloupes and watermelons. During the summer, and especially during the hottest months, infant mortality increases by leaps and bounds. If the babies can be put on milk diets under the care of a visiting nurse, they seem to do quite well, although it is necessary for the nurse to repeat her instructions many times."

Wood fears that combining Mexican and American food habits will harm Americans. "When the Mexicans intermarry with Americans, the result of the cross dietary is that often there is double the amount of fat taken at the meal by the American. The Mexicans put their fat *into* the food, while the American puts his *on* the food. Therefore if he eats bread and butter, or potatoes with butter and green peppers fried in oil and rice, he is getting more fat than a Mexican would get. He would eat his bread without butter, and would not eat potato and butter with peppers and rice. As the Mexicans come north or intermarry, it would be better for the children and adults to learn to eat the simpler foods of the American people, boiled or baked, with less spice or fat."

Ellis provides a tutorial on proper nutrition. She begins by breaking down four overlapping but distinct categories of foods: "(I) body regulators (water and minerals), (II) body builders (water, fruits, vegetables, cereals, eggs, and milk), (III) body regulators and energy givers (1. Carbohydrates—sugar, cereals, root vegetables, starchy foods 2. Fats—cream, milk, butter, oil from meats 3. Protein—eggs, milk, beef, cheese, legumes, fish), and (IV) Vitamines (A, B, C, and D as well as foods rich in iron, particularly in a child's second year)."[26] She then offers six soup recipes using milk, before providing pages of dessert recipes—for ice cream, oatmeal cookies, pumpkin pie filling, lemon pudding, sponge cake, jellies, candies, stuffed fruit, fudge, creams, taffy, and panocha—an outdated English word for molasses candy that also happens to be Spanish slang for "vulva."

Taking on the most important meal of the day, the school lunch, Ellis illustrates its significance with a full-page picture of a smiling boy clutching a lunch box captioned "This Boy Has a Good Lunch, Is Happy and Well-kept." He also "ranks well in his lessons." The connection between diet and morality is reinforced with a section titled "Nutrition and Crime." Despite Mexicans' almost inevitable criminal tendencies, Ellis believes that if "we can teach the girls food values and a careful system of budgeting; how to plan in prosperity for the day of no income and adversity, we shall avoid much of the trouble mentioned here, in the future. Children will not come to school then with no breakfast."

The burden falling on Mexican girls goes well beyond the kitchen. "Employers maintain that a man with a home and family is more dependable and less revolutionary in his tendencies. Thus the influence of the home extends to labor problems and to many other problems in the social regime. The homekeeper creates the atmosphere, whether it be one of harmony and cooperation or of dissatisfaction and revolt. It is to be remembered that the dispositions, once angelic, become very much marred with incorrect diet and resultant digestive disturbances." Ellis's analysis aligns with the interests of employers who advocated for Americanization programs as a method to discipline and control Mexican workers.

To help Mexican girls shoulder this weighty responsibility, Ellis suggests a Christmas dinner project. The occasion will consist of "pleasant conversation in English" between the girls. In one variation of the assignment, "the girls entertain the boys of their class." Ellis also recommends teaching Mexican girls the art of table service. This is important to do at school because "the background of the American and that of the Mexican girl differ. The former has learned the little courtesies of table etiquette in the home, but the latter, who may not have had a table in the home, must obtain her knowledge in the school room." Ellis's observation may have sprung from the reports of home teachers who visited poor families in shelters where two-by-fours stood in for tables, shelves, and beds.[27]

Ellis goes into painstaking detail about table settings and their functions. "The knife is used to cut and spread food. The fork is used to pick up and transport food. Nearly all foods should be eaten with a fork. The spoon is used to stir liquids and transport softer foods to the mouth. . . . The glass holds pure water, which should not be gulped down but drunk quietly and slowly. The napkin serves to protect the clothes of the individual."[28] The ideal hostess has emotional, as well as practical, responsibilities. "Conversation should be within the comprehension of every member of the table. If it lags or becomes controversial the hostess should lead it away from boring or exciting subjects. . . .

She should steer away from all embarrassing subjects." Ellis does not provide a list of these.

This home training would also be useful for future employment. "Mexican girls need a great deal of training in serving and table etiquette, as being a waitress may be their method of obtaining a livelihood. Sloppy appearance and uncleanliness of person would not be tolerated in a waitress and would be the cause of no position or of losing one already obtained."

Arizona cities Tucson, Yuma, and Phoenix ran evening Americanization programs labeled "The Mother's Club." They offered mothers an opportunity to get out of the house, deposit their children at the door with a day care worker, then enjoy free snacks—in exchange for listening to Americanization lessons.[29] In El Paso, Texas, the Women's Missionary Society set up a settlement house to introduce Mexican women to new foods in a "cooking class, where merry girls made pies quite "'good enough to eat'"—to satisfy the growing demand of the men in their homes for "American cooking."[30] The missionaries set out to remove all obstacles to their subjects' Americanization. "'I can't cook that way,' said a mother, 'I haven't any stove.' 'We'll fix that,' said the boys. And they came from their work that night, carrying an American stove on their shoulders."

Consuelo Lerma, who was born in New Mexico, worked for the Home Education Livelihood Program, a state-sponsored Americanization program that taught sewing skills to the wives of *braceros*, seasonal agricultural workers, and other migrants in the 1950s. Despite the focus on sewing, food played an integral part in the program. At Thanksgiving, Lerma taught her students how to stuff turkeys, prepare dressing, and bake lemon and pecan pies. In return, the wives taught her how to make tamales. "They made sweet tamales, which I had never eaten, and they used sugar, and raisins, and pineapple, a can of pineapple. They were delicious for breakfast, for coffee. I had to buy the masa already ready. They were really good.

"When I would go and knock on doors in the morning, they would, the *braceros*, some of them, would come home for lunch, and I could smell the girls making these homemade tortillas, corn tortillas, and everybody was fixing lunch. If I'd go knocking doors between 10:00 AM and 11:30 AM, I could smell their *sopa de arroz* cooking and their food. And in the summer, they used to have corn.

"They invited me, so when my supervisor walked in, I'm sitting, eating corn on the cob. (laughs). Then she says, 'Now, Mrs. Lerma, it's not, this is not the policy . . . you don't eat any of their food, because you could get sick.' I said, 'Sick? Those are boiling.' I started talking back to her, and she started laughing, 'I know this taste good, but it's the policy, you don't eat food in their house.'"[31] Lerma knew the food was fine and wouldn't make her sick, but she had to stop eating it to keep her job.

Americanization programs existed in a bubble far from reality and did not, by their own standards, succeed.[32] Their underlying goals were to teach their targets "the fundamental principles of the American system of government and the rights and duties of citizenship."[33] But poverty frustrated their mission. Their efforts fell short in the face of the lived realities of immigrants crowded into communities with few resources to support the changes to domestic practices that home teachers prescribed.

Instead of assimilating, fewer Mexican immigrants chose to naturalize during this period. They remained politically loyal to Mexico. Mexican communities grew and sustained their culture and language. Mexican women entered the workforce, because they had to, not because they wanted to. Americanizers assumed that newly educated mothers would and could embrace food habits that would hasten their families' journeys to become real Americans. But Mexican mothers and daughters could not control the price of food or their access to it.


"IF A MEXICAN woman had a bushel of money she would still feed those kids tortillas and beans."[34] This reprimand, offered at a hearing to decide whether the federal government should create a program to meet the nutritional needs of poor women, children, and infants, was key to winning over skeptics. (A similarly successful argument that helped decide in favor of the legislation attacked Black women's fondness for grits). That it was patently incorrect went unnoticed—tortillas and beans form a complete protein and are an excellent source of nutrition.[35]

This was the Special Supplemental Nutrition Program for Women, Infants, and Children (WIC), which launched in 1974 and gives participants vouchers or checks every month to purchase specific foods intended to enrich their diets, including tortillas and beans. The assumption that WIC would serve mainly Black and Latina women led to some of the program's more bizarre—and degrading—components, among them an unnecessary physical examination by a doctor to diagnose whether they are at "nutritional risk."[36] (SNAP, the USDA's other program that provides food assistance to households based on income levels, does not require participants to jump through these kinds of hoops.)

About 42 percent of WIC users are Latina, although Latina mothers only make up roughly 18.5 percent of the U.S. population.[37] The belief that Latinas are ignorant about proper diets persists, fifty years after the program's inception, keeping it palatable to policymakers and justifying food restrictions that steer participants toward subsidized commodities.

Narrowing WIC users' choices to non-organic, low-end products (including low-end baby formula) forces participants to select foods that contain higher amounts of corn syrup and soybean oil.[38] Similarly to the Food Distribution Program on Indian Reservations, WIC's restrictions allow the USDA to use the program to get rid of commodity surpluses. Its offerings support agricultural interests but hurt the people who the program claims to serve. When an infant formula shortage hit in 2022, WIC's strict limitations on formula choice left many families without any means to feed their babies when the brand endorsed by their state became unavailable.

Latine households also receive SNAP benefits in large numbers, but these numbers should be higher.[39] Only half of Latine SNAP-eligible households participate in the program, and even fewer eligible noncitizen households participate. More than four million food-insecure Latine households don't or can't take advantage of the program. Some people fear that accessing public benefits will affect their immigration status, a concern that the Trump administration justified with its public charge inadmissibility rule, which denied entry to immigrants deemed likely to rely on public benefits. Although the rule became inactive in 2019, its specter continues to loom large. Some eligible people don't participate because they stumble over the complex SNAP forms and can't get help.

The USDA's control over the foods that WIC and SNAP offer does not make recipients healthier, although when they are allowed to spend their benefits at farmer's markets, they buy more nutritious foods.[40] Latine households that don't depend on USDA nutrition programs have better diets and health outcomes.[41] Corporate profits rather than health considerations play a significant role in shaping USDA nutrition.

BEYOND AMERICANIZATION PROGRAMS, public schools have functioned as a site for policing Mexican children's diets. In Rudolfo Anaya's 1972 novel about a Mexican boy adapting to life in New Mexico, *Bless Me, Ultima*, Antonio recounts his experience in his new school. "At noon we opened our lunches to eat. Miss Maestas left the room and a high school girl came and sat at the desk while we ate. My mother had packed a small jar of hot beans and some good, green chile wrapped in tortillas. When the other children saw my lunch they laughed and pointed again. Even the high school girl laughed. They showed me their sandwiches which were made of bread."[42]

Thirty years later, schoolgirl Lara was subjected to food that repelled her at free lunch. First she learned that being in an ESL classroom meant that everyone, including her teacher, assumed she got free lunch.[43] The label and stigma stuck. "Even when you moved out of the ESL program . . . people associate you with the program." The free lunches disgusted her. "Milk is not a drink in Mexico . . . you don't eat milk with your food. You don't! You would eat milk in the morning with platanos. . . . But never, ever with your food. You only drink milk [in the morning] or at nighttime before you go to bed."

Jorge brought his mother's food to school but wished he didn't. "My

mom used to send me to school with tacos. Basically they were flour
tortillas and my mom would make an omelet with beans, and eggs, or
sometimes chorizo, or sometimes *papas*. Three or four small little tacos,
in a Rainbow Bread plastic bag . . . I don't remember having a back-
pack. . . . But what I remember is being embarrassed that . . . one—I
had Mexican food, and two—that I had it in a Rainbow—Bread—
plastic—bag. . . . Because all the kids, the thing with the white kids, if
they had paper bags, they were like these classic, brown paper bags,
but most of them had lunch pails. The big thing was lunch pails . . .
like Superman, or Spiderman, or the girls had different characters. . . .
I remember eating, trying to hide it, eat my food in one corner, and not
get too much attention.

"I wanted to be part of these group of kids—white English-speaking
kids. . . . I wanted the peanut butter and jelly, I wanted the bologna
sandwich. So at some point between 3rd and 6th grade, I had nothing to do with the Mexican food. . . . I remember the total driving of
school . . . was to become American . . . the way I interpreted it . . . one
was not to speak Spanish . . . and in the other area was that I wanted to
bring bologna sandwiches."

Children learn to change their tastes and habits as a social survival
strategy, and American food is a more affordable status symbol than
brand-name clothing or accessories. Rejecting traditional foods in
favor of U.S. favorites can offer a shortcut up the school social ladder, but it can also wreak havoc at home. "I try to prepare something
healthy at night because my kids eat poorly at school. Yes, my kids
prefer *chatarra*"—trash—"but at home I can control it: I don't let them
eat it."[44] "At school they give the kids pizza, Yoggie's, Macaroni Cheese,
that is that quick pasta, and that is where it gets hard, because we have
the children used to home cooked food, but then the American food
is at school."[45] "School food isn't nutritional at all, you know? So, they
spend a lot of time at school, of course they get used . . . to what they
get at school, more than at home. School food is basically comida
chatarra."

Lady struggled with the change in her son's eating habits, complaining that he became "really picky here. He won't eat the same

things he ate in Colombia. He used to eat fruits and veggies and here, nothing . . . I can't get him to eat the same things. I guess it's the taste that's different. He used to eat meat in Colombia, but he won't touch it here, and he does eat chicken but not like in Colombia. His appetite changed. . . . I am bringing my child to the doctor because his appetite has decreased and he won't eat Colombian food. All he wants is pizza or a hamburger. In Colombia, he did not know what that was—only on rare occasion did he eat that. At school, he has to eat lunch there and so he won't eat the food at home, only American food."[46] Unhealthy snacks meant to supplement school lunches can also cause problems. "Kids aren't eating their school lunches, and I think it is because snacks are sold. If they were eliminated, kids would eat the food."[47]

"My son who goes to school does not want Mexican food. He wants American style foods. He wants sandwiches, macaroni and cheese, hamburgers, and fried potatoes."[48] This can lead to double cooking duty. "They asked me to prepare meals that they eat at school, and I prepare different meals for them. I have to give him the same meals that are prepared at school. I prepare Mexican style soup, and he does not like it. He wants to eat sausage and ham. He does not like the meals I prepare. Sometimes I cook meat soup, or what we call cocido, and I cook it just as I did in Mexico, with potatoes and carrots, but my children only eat the meat and not the juices (spicy stock), carrots, or the potatoes." "Only my husband and I eat Mexican food, and my kids eat American food."

THE STANDARD AMERICAN diet is very familiar to some Latine immigrants:[49] American imperialism has exported fast and unhealthy food that infiltrates other countries' diets[50] with an endless supply of cheap, ultra-processed junk foods. But still, low-income immigrants report a sharp decline in their diets after moving to the U.S. A 2013 study of a low-income Spanish-speaking neighborhood listed the most frequently purchased food items as malt beverages, sugary cold cereals, sugary drinks, fruit drinks, instant ramen noodles, and salami.[51] Another study found that Latine immigrants eat "fewer complex carbohydrates and more simple sugars, fat, white sliced bread, vegetable salad, mayonnaise, flour tortillas, sweetened beverages, snacks, sweets, and meats."[52] The top five foods consumed by Latine children who live in a household with at least one U.S.-born person are soda, low-fat milk, pizza, ketchup, and white bread. That, in a nutshell, is the standard American diet (also known as SAD).

The dietary acculturation that makes immigrant diets decline rapidly after arrival in the United States often stems from time and budget constraints.[53] U.S. work norms and demands steal the time that would make healthy eating possible. "The problem here is that there is more work than life."[54] "All I do is work. . . . I leave at 6:00 am and get home at 3:30 and start housework. I don't have anyone else to help us with the house chores. In Colombia, my job was to take care of the kids. I did not have to worry about what to make for dinner or about laundry because someone else would always help me. . . . Here I have to work and do everything else all by myself."[55]

"In Mexico (women) did not have to work, but here you have to work. Because of this, sometimes you have to buy easy things to give to the children. You arrive from work tired. In Mexico, you attended to your kids more. Here there is not time."[56] "I look for the quickest thing. . . . One has to work until four, five, six o'clock in the afternoon. In my country (Nicaragua), we ate three meals at specific times of day; here this has all fallen to the side because of the system of work."

"I had a lot of time to dedicate to cooking, sewing, to preparing the food for the family. Here, everything has changed. Work has changed everything." "A person has to work twelve, fourteen, fifteen hours, not just to support his family in the U.S. but also to send money to his home country. We do not enjoy the benefits of a citizen or resident, who has health insurance; we have to save money. The Hispanic is forced to work sixteen hours, more than normal, and this results in neglect of the family life."

This new life can have a profound impact on family relationships and gender roles. "There have been some changes, such as my husband does the cooking now. He barbecues a lot of meat and fish."[57] "I still do most of the cooking, but my husband helps me out during the week when I am working. He feeds the family." Many Latino immigrant men eat less healthily than women:[58] some claim that food is simply not their department;[59] others blame the power of fast-food advertising. Even when men know that dietary changes would be good for their health, there is resistance because they consider dieting to be something that is only for women.

The American idealization of thinness can also cause Mexican women to eat less than they did back home, even though the idea that everyone should be skinny is unrealistic, unhealthy, and incompatible with the standard American diet.[60] Eugenia Delgado, who left Mexico for Minnesota, gained seventy pounds during her first two years in the United States. "In Mexico, you walk," she said. "Now, I only walk to the garage and then I get to the store and I'm looking for the closest parking and I don't want to walk no more. We got lazy here."[61] Eugenia is far from lazy. She works long shifts at a food processing plant, so convenience often wins over cooking. When she works the 2 a.m. to 2 p.m. shift, she leaves work exhausted.

Immigrants also experience profound changes in food quality after they cross the border. Elena, the Columbian mother separated from her daughter in Patricia Engel's novel, *Infinite Country*, heard horror stories before she began her journey north. "Before they left for Texas people warned Elena everyone gets fat in the north. Chemicals replace natural ingredients, so bread is not bread by the time one eats it. Meat from hormone-reared animals, mutant produce, colorful and rotund yet flavorless. Where fresh was expensive, and cheap was a tasty poison packaged as a meal."[62]

The differences are striking. "Food is artificial here. Fruits in the U.S. do not have flavor or aroma. Milk and butter here are not milk and butter."[63] "In my country (El Salvador) there was less food, but the food we had contained more 'proteins,' it was more nutritious, because it was more natural." "In the food stores in Mexico, you can find everything fresh, just made. I think that everything has preservatives here, well more in frozen foods. When we go to Mexico, we take with us some frozen foods because it is effortless. People here live their life hurrying. It is much easier to buy frozen foods and cook them in the microwave, so they will have more time to get ready for the next day. In Mexico, it is not like that."[64]

"We are accustomed to eating fresh foods rather than canned. I want to prepare foods the way I like them, but here, everything is canned." "Everything was fresh; we had no need for the refrigerator, not even for the meats." "That's the good thing about Mexico ... you may be poor but the nopales are more natural. The fruit that we eat is fresher than here."[65]

Household budgets, shaped by factors like employment opportunities, housing affordability, and social welfare programs, probably have the biggest impact on food choice, and processed junk food is cheaper than healthier options. "Here it is expensive to eat healthy; the cheap foods make a person fat."[66] "We ate seafood in Mexico, but here it's expensive. [The biggest influence] is usually about price."[67] On the other hand, in the U.S. "the meat is much less expensive than in Mexico, although it is still quite expensive. In Mexico, we used to eat a lot of vegetables and meat only once or twice a week. Here, we eat meat almost daily."[68]

As Tere notes, "I head to the supermarket and check the prices and say, 'this is cheap and easy, I am going to buy this.'" "Most of the times we don't make enough money so we go find what is cheap and you all know that fruits and vegetables are not cheap so sometimes we can't afford to buy them."[69] "It is difficult—fruits and vegetables don't make you feel full, so if I have to spend $1 to buy an apple I rather spend that $1 in a hamburger, is the same price but the hamburger makes you feel full."

Lady, after three years in the U.S., relies mostly on the food that her neighborhood stores stock. "Some things are expensive in some stores and you have to go to other stores but sometimes you don't have a ride or car."[70] Some families use SNAP to increase their food choices. "In my country people eat what they can afford: potatoes, eggs, beans, and rice. Mexicans live off of these. Here in the U.S., the government helps you if you can't afford to buy your own food."[71] Government support can also make foods that people ate back home only on special occasions, like tamales at Christmas, available and affordable year-round.

The "festival foods hypothesis" offers another explanation for why some immigrants' diets and health decline in the U.S.[72]

Fast-food restaurants, sites of family celebrations back home, are easier and cheaper to access in the U.S. "Here, I eat a lot of burgers and fries. I usually eat at several of the local fast-food places. I like them a lot, but I know that they have plenty of fat, and generally, after I eat them, I feel sick. I feel better when I eat other kinds of meals."[73] "My kids ask me for hamburgers, so I take them to a fast food restaurant."[74] "Because of the kids . . . It is what they want to eat, or pizza, it is fast, and we can take it home."

Sometimes food produced in the United States is less healthy than the same food is in other countries. For example, the way U.S. dairies process milk triggers lactose intolerance for many Latine consumers.[75]

Lard, which is widely used in Mexico, has a bad reputation in the U.S. "It's hard because of my culture, I've always been told that cooking with lard is good because it adds flavor to our food, and then they try to tell me that is not good and that I have to switch to oils. It is difficult to make this change happen."[76] "I can't imagine cooking with oils instead of butter or lard. For example, if I cook charro beans with oils I'd have to use the whole bottle; if not, you know that it wouldn't have any flavor." Conversely, food deemed healthy is often bland or boring for Mexican palates. "Simple steamed chicken, without oil or anything, vegetables with few spices and rice. Vegetables that have no fat or seasoning and more vegetables than tortilla."[77]

Back home, immigrants might have grown herbs and vegetables in their gardens and shared with their neighbors. These types of ingredients, which provide flavor, are almost impossible to find in the U.S. because they are not mass-produced or exported.

The shopping experience also dictates consumption. Corner stores, liquor stores, dollar stores, and cheap supermarkets offer a profoundly different experience from the outdoor markets common in Mexico. Shopping in the U.S. is less of a social activity, and farmers' markets, where they exist, primarily serve wealthy white communities.[78] Outside of cities, healthy food sources can be insurmountable distances away. Signs advertising farm stands may only be in English.

Generally, grocery shopping is a time-consuming activity that must be done weekly, not daily. "For me the hardest part is when we shop for 10 or 15 days, you know that fruits and vegetables don't last that long so we don't buy them."[79] "We go shopping every two weeks and fruits and vegetables won't last that long, so I consume fruits and vegetables for the first couple of days after going grocery shopping, but after that I don't." Sterile plastic packaging offers no way to judge or enjoy the smell, feel, and taste of food. To substitute for this visceral experience, food corporations spend billions on packaging and marketing to make their products look appealing.

IN ONE STUDY, Latine Americans perceived as white self-report having excellent or very good health compared to those perceived as Latine.[80] This suggests that racism is a direct cause of poor nutrition, whether it operates through fewer opportunities, a more difficult climb up the social ladder, or biased health care and treatment. In response, food activists have called for a reclaiming of their ancestors' healthy eating habits. Advocating for a defiant return to Latine dietary roots, the *Decolonize Your Diet* manifesto reminds readers of the spiritual and health benefits of ancestral food consumption. This return can be simple yet meaningful. "Cooking a pot of beans from scratch is a microrevolutionary act that honors our ancestors and the generations to come."[81]

To counter food oppression, Mexican feminist activist La Loba Loca shares *abuelita* knowledge, "bodies of knowledge that have been oppressed, stolen, silenced, gone underground, hidden themselves in between spice jars in kitchen cabinets, locked away but remembered and restored when necessary."[82] Jenny Silva, Malinalli Superfoods co-owner, draws on the spirit of the Chicano *rasquache*, the underdog, as inspiration for her business selling traditional remedies in East Los Angeles. "We are bringing back this health to our communities because there are no health stores near us." She seeks to dispel the myth, common even in her community, that Latine health food is a contradiction in terms.

Indigenous activists in Mexico have led food resistance movements that may spill over into the U.S. Through 1994's North American Free Trade Agreement, U.S. food companies gained unrestricted access to Mexico, sparking a massive increase in obesity and diabetes diagnoses.[83] To combat this, in the summer of 2020, Indigenous people in Oaxaca used a blockade they had originally constructed to keep their communities safe from Covid-19 to block trucks loaded up with junk food.[84]

The state governments of Oaxaca and Tabasco followed these activists' lead by banning sales of junk food and sugary drinks to minors. State legislators sought to put food decisions into the hands of parents and caretakers.[85] Next, the Federal Senate passed the Ley Chatarra, prohibiting junk food in school meals and for sale near schools in stores or vending machines. The Ley Chatarra also requires a new front-of-package warning system that highlights the health effects of processed foods high in sugars, calories, salt, and saturated and trans fats.[86]

At a World Trade Organization meeting in August 2020, the United States, in concert with nine food industry groups, urged Mexico to delay implementing the Ley Chatarra.[87] Canada, the European Union, and Switzerland—home to Nestlé, the world's largest food and beverage corporation—joined the U.S. in opposing Mexico's public health efforts. Indifferent to Mexico's epidemic-level rates of obesity and diabetes and how those conditions worsened the effects of Covid-19, these countries objected to the new nutrition standards as too high. The U.S. delegation expressed concerns about the impact of Covid-19, but they were not related to the pandemic's harm to people's health. Instead, it bemoaned the fact that Covid-19 "placed significant pressure on the food and beverage industry."[88]

# 4

# The Unbearable Whiteness of Milk

4chan is an imageboard website, a place where people can share anonymous images and text, favored by white supremacists. In 2017, a 4chan user posted a map titled "themilkzone" showing the parts of the world where people can digest milk without pain or discomfort. A user named Enter the Milk Zone responded to the post with a poem: "roses are red/barack is half-black/if you can't drink milk/you have to go back." Another user asked, "why is that map so much better than usual." Anonymous posted a picture titled "WHITED" of two white men on a boat displaying their muscles next to the words "Milk make man big and strong."

Next to the map, a user put up a picture called "milkpride" of neo-Nazi protesters outside actor Shia LaBeouf's 2017 anti-Trump installation at Queens, New York's Museum of the Moving Image. The shirtless demonstrators chugged jugs of milk, letting the white liquid stream down their naked chests. They claimed they were there in opposition to "the vegan agenda." Their protest continued a long tradition of associations between milk's whiteness and racial purity. Biochemist E. V. McCollum was likely the first person to speak publicly on the topic in the early twentieth century. But long before him, colonizers transformed people's diets to try to pass on milk's white color and what they believed to be its civilizing effects.

Africans drank milk at least six thousand years ago, before humans developed the enzyme lactase, which breaks down lactose.[1] Before anthropologists discovered this fact in 2022, historians believed that milk drinking originated in Scandinavia and Northern Europe. It appears that descendants of Nordic milk drinkers developed the gene that allows for lactose digestion while most people of African descent did not. People who do not retain the enzyme lactase into adulthood experience pain, diarrhea, and other uncomfortable digestive symptoms when they drink milk.

Since Europeans first ventured to colonize land and subjugate its peoples, milk and whiteness have been intertwined. Europeans encountered dairy practices in Africa that were unfamiliar to them: allowing cows to graze naturally, sharing milk with calves, and drinking it at times that accommodate calves' natural feeding rhythms. These migratory and pastoral methods maximized milk's health benefits without harming humans, cows, or calves.[2] Colonizers insisted that the milk produced this way was inferior to the milk that they drank at home, but in fact, the opposite was true. But milk consumed using these natural methods is not the bright white shade familiar to colonizers.

Also, acknowledging the superior eating habits of the people they sought to dominate would have undermined colonizers' justifications for land theft and agricultural assimilation. So, instead of learning and adopting local practices, Columbus and other colonizers sent cows across the seas,[3] confining them to small spaces, severely restricting their movement, separating calves from their mothers, and drinking their milk at any time they wanted it. Milk consumption and production became emblematic of civilization.

In the United States, enslavers knew that Africans could not digest the milk produced locally. A 1977 *Journal of Social History* article references publications written by enslavers that advised providing only "soured" milk to help avoid stomach problems.[4] A 1978 *Journal of Interdisciplinary History* article similarly claimed that in 1860 enslavers believed that drinking milk made their enslaved workers sick and lowered their productivity.[5]

At the same time, Indigenous peoples rejected settlers' milk-drinking habits because the reaction it caused in their bodies made milk feel like poison. Indigenous parents' decision not to feed their infants milk elicited derision from white officials. They deemed the Mojaves "willfully ignorant," "hopelessly lazy," and "practically doomed" to high infant mortality and tuberculosis rates.[6] In 1912, angry about the Mojaves' resistance, August Duclos, a superintendent within the Office of Indian Affairs, complained about their "most pernicious habit of feeding infants coffee and tea."[7] The office's rules for the Indian School Service commanded that "coffee and tea must be furnished sparingly; milk is preferable to either, and the children should be taught to use it."[8]

The Mojaves' instinct to avoid milk was, however, sound. Early efforts to transport milk from rural farms to urban centers so that city dwellers could drink it caused immeasurable heartbreak. In *Nature's Perfect Food*, Melanie Dupuis describes how an estimated 49 out of 100 urban children who drank milk before 1895, when pasteurization became common, died from contamination.[9] Unrefrigerated milk spoiled within hours. Cows' milk also carried tuberculosis, one of the two leading causes of death in the early 1900s. Indigenous parents' refusal to use milk as baby food was a lifesaver.

Nutritional scientist E. V. McCollum was a pioneer of dairy boosterism. He gained renown by inventing the use of rat colonies for experimentation in 1908. In his early feeding trials, he discovered that young rats that consumed fat from butter or egg yolk thrived compared to those fed olive oil or lard. When H. L. Russell, dean of the Wisconsin College of Agriculture, got wind of this finding in 1912, he celebrated its potential to increase dairy sales. McCollum also labeled milk and leafy vegetables "protective foods" because "they were so constituted as to make good the deficiencies of whatever else we liked to eat."[10] In other words, drinking milk could compensate for other dietary sins.

After milk caused an outbreak of foot and mouth disease in 1915, dairy was badly in need of a champion. The USDA, committed to supporting the dairy industry since its founding in 1872, had already invested heavily in mass production and quality improvement to facilitate the movement of milk from farms to cities. On a mission to alter public opinion, the agency churned out publications touting dairy's health benefits. A 1917 USDA pamphlet on the five food groups subtitled its chapter on milk "The Best Food We Have" and implored readers to "GIVE YOUR CHILDREN MILK."[11] "Buy more milk and less meat and your family will be better fed. Look at children who do not get milk but get tea and coffee instead. Aren't most of them pale and sickly? There are always very many sick children in cities and in countries where milk is scarce. When prices go up and mothers start to economize on milk more children become sick. Do not let your children run this risk. Give them fresh clean milk and help them to grow up strong and well and win in their fight against disease. Save on other things if you must but not on milk, your child's best food."

For his part, McCollum wrote a series of essays praising milk's nutritive value in *Hoard's Dairyman*, the nation's leading dairy industry publication. McCollum also proposed the establishment of a National Dairy Council to promote milk across the country. His industry advocacy captured the attention of Herbert Hoover, who was then director of the U.S. Food Administration. Hoover appointed McCollum to his Advisory Committee on Nutrition during World War I, giving him a national platform.

McCollum published *The Newer Knowledge of Nutrition: The Use of Food for the Preservation of Vitality and Health* in 1918. The book ends with the claim that "Milk is our greatest protective food, and its use must be increased." Well-versed in DC politics at this point, McCollum dispenses economic advice along with his nutritional bon mots. "The price must be allowed to go up, so long as the cost of production makes it necessary, and up so far as is essential to make milk production a profitable business. Unless this is done, the effects will soon become apparent in the lowering of our standards of health and efficiency."[12] Tying together the health of the population and the industry was an ingenious way to ensure the dairy trade's survival.[13]

Hoover sent McCollum on a national tour to teach regular folks how to improve the typical American diet. On this tour, he linked milk to whiteness, attributing the superiority of the product to its European roots. "The people who have achieved, who have become large, strong, vigorous people, who have reduced their infant mortality, who have the best trades in the world, who have an appreciation for art, literature and music, who are progressive in science and every activity of the human intellect are the people who have used liberal amounts of milk and its products."[14] This speech appeared in several National Dairy Council pamphlets.

An admiring biographical article about E. V. McCollum laments that he prescribed large quantities of daily milk intake, a pint for adults and a pint and a half for children, "years before it was discovered that some older children and adults, especially those with dark skins, do not tolerate milk well, but often develop gastrointestinal distress after drinking several ounces of milk."[15] The authors, writing in 1980, advise pressing pause on daily milk recommendations in light of this "news." But at that point, the knowledge that some populations could not easily digest milk was at least a century old.

McCollum's early association of milk with whiteness, intelligence, strength, and refinement helped drive up the number of milk converts. Milk production increased by a third between 1919 and 1926. Cities began running Milk Weeks and boxing matches to raise money for milk funds. The press took notice. According to a 1922 article in *The Farmer's Wife*, "Any person in Thurston County who did not know that a milk campaign was going on, must have been blind and deaf. Milk signs and milk slogans assailed eyes and ears at every turn. Fifteen store windows carried displays emphasizing the importance of milk; at intersections were huge milk bottles pointing out that the 'milk way' was the 'best way'; streetcar banners, milk bottle 'stickers' for automobile windshields, and placards in restaurants all carried their milk message." During Milk Week, more than ten thousand people listened to talks stressing milk's important role in building healthy bodies. Milk Week events appealed to adults with a Milk Bar offering milk-based cocktails: "Guernsey Highball: ¾ cup milk, 2 Tablespoons vanilla syrup. Jersey Fizz: ¾ cup milk, 2 Tablespoons pineapple syrup. Timonium Racer: ¾ cup milk, 2 Tablespoons mint syrup. Buttermilk Highball: ¾ cup milk, 2 Tablespoons sugar, 2 Tablespoons lemon juice."[16]

One report highlighted the link between milk and whiteness by accusing a group of Black children of stealing or hoarding free milk during their county's event. "Several small negroes brought quart bottles which they hid behind the milk booth. They took their places in line, received their individual glasses of milk, went around the booth, emptied the milk into the bottles, and started in all over again. By 'repeating' a sufficient number of times they were able to fill their bottles as well as themselves."

Herbert Hoover personally praised milk's nutritional qualities. He stressed that people "cannot survive without the use of dairy products." He had no sympathy for aversion to milk and seemed unaware of the existence of a biological intolerance. His boosterism appeared alongside endorsements in the *Farmer's Wife*. "In many families, there is plenty of milk available but the children do not drink it 'because they do not like it.' In practically every case this is a matter of habit. In such cases, the required amount of milk can be put into their diet in other forms such as milk soups, custards, whips, and so forth. Thousands of children who did not 'like' milk at home have found that they do like it as soon as it is introduced into the school and public opinion among their playmates makes it 'the thing' to drink a given amount daily."

*A History of Agriculture of the State of New York*, published in 1933, explicitly linked milk and whiteness. The text declared that "a casual look at the races of people seems to show that those using much milk are the strongest physically and mentally . . . the Aryans seem to have been the heaviest drinkers of milk and the greatest users of butter and cheese, a fact that may in part account for the quick and high development of this division of human beings."[17] At the 1933–34 Chicago World's Fair, the USDA set up a 15,000-square-foot building with a banner boasting, "Dairy Products Build Superior People."[18] An ad campaign called "Milk Made the Difference" compared the bodies of pigs, dogs, rats, chickens, and people who drank more milk with ones who drank less. Those who drank more milk were bigger.

DURING THE DEPRESSION, when milk supply exceeded demand, the government bought milk to keep its price stable and support dairy farmers. Then, trying to find a way to store or get rid of the surplus, it started stockpiling cheese, which lasts longer than milk. American cheese, a processed blend of cheddar, Colby, curds, and emulsifiers created by the Kraft company in 1916, keeps the longest. It is bright orange and comes in large blocks. The government bought so much American cheese that it eventually filled every cold storage in the country. But there was still more excess milk. The USDA rented half an acre in a Kansas cave and filled it floor to ceiling with blocks of cheese. At its height, the U.S. had two pounds of stored cheese for every resident. Unable to store any more, it bought dairy farmers' cattle to stop them from producing.

Another outlet for surplus dairy, school milk programs, began as a twinkle in E. V. McCollum's eye. McCollum urged the National Dairy Council to focus on teachers and women, who ended up spearheading local dairy councils, as he predicted they would. These councils ran "milk-for-health" campaigns consisting of dairy-themed songs, stories, and plays aimed at children. They conducted check-ins, measuring children's weight to create before-and-after snapshots of how drinking milk affected their growth. The USDA relied on these snapshots to claim that drinking milk reduced children's undernourishment by 12 percent. These results inspired schools to introduce milk as a staple in their lunches.

Chicago was home to the first federal school milk program. Fifteen elementary schools in Chicago's low-income districts received subsidized government milk in 1940. The families who could afford to paid for their children's half pints. Donations covered the cost for families who could not. A New York program followed on Chicago's heels. Next were Omaha, Nebraska; Ogden, Utah; Birmingham, Alabama; St. Louis, Missouri; and Boston, Massachusetts.

Dairies bid to participate in these USDA-run programs and received one cent for each half pint of milk. If a school did not collect enough money from students and donations to pay the dairy, the government made up the difference. The 1954 Special Milk Program expanded this service to public schools and day cares across the country. Over the next two decades, schools went from serving students 228 million half pints of milk a day to 2.7 billion in the 1970s. During this time, the public school population became less and less white.

When inflation skyrocketed and the economy went into freefall in the middle of the 1970s, the USDA turned to its nutrition programs to dispose of excess cheese. Despite most Indigenous peoples' inability to digest milk, commodity cheese became the centerpiece of the Food Distribution Program on Indian Reservations. In "Commod Bods and Frybread Power," Dana Vantrease offers examples of commodity cheese's special place in Indigenous culture and identity.[19] Musician Wade Fernandez, a member of the Menominee tribe, has a track on his award-winning album *Song of the Black Wolf* titled "Commodity Cheese Blues." Its first verse laments, "I went downtown to the commod shop/Met the blues 'cause they were out of stock. Tell me please when I'll get my commod cheese."

Nicknamed "pasteurized gold," the bright orange cheese bricks sometimes operate as currency. "Visa cheese" refers to "a mode of exchange in which a block of commodity cheese can purchase other goods or services." The irony of this treasure is not lost on critics. In 2006, an *Indian Country Today* article observed, "Some Lakota still say to this day that the only brick of gold the Lakota people got out of the Black Hills is the brick of cheese rationed out on commodity day."

Funneling surplus cheese into nutrition programs like FDPIR and school lunches was still not enough to save the dairy industry, which accounts for 3.5 percent of the U.S. gross domestic product—half a percentage more than the auto industry. President Jimmy Carter vowed to increase the price of milk by six cents a gallon in 1977 and committed to buying as much dairy as necessary to make that happen.[20] When government-purchased cheese began to mold, a plan to get it out of storage became urgent. In 1981, a USDA official told the *Washington Post*, "We've looked and looked at ways to deal with this, but the distribution problems are incredible. And you cannot permit a disruption of sales. Probably the cheapest and most practical thing would be to dump it in the ocean."[21]

Instead, in 1981, President Reagan's administration came up with an idea that would solve the problem without affecting the demand for or price of cheese. Through the Temporary Emergency Food Assistance Program, Reagan created the Dairy Distribution Program, sending forty-foot semi-tractor trailers with twenty pallets of cheese in each truckload to poor neighborhoods around the country.[22] Because it was hard for community organizations to store it in that quantity, the cheese often went moldy.

Inevitably, government cheese entered popular culture as a marker of poverty. A series of skits on the comedy show *In Living Color*'s fifth season, which aired in 1993–94, featured a Black version of *All in the Family*, a 1970s sitcom about a white working-class family. On *In Living Color*'s "All Up in the Family," Archie comes home from work expecting Edith to have dinner waiting on the table.

ARCHIE: Edith! What's for dinner?

EDITH: Oh, Archie, it's your favorite! Macaroni and the government cheese!

ARCHIE: Aw, geez, Edith! You know what the government cheese does to me! I spend more time on the throne than Queen Latifah!

In his 1997 *It's Showtime at the Apollo* performance, "That's Deep," comedian Steve Harvey reminisced about eating government cheese. "I'm thirty-eight years old. I've been poor thirty-six of those years. . . . When you're poor, a lot of stuff means something to you that doesn't mean much to other people. Like free. Oh, free go deep with us. We will line up for some free. Don't sit there looking like you don't know what I'm talking about. Cause you would line up for some free. Don't sit there looking like you don't know what I'm talking about, come on now—don't make me say cheese. Don't make me say cheese. Oh, you didn't line up for some cheese before? Oh, I didn't been in the line for some cheese all day? I've been in the line all day."

"I'm going to tell you something about government cheese," Harvey promised. "I said it right. GUV'MENT cheese. Not government. Guv'ment cheese. Guv'ment cheese make the best grilled cheese you done ever had in your life. Oh, you can't eat a better grilled cheese than guv'ment cheese. But you got one problem. You got to cut it though. Oh, this ain't no Velveeta. This ain't individually wrapped. You got to put some pressure on the butcher knife to cut some guv'ment cheese."

Harvey demonstrates by placing his knee on his hands to try to push an imaginary knife through an imaginary block of cheese. His sketch highlights that government cheese did not always live up to the USDA's requirements that it slice and melt easily: "The cheese shall have been tested for meltability in accordance with AMS Methods of Laboratory Analysis, and shall be at Number 3 or higher."

Fifteen years later, in "Money Trees," hip-hop artist Kendrick Lamar raps, "Pots with cocaine residue, everyday I'm hustlin' / What else is a thug to do when you eatin' cheese from the government?" Rapper Jay-Z delivers a similar message in "F.U.T.W." (Fuck Up The World). "After that government cheese, we eatin' steak. / After the projects now we on estates / I'm from the bottom, I know you can relate." Government cheese prompts complex responses in those who grew up eating it. In her youth, writer Bobbi Dempsey assumed the cheese was an attempt to "kill off us people on the brink by stuffing us with enough fat and cholesterol to give us heart attacks before we hit high school."[23] But it also triggers feelings of nostalgia.

Donnie Wahlberg, a founding member of the boy band New Kids on the Block, owns the burger chain Wahlburgers with his brothers Mark, actor and frontliner of another '90s group, Marky Mark and the Funky Bunch, and Chef Paul. Donnie shares, "We grew up on food stamps, at times on welfare, and we had to go to the government food line and get free cheese and peanut butter." He insists "that government cheese, there's nothing like it. For a hamburger, there's nothing better."[24] In 2014, Wahlburgers tweeted a picture of a cheeseburger captioned, "Yes, that is government cheese. That's the way we like it. You too?"[25] By 2022, according to the chain's website, Wahlburgers had switched. "Today . . . we use a premium American cheese to top our burgers, but give a wink and a nod to where we came from. Growing up in a house with nine kids, things were tight. Back then, blocks of cheese, known as 'government cheese,' were given out to folks who needed a hand up. And we were so thankful." Being white, the Wahlbergs were less likely to suffer the pain and discomfort that other families experienced trying to digest dairy, parodied in the "All Up in the Family" skit.

Boxing promoter Joe Mora founded Chico's Tacos, an El Paso,

Texas, institution, in 1953. Chico's signature dish is three flautas—rolled tacos or taquitos stuffed with ground beef and onions and then deep fried—bathing in a soupy tomato sauce topped with mounds of finely shredded government cheese. Mora created the dish as a teenager while caring for his siblings when his parents were at work.[26] A 2009 *Playboy* article described a midnight visit to Chico's by city representative Susie Byrd.[27] "The secret of Chico's," Susie Byrd told the *Playboy* journalist, "is I think that this might be government cheese!" City Commissioner Valerie Escobar chimed in, "It's that good welfare flavor."[28] El Pasoans criticized Escobar for the quip, declaring her unfit to run for county judge. AM radio talk shows mocked her. Escobar denied making the comment.

Despite the negative association between benefits and Chico's cheese, Chico's devotees were outraged when Chico's replaced it in 2016.[29] A community petition tried to reinstate the old cheese. "Chicos Tacos has never been the same since they have change the cheese. We are begging to bring the government cheese back to make Chicos Tacos great again."[30] A Facebook comment on the El Paso History Alliance page appealed to Joe's brother and partner. "Bernie Mora please please bring back the original cheese. How can someone say it was discontinued when WE all know it's Government Cheese!!!! It's just not the same."[31]

This passion reflects people's complicated feelings about the cheese. *Vice* magazine noted, "There's a special *je ne sais quoi* that accompanies the fact that your food is being made by Uncle Sam—often contempt, or associations with hard times. Recollection of the food transcends its gustatory characteristics; government cheese represents times of poverty, when its consumers were forced to rely on federal handouts to fill the dinner table."[32]

Although commodity cheese remains a vital part of the Food Distribution Program on Indian Reservations, other forms of government cheese handouts died out at the end of the 1990s. Then in 2016, the USDA revived the program to deal with a 1.2 billion-pound dairy surplus. A fall in demand for dairy exports collided with consolidation of the dairy industry and technology that made dairy farmers more productive. The USDA responded by buying $20 million worth of cheese to give to food banks while dairy farmers dumped forty-three million gallons of milk down the drain.[33] Instead of allowing the market to shrink in response to reduced demand, which would have led to farm closures, the USDA gave dairy farmers $11.2 million in the form of subsidized insurance.[34]

The influx of milk products to government programs and food banks disproportionately harms Indigenous, Black, and Latine people, who participate in these programs at the highest rates and experience higher rates of dairy-related harms than white people. People who do not retain the enzyme lactase into adulthood experience pain, diarrhea, and other uncomfortable digestive symptoms when they drink milk. Approximately 80 percent of Indigenous and Black people, between 50 and 80 percent of Latine adults, 90 percent of Asian Americans, and just 5 percent of Northern Europeans cannot digest lactose.[35] The condition is labeled "lactose intolerance," but with most of the population losing the enzyme lactase after childhood, it would be more accurate to label people who retain it "lactose persistent" instead of pathologizing its absence. Characterizing lactose intolerance as abnormal makes the white experience the baseline, with any departure signifying an inferior and undesirable condition.

Beyond the harm done by consuming indigestible lactose, milk products contribute to the development of type 2 diabetes and obesity, experienced disproportionately by Indigenous, Black, and Latine people—the populations mostly likely to experience food insecurity and use food banks. Medical and scientific research also links milk to increased risk of prostate, pancreatic, breast, and ovarian cancer, as well as heart disease, diabetes, multiple sclerosis, high blood pressure, and high cholesterol, which open the door to even more types of cancer.[36] Black, Indigenous, and Latine people get these diagnoses at higher rates than white people and die from these conditions more often.[37] They receive cancer diagnoses at a later stage, giving them fewer and less effective treatment options.[38]

At the height of the Covid-19 pandemic, while medical experts advised people in these communities to improve their eating habits to prevent the worst cases, the government dumped more and more cheese at emergency food banks.

IN THE EARLY days of mass marketing, milk advertisers directed their efforts exclusively at white consumers. The first campaign linking milk and whiteness was a 1905 "Coffee and Milk" Milkmaid ad in the United Kingdom featuring a smiling Black boy in ragged clothing representing coffee sitting on a wooden crate next to a cherubic, prettily dressed white girl, representing milk. From then until the late 1940s, milk advertisements only used white models.

That changed in 1946, when Pet Milk company began appealing to Black consumers to buy its evaporated milk (marketed as infant formula) through a campaign featuring the Famous Fultz Quads. Annie Mae Fultz, a Black and Cherokee woman married to a tenant tobacco farmer, lost the ability to hear and speak in childhood. She already had six children when, in May 1946, she gave birth to the first recorded Black identical quadruplets, four sweet sisters who became instant celebrities. Annie Mae's doctor, Fred Klenner, who named the girls after his relatives, started doing vitamin C experiments on them on the day they were born, and held a bidding war for formula companies seeking to use them in their marketing materials. The photogenic, light-skinned sisters became Pet Milk poster girls, advertising evaporated milk as formula and an essential baking ingredient over the next eighteen years. Pet Milk's groundbreaking ads represented the first national corporate campaign designed to sell anything other than alcohol, cigarettes, or beauty products to Black consumers.

Carnation advertised its evaporated milk to Black consumers with another set of Black quadruplets, the Tigner Quads, also born in 1946. The company planned a major campaign featuring the siblings but could only run one ad after the quadruplets' parents separated and the state assigned the children to different foster institutions. In 1949, Pet Milk launched a "Happy Families" campaign showing prosperous Black middle-class homeowners with stay-at-home mothers. These ads responded to a call by Black marketing experts to portray Black consumers as socially and financially equal to white consumers, even if that did not always reflect reality. The same year that a "Happy Family" ad celebrated a move to a new house in Birmingham, Alabama, for John and Helen Norman and their twins, there were six bombings of Black homes in the city.[39]

The first multicultural ad for fluid milk appeared in the 1950s. The ad was a bold departure from previous milk campaigns because it portrayed children of different races consuming the beverage together. Interracial mixing was taboo at that time. *Loving v. Virginia*, the Supreme Court case that invalidated laws against interracial marriage, was still a decade away. The radical Hood Dairy poster shows a group of children under the caption "Vitamin-rich milk and nourishing foods are the foundations for a strong America." A Black boy in a pink shirt and an orange tie whistles appreciatively at a tall glass of milk. Although his presence signaled progress in terms of inclusive marketing, the whistle evokes the false accusations of Black men and boys whistling at white women that led to lynchings. Behind the Black boy, there is an Asian-looking boy. There are three white boys to his left. On the right side of the glass, there is a white girl standing by herself. The ad reflects a desire to expand the market for milk even at the risk of the backlash that Hood might face.

In the UK, inclusion initially relied on stereotypes that reinforced the idea that white people consumed milk in a civilized way. A 1953 UK National Milk Publicity Council ad shows an almost-naked Indian man with a long white beard sitting on a spiked board while sipping milk from a bowl with a monkey watching him. The text says, "The devout Hindu Doth meat eschew; HE'LL live on milk and so could YOU." In the bottom left of the poster, in contrast with the barely clothed man, a dimpled white boy sporting a tie smiles while holding up a glass of milk with a straw in it. On the right, a white girl in pigtails tied with ribbons sips on her glass of milk through a straw.

Sealtest ran the first ad for fluid milk designed to appeal to Black consumers in *Ebony*, a popular African American magazine, in 1963. Under six different squares, each containing a Black adult drinking milk, the tag line reads: "That old time flavor—glass after glass after glass." Another Sealtest milk ad shows a Black girl pouring milk for her younger brother and declares, "Your family deserves the best!" While hundreds of ads directed toward white people ran during these decades, Pet Milk, Carnation, Hood Dairy, and Sealtest produced the only ones targeting Black consumers. Most companies feared that associations between their products and Blackness would cost them too great a share of the white consumer market.

In the early 1970s, UK milk company Unigate ran a series of humorous ads warning consumers to drink their milk quickly before "the Humphreys" stole it. The Humphreys are invisible creatures carrying long red and white swirled straws. One of the ads features Unigate's first Black model, boxer Muhammad Ali, famous for his rhyming boasts. It was the first UK milk ad to appeal to Black consumers. Ali says, "Here's a message for my English fans. Your milk quenches my thirst. But you got to drink it quickly or a Humphrey will drink it first. And everybody know that I am the greatest. That's in the boxing ring. But when it comes to drinking Unigate milk, a Humphrey, he's the king. So, when I'm enjoying a Unigate pint I watch my left and my right. Because if a Humphrey comes near my milk there's gonna be a fight." In the early 1980s, as part of the popular UK "Milk Gotta Lotta Bottle" campaign, a Black male bodybuilder lifts a barbell weighted down by golden crates filled with milk bottles. These ads, while signaling racial progress by featuring Black models, still relied on the stereotype that Black people are either athletes or entertainers.

In the 1980s, a dynamic ad campaign with the tagline "Milk: It Does the Body Good" revived falling milk sales. The campaign's message echoed early E. V. McCollum and USDA claims about milk's protective aspects that characterized the industry's continued efforts to persuade the public that milk is healthy, despite the fact that it makes so many people feel sick. Demand continued to drop, prompting the USDA to start a check-off program, designed to improve a product's market position, using funds collected from dairy farmers. In 1995, the brand-new USDA Dairy Marketing Inc. launched the award-winning "Got Milk?" milk mustache campaign. In the first spot, Black model Naomi Campbell sports a milk mustache (an illusion created by spreading white glue above her upper lip) next to the caption, "Milk, What a Surprise!"

Over a span of twenty years, 350 milk mustache ads followed. The campaign ushered in a new era of milk marketing using Black, Asian, and Latine celebrities. The "Got Milk?" A-list includes tennis superstars Venus and Serena Williams and singers Beyoncé and Solange Knowles with their mother, Tina. Other mustachioed superstars included singers Rihanna, Chris Brown, Jennifer Hudson, and Usher; actors Sofia Vergara and Salma Hayek ("Toma Leche?") and Taye Diggs with his son; models Tyra Banks and Iman; figure skater Kristi Yamaguchi; basketball players Dennis Rodman, Patrick Ewing, Nikki McCray, Lisa Leslie, and Sheryl Swoopes; football player Terrell Davis; boxer Oscar De La Hoya; action film star Jackie Chan; hip-hop artist Nelly; and comedians Bernie Mac and Whoopi Goldberg. These ads reflected USDA-driven efforts to expand the milk market beyond white consumers even though the agency knew that drinking milk made most people who are not white sick.

Goldberg, who was lactose intolerant, initially did not participate but got on board when "Got Milk?" started advertising lactose-free milk. Forty years after the Unigate Humphreys ad, Muhammad Ali and his wife donned milk mustaches for the campaign. When Spike Lee, a film director known for his provocative, anti-racist work, appeared in an ad, critics responded with poetic commentary. "Spike's a famous director and Knick fan, With a message for each African-American. Ninety percent of blacks cannot tolerate lactose, so why does Spike endorse taking dose after dose? Lee poses with glue applied to his face, and in doing so betrays nine out of ten of his race."

The USDA's "Got Milk?" campaign went beyond the milk mustache, introducing White Gold, an icon of masculine whiteness, to the world in 2008. White Gold is a rock star with fabulous hair, a thick mustache made popular by 1970s porn stars, gleaming white teeth, and white painted nails. He has two Black female backup singers, the Calcium Twins. The twins worship White Gold and attend to all his needs. In the original print ad, White Gold stares sultrily at the camera while the twins stand defiantly behind him. The ad asks, "Is it me or do you love my hair?" White Gold's flowing locks are a visual representation of the claim that drinking milk makes your hair healthy. Further down, in smaller print, he admits, "The best I can give is 2 percent." This quip referencing 2 percent milk positions White Gold as the embodiment of milk. In another, sexually charged ad, the twins gaze up thirstily while milk cascades into their raised hands beside the caption "Pour the Milk Sister."

The "White Gold" campaign reaffirmed the link between milk and whiteness that the ads featuring Black, Latine, and Asian celebrities temporarily disrupted. In a TV commercial, White Gold flaunts his entitlement by using a slur against disabled people while describing an episode from his childhood. "I was painting as a kid and everybody said, 'Uh . . . I like your picture—I like your pictures, you know, what is it?' And I said, 'Well, it's a masterpiece.' And a lot of people thought I was retarded because there was nothing on the paper. I said, 'Well, I do everything in white.'"

Another White Gold video shows his gratitude for milk's ability to relieve him of dealing with the twins' premenstrual symptoms. He asks, "Do you remember when we, well, there was a tube ride on the red river and it was that time of the month?" Calcium Twins: "Mmhmm." White Gold: "Do you remember when I told you that milk would help?" Calcium Twins: "Yes." White Gold: "Didn't it?" Calcium Twins: "Yes!" White Gold: "Yeah, it helped me to get through that time. Milk helps PMS be not so bad for me and you guys, right?"

The California Milk Processor Board ran a similar series of ads in 2011, one featuring a comically beleaguered Black man who stares at the camera while holding up identical milk cartons, one in each hand. His eyebrows are raised in disbelief to match the caption, "I'm sorry for the things—or thing—I did or didn't do." Under him, there is a banner that reads, "Everything I do is wrong.com" and beneath it, "Milk can help reduce the symptoms of PMS." After a swift backlash against the Angry Black Woman stereotype invoked by the ads, the milk producers yanked them but expressed only half-hearted atonement. Claiming that some people found the ads "funny and educational," the board apologized to "those we offended."[40]

White Gold's popularity was not affected. DMI released two music videos, "One Gallon Axe" and "Tame the Tiger," along with its pièce de resistance "Battle for Milkquarious," a twenty-minute video that DMI pronounced, "the most amazing rock opera ever made about milk." In it, White Gold battles The Evil Mysterious for control of Milkquarious. White Gold must rescue his milktastic counterpart, white woman Strawberry Summers, from his villainous adversary. Summers is the only girl in the galaxy with "as much milk-enhanced hotness" as White Gold himself. Along the way, White Gold meets Jug Life, a tattooed Black man with excellent fighting skills who drinks chocolate milk. Jug Life, like many Black characters, is expendable: White Gold sacrifices him to monsters so that he can continue his quest to defeat The Evil Mysterious.

Following White Gold's success, DMI added another ad to the "Got Milk?" campaign that equated milk with whiteness, 2010's "Mootopia." A black-and-white spotted cow reclines in an idyllic field in front of a white waterfall and beside a white lake. A white woman in a white dress lies sleeping in the crook of the cow's body. Small white clouds above her head lead to a bigger white cloud, where she dreams the scene that she is in, in an endless loop.

In contrast with the peaceful white woman, another "Got Milk?" ad shows a scruffy, stressed-out Black woman approach a sullen Black girl sitting in a shopping cart in the milk aisle. Woman: "I'm you, from the future." Girl, disappointed: "You're me?" Woman, shrugging apologetically: "I know. Drink this." The girl drinks, and suddenly the woman's disheveled clothing falls away from her body revealing athletic wear. She begins to run. "It's working, keep drinking!" She throws a javelin and a shot put and sprints to the podium to accept first prize. "We did it!" Her younger self looks on amazed as her mother throws carton after carton of milk into the cart.

"Toma Leche?" is the Spanish version of "Got Milk?," aimed at Latine consumers. Many "Toma Leche?" spots emphasize the importance of family. Advertisers tried to evoke and trade on the distress of separated immigrant families by telling stories that would remind them of their lives back home. A 1996 advertisement, tagged "Familia,

Amor y Leche"—family, love and milk—features a grandmother cooking traditional milk-based desserts with the caption, "Have you given
your loved ones enough milk today?" The campaign also teamed up
with Latina mom bloggers to spread milk gospel in their communities.[41]

A 2001 "Toma Leche?" ad appropriated the Mexican legend of La
Llorona, a ghoulish weeping ghost who roams the earth each evening
looking for her children. In the ad, La Llorona wafts through a family
home late at night searching for milk. When she reaches the fridge, her
weeping stops. She excitedly grabs the milk carton but then, finding it
empty, returns to her wailing despair. The ad uses deprivation marketing tactics: instead of trying to convince consumers of milk's upsides, it
frames the lack of milk as a problem that parents need to solve.

"Toma Leche?" ads draw on folk beliefs about milk's magical qualities. They reinforce the notion that drinking milk before bed will help
children sleep better and have good dreams. In a dentist's office, teeth
on a poster come to life to dance and sing because milk is good for
them. A woman running in the forest suddenly levitates because milk
has given her beautiful hair. The "Mucho Màs Que Leche"—Much
More Than Milk—campaign shows athletes fueled to perform incredible feats by chocolate milk instead of Gatorade.

El Maestro Del Vaso Medio Lleno—The Master of the Glass Half-
Full—introduces the Most Positive Man in the World. After spending
his life as a staunch pessimist, he meets a guru who shows him a glass
of milk that is never empty, no matter how much he drinks from it. The
man transforms into an eternal optimist who butters his bread on both
sides, then throws it to the ground, where it stands up straight, neither
side touching the floor.

DMI promotes more than just milk. In 2008, it teamed up with
Domino's pizza to create the "American Legends" seven-cheese pizza
line, which offers 40 percent more cheese than the company's other
pizzas. To launch this product, DMI financed a $12 million marketing
campaign that included a prime ad spot during the 2009 Superbowl.
DMI also worked with Taco Bell to create the steak quesadilla, which
has eight times more cheese than other Taco Bell offerings. DMI is

responsible for Pizza Hut's Cheesy Bites pizza, Wendy's dual Double Melt sandwich, and Burger King's Cheesy Angus Bacon cheeseburger and Tendercrisp chicken sandwich.

DMI's partnerships with fast-food companies were not public knowledge until the *New York Times* ran a front-page exposé by Michael Moss in 2010, "While Warning About Fat, U.S. Pushes Cheese Sales."[42] The article compares DMI's annual budget—over $141 million that year—to the $6.5 million allocated to the USDA's Center for Nutrition Policy and Promotion, a division tasked with promoting healthy foods. In 2008, the USDA paid DMI's chief executive, Thomas Gallagher, a salary of $633,457. Gallagher earned his keep by generating a cheese sales growth of almost 30 million pounds, slowing the steady decline in milk consumption by focusing on marketing initiatives aimed at school-children. In 2015, DMI helped McDonald's switch from margarine to butter, increasing butter consumption by about 600 million pounds.

DMI is responsible for the dairy-heavy coffee beverages that McDonald's serves and Pizza Hut's pan pizzas, which feature 25 percent more cheese than its original pizzas. DMI's 2020 partnership with Pizza Hut included a giveaway of free pizzas for 500,000 high school graduates homebound due to Covid lockdowns, announced on Jimmy Fallon's *Tonight Show*. DMI also helped promote Taco Bell's Grilled Cheese Burrito. "The first thing you'll notice is the impressive pressed-cheese exterior with all its melted, grilled goodness. Then, after biting in, your taste buds will be swept away by the nacho cheese sauce and shredded cheeses on the inside. . . . The Grilled Cheese Burrito makes a statement that cheese is meant for literally everywhere. . . . A world with more cheese in it is a good thing. And a world with more cheese on it is a game-changer."[43]

Eating more cheese triggers serious health consequences and incorporating more of it into fast food disproportionately affects low-income Black, Latine, and Indigenous consumers.[44] Fast food is a larger part of their diets, although white people eat more fast food by volume. Despite racial disparities in all dairy-related diseases, the USDA, through DMI, creates marketing schemes designed to increase intake of harmful products. Instead, the government should eliminate all its partnerships with all fast-food companies.

THE USDA HAS poured billions of dollars into race-targeted advertising because it works. Poor nutrition has overtaken smoking as the leading cause of premature death in the United States. There are racial disparities in these death rates and in every food-related illness and condition. These deaths and disparities are not inevitable. To reduce or eliminate them, the government could get out of the business of milk marketing. It could make it harder for companies to use racially targeted ads by either prohibiting or restricting them. At the very least, it could require industry-created guidelines that explain the ethical issues surrounding race-targeted marketing. At that point, concerned consumers could use their dollars to show support for companies that try to reduce racial health disparities. The government could also require warning labels on dairy products like those that appear on cigarettes.

In a rare moment of oversight, the Federal Trade Commission stepped in to stop a DMI campaign that claimed that drinking milk causes weight loss. The Physicians Committee for Responsible Medicine (PCRM), a nonprofit organization of over 17,000 doctors, appealed to the FTC to shut down "Milk Your Diet! Lose Weight!" and "3-a-Day. Burn More Fat, Lose Weight" in 2005.[45] After the FTC met with the USDA, the agency decided to discontinue all advertising and marketing activities linking milk with weight loss "until further research provides stronger, more conclusive evidence." The USDA never made those claims again because the research never supported it.

Instead, a meta-analysis of twenty-nine studies showed that milk has no effect on weight in children or adults. In another study, researchers observed that, counterintuitively, drinking reduced-fat milk actually led to more long-term weight gain than drinking full-fat milk.[46] Even a study paid for by the USDA showed no weight loss associated with milk. But that did not stop DMI from using the false weight-loss claim to argue against a reduction in the amount of milk included in emergency food assistance programs.

The PCRM and FTC have butted heads over related issues. The PCRM filed a lawsuit against the commission in 2020 because it failed to respond to the organization's petition to require warning labels on cheese products. Based on several studies linking dairy consumption to an increased risk of breast cancer, the suggested label would have read: "Dairy cheese contains reproductive hormones that may increase breast cancer mortality risk.'" In Canada, dairy producers received an exemption from these types of labeling laws after persuading lawmakers that their products' calcium-content benefits outweigh their health risks.[47]

Clinical studies contradict these industry claims. Exercising, reducing sodium, and eating less animal protein and more foods like beans, kale, and broccoli build bone density better than consuming dairy does. The calcium in cow's milk comes from the grass and grains that the cow eats. Humans can get their calcium directly by eating similar foods. The calcium study that forms the basis for U.S. milk recommendations tracked only 155 people for two to three weeks.[48] A newer study, which had 10,000 participants, found no relationship between calcium intake and bone density. Adding milk to the diets of children entering puberty did not affect their bone mineralization. Instead, a study of two large cohorts showed that drinking more milk than usual as a teenager *increased* the rate of hip fractures for men at a rate of 9 percent higher risk for every additional glass of milk they drank per day.

Even without proof that milk is good for bones, the USDA continues to claim that it is an essential component of the daily diet. In *Re-Imagining Milk: Cultural and Biological Perspectives*, Andrea Wiley describes how the USDA encourages people who are lactose impersistent, a term she prefers to intolerant, to drink milk.[49] Instead of suggesting substitutes that have the same nutrients as dairy but do not cause pain or discomfort, the USDA offers "tips for tolerance." These tips include drinking small amounts of milk with meals throughout the day, drinking lactose-free milk, and taking pills to ease digestion.

The USDA's MyPlate diagram, which illustrates the federal dietary

guidelines, is a circle with four color-coded sections. Grains (orange) and vegetables (green) are of equal size and larger than fruits (red) and protein (purple), which are also of equal size. On the top right corner there is another, smaller circle, labeled dairy (blue). Dairy is the only food category with a separate, special place on the diagram. The 2020–25 federal dietary guidelines recommend three servings of milk a day,[50] which is twice the amount that people in the U.S. currently consume.

Regulations require the guidelines to reflect the latest medical and scientific research. They do not. Instead of suggesting alternatives that would reduce illness and improve the digestive health of many people, they recommend choosing fat-free or low-fat milk instead of full-fat milk. This advice defies nutrition science because full-fat milk is no worse than the other versions and might even be better. The recommendation, along with a 10 percent recommended daily cap on saturated fats, simply reflects a compromise with the dairy industry.

The guidelines also intentionally confuse readers by using three different terms for saturated fats: "solid fats," "saturated fatty acids," and "trans fatty acids." The section designed to help people reduce their saturated fat intake is unclear. Instead of straightforwardly stating that most saturated fats come from dairy products, the guidelines contain rambling sentences that identify broad categories of foods to avoid. For example, they state that most saturated fats come from "sandwiches." This begs the question: Is a hummus and cucumber sandwich on whole wheat equivalent to a meatball sub with extra cheese on a hoagie?

The National Academy of Sciences, Engineering, and Medicine conducted the first major peer review of the guidelines process in 2015. The academy's resulting report revealed that the guidelines rely on outdated and selective sources to reach their recommendations. The guidelines committee's methods were impossible to reproduce—a methodological red flag in any scientific field. The report recommended extensive reforms to increase the committee's scientific rigor and transparency.

The committee rejected most of the report's suggestions. Although it might be surprising that the government would ignore the academy's

input, the guidelines committee includes representatives from Nestlé, the world's largest food company; Merck pharmaceutical company; Conagra packaged foods company; Danone/Dannon yogurt company; and Monsanto. Committee members have repeatedly refused to disclose financial conflicts of interest. Four out of the six members on the Birth to 24 Months Subcommittee have ties to formula and baby food companies. These links between the government and the formula industry help explain why the WIC program is the largest formula purchaser in the U.S.

Instead of simply lowering their dairy recommendations, the guidelines outline steps to reduce the potential harms of saturated fats. "Strategies to lower saturated fat intake include reducing intakes of dessert and sweet snacks by consuming smaller portion sizes and eating these foods less often. Additional strategies include reading food labels to choose packaged foods lower in saturated fats and choosing lower fat forms of foods and beverages." The emphasis on choice here is key. Many people who survive on SNAP or WIC benefits don't have genuine choices. Indigenous people who get FDPIR boxes of commods have only one choice: take it or leave it. Millions of public-school students can either eat what the lunchroom offers or go hungry.

Only two groups were happy with the 2020–25 guidelines dairy recommendations: the International Dairy Foods Association and the National Milk Producers Federation. The American Dairy Coalition was not. It wrote a scathing letter to the Health and Human Services secretary in July 2020 after it found out about the new saturated fats cap. The cap prevents schools and other institutions from serving full-fat milk, cutting off some of the product's most lucrative markets and forcing producers to remove the product's natural fat. The question of what happens to it after that helps explain the 1.4 billion pounds of cheese in cold storage.

Perhaps the most vehement opposition to the 2020–25 guidelines came from the PCRM. The organization objected to the committee having ignored the research linking dairy to increased risks of breast, ovarian, and prostate cancers, asthma, cognitive decline, and early death. The PCRM also pointed to milk's weak or nonexistent potential

to increase bone strength, which undermines the committee's strongest argument for its recommendations. The PCRM urged the committee to include language in the guidelines saying that milk products are not necessary for a healthy diet and that they particularly harm Black and Latine communities.[51] The American Medical Association took a similar stance. In 2018, it passed a resolution recommending that the guidelines make dairy optional because of racial disparities in lactose intolerance.

In April 2021, three doctors sued the USDA for issuing guidelines that contradict scientific and medical knowledge; harm the 25 percent of Americans that are lactose intolerant; and protect meat and dairy interests instead of the population's health.[52] Although 60 percent of people in the U.S. have at least one diet-related chronic condition (including heart disease, obesity, and diabetes), the guidelines fail to address how nutrition might worsen or improve these conditions.[53]

Since the first dietary guidelines for Americans came out in 1980, childhood and adult obesity have tripled.[54] Instead of responding to that change in the nation's health profile, the guidelines have successfully propped up a failing milk market. While Black, Indigenous, and Latine communities absorb the costs of that choice, some dairy corporations hedge their bets by including dairy-free alternatives among their products.[55] The USDA also stands to gain from the sale of soy milk because soybeans are another subsidized commodity.[56] Promoting it as a dairy alternative would decrease the soybean surplus but risk alienating the dairy industry.

The guidelines have an oversized impact on poor people's diets because they govern USDA nutrition programs, including school lunches and WIC. Dairy products are available to WIC participants but not in their healthier, organic versions, which are less likely to contain harmful chemicals. Milk contains pesticides, carcinogenic (cancer-causing) polychlorinated biphenyls (PCBs), and dioxins. People ingest almost all PCBs and one-quarter to one-half of dioxins through dairy products, which can lead to damage in the immune, reproductive, and nervous systems. Melamine, which harms the kidneys and urinary tract, and aflatoxins, which are carcinogenic, also show up in milk.

Despite these dangers, 2014 USDA guidelines require WIC state agencies to "ensure that participants and caregivers receive education that stresses the importance of milk over milk substitutes." They further instruct that "Lactose-free or lactose-reduced fortified dairy products should be offered before non-dairy milk alternatives to those participants with lactose intolerance that cannot drink milk."[57] SNAP recipients can theoretically choose organic dairy products, but their limited budgets put those products out of reach. For most families, SNAP benefits don't last until the end of the month, making the cheapest foods their best or only choice.

ALTHOUGH THE USDA disproportionately provides milk to Black, Indigenous, and Latine people, the alt-right has ramped up its association between milk-drinking and white superiority, based on its view of lactose intolerance as a biological weakness. After the neo-Nazi milk-chugging protest at Shia LaBeouf's art installation, headlines announced "Milk Is the New, Creamy Symbol of White Racial Purity in Donald Trump's America,"[58] "Secret Nazi Code Kept Hidden by 'Milk' and 'Vegan Agenda,'"[59] and "Got Milk? Neo-Nazi Trolls Sure as Hell Do."[60] White supremacist leaders reacted to this press by doubling down. Richard Spencer, head of the alt-right National Policy Institute, and Tim Treadstone, far-right media personality known as Baked Alaska who took part in the Capitol riots on January 6, 2021, added a glass of milk emoji to their twitter handles. In Jordan Peele's 2017 Best Picture–nominated film *Get Out*, a white supremacist eats dry Fruit Loops out of a bowl while sipping milk from a straw to preserve the drink's purity. Actor Laurence Fox added the glass of milk emoji to his twitter handle during his 2021 London mayoral run.

Responding to dairy's sudden resurgence in hate group discourse in 2017, *Wired* ran an article called "The Alt-Right's New Ploy? Trolling with False Symbols."[61] The piece frames the milk and white supremacy association as part of a bigger trend of alt-right internet trolls co-opting seemingly innocuous symbols to confuse liberal "normies'" and "snowflakes." *Wired* argues, "The alt-right is attempting to normalize itself and its ideas. If anybody who drinks milk might be a Nazi, the idea of someone being a Nazi starts looking more pedestrian." While this might be true for some symbols, milk has a very different history from white nationalist symbols Pepe the Frog and the OK sign, which arose in the twenty-first century.

"Milkshaking" became a new act of protest in the UK in 2019. Opponents of the far-right Brexit party began publicly dumping milkshakes on party members' heads.[62] Fearing a frozen bath for party leader Nigel Farage during his visit to Scotland, police asked an Edinburgh McDonald's outlet to temporarily stop selling milkshakes. Some commentators explained the choice of milkshakes as a matter of convenience. "Holding a milkshake was less conspicuous than clutching an egg."[63] But others admired the co-optation of the white supremacist dairy obsession. "It turns a symbol used by the alt right—milk—to symbolize 'whiteness' and to mock ethnic groups with a greater predisposition to lactose intolerance, into an image of dramatic opposition," wrote the *New York Times*.[64]

While mocking may be relatively harmless, government programs that push milk to the most vulnerable populations for the purpose of boosting Big Food and Ag companies send a clear message: Corporations' profits matter. Black, Indigenous, and Latine lives don't.

# 5

# School Food Failure

Maryn Holler posted a photo of her lunch at Apollo High School in St. Cloud, Minnesota, on Facebook on September 13, 2019.[1] Above the picture of a hot dog bun (with no hot dog), dabbed with melted cheese, a pool of marinara sauce, and a few baby carrots, she wrote, "Alright so I paid for this to eat at lunch today. I thank God everyday that my family has the money where I get to go home and eat actual food. There are kids at this school who this is ALL THEY GET TO EAT, and we were given a hot dog bun with cheese. It's honestly sad to know that we go to school and pay around 3 dollars for something that cost .50 cents to make."

About a year later, during the Covid-19 lockdown, a parent posted a picture of the Buffalo school district's takeaway lunch: a shriveled hot dog on one side of the tray (with no bun) and nine tater tots on the other side. For families who lost jobs during the pandemic and faced miles-long lines at food banks that often ran out, these sad school lunches were sometimes the only food their children ate all day.

WHEN SOCIOLOGIST ROBERT Hunter published the first general statistical survey of the poor, *Poverty,* in 1904, the lunch program provided by New York's Children's Aid Society for vocational students was the only one of its kind.[2] Hunter laments, "It is utter folly, from the point of view of learning, to have a compulsory school law which compels children, in that weak physical and mental state which results from poverty, to drag themselves to school and to sit at their desks, day in and day out, for several years, learning little or nothing."[3] School meals were the solution, he claimed.

"If it is a matter of principle in democratic America that every child shall be given a certain amount of instruction, let us render it possible for them to receive it, as monarchial countries have done, by making full and adequate provision for the physical needs of the children who come from the homes of poverty," he wrote in *Poverty*. Socialist writer John Spargo built on this argument in his 1906 work, *The Bitter Cry of the Children*. "Not less than 2,000,000 children of school age in the United States are the victims of poverty which denies them common necessities, particularly adequate nourishment.... Such children are in very many cases incapable of successful mental effort, and much of our national expenditure for education is in consequence an absolute waste."[4]

Responding to these calls, Philadelphia, Boston, Milwaukee, New York, Cleveland, Cincinnati, St. Louis, Chicago, Los Angeles, and some rural school districts launched school meal programs. Charities sometimes supplemented state budgets allotted for the food, but it wasn't enough to meet the demand. School boards, parent-teacher associations, mothers' clubs, and other civic and social entities initially ran these programs without any help from the federal government. Then, after Congress enacted New Deal laws to cope with the massive unemployment of the 1930s, various bodies—the Civil Works Administration, Federal Emergency Relief Administration, Reconstruction Finance Corporation, and Works Progress Administration—assigned unemployed women to school kitchens to help manage the increasing need.[5] The National Youth Administration added unemployed young people as part-time helpers or put them to work building tables, chairs, and other lunchroom equipment.

School meals and agricultural commodities became bedfellows in 1935 as part of Congress's efforts to get rid of the surplus subsidized foods that were flooding the market and depressing prices.[6] Some surplus foods left the country as exports. At home, the government looked for opportunities to channel surplus commodities to people who could not afford them otherwise. Schoolchildren fit the bill—they could consume these goods without ever affecting their price. The first foods that the government bought through the Federal Surplus Commodities Corporation were pork, dairy products, and wheat, fueling a fast-growing program—from 3,839 participating schools in 1937 to 14,075 in 1939.

To be eligible for this windfall, school representatives had to agree not to spend less money on commodities than they would have done if they were not receiving any of them for free. Schools also had to promise to hide the identities of students receiving free lunches. It was clear that free meals combined with children's cruelty could lead to bullying or, worse, hunger if students chose not to eat to avoid their peers' mockery.

Everything changed after the U.S. entered World War II. Suddenly, surplus food went to U.S. soldiers and allies overseas. WPA labor dried up. But the war effort ultimately gave school meals an unexpected boon. In 1945, former school principal General Lewis B. Hershey, head of the Selective Service, testified to the House Agriculture Committee (HAC) that poor diets accounted for 40 percent of all draft rejections. "Whether we are going to have war or not, I do think that we have got to have health if we are going to survive."[7]

Heeding Lewis's warning, the USDA created the National School Lunch Program (NSLP) in 1946 "as a measure of national security."[8] Under the NSLP, the federal government sent commodities to schools, along with a small amount of funding to buy other foods. Families who could afford to pay for meals covered the rest of the expenses. This Department of Defense–inspired program eventually directed billions toward both school meals and the agricultural sector. The House Agriculture Committee, like Americanizers and Indian boarding schools before them, believed that school food also served a cultural purpose. The committee insisted that students who ate lunch at school would bring valuable nutrition knowledge back to their families.

Based on rudimentary nutritional research, the secretary of agriculture designed three NSLP lunches, designated Type A, Type B, and Type C. Type A lunches were 8 ounces of whole milk, 2 ounces of protein-rich food, 3/4 cup of vegetables or fruit, one portion of a bread product, and 2 teaspoons of butter or fortified margarine. Type B lunches were for schools that did not have proper cooking facilities—they consisted of the same portions of bread and milk but only half portions of the other foods. Type C, intended for students who could supplement the meal with something from home, was one half pint of whole milk. Regulations required school milk to meet the local minimum standards for sanitation and butterfat content. If the available milk did not meet these standards and schools could not serve it, the USDA would reduce lunch reimbursements by two cents. If milk was available but not served, the USDA would not reimburse meals at all.

These menus remained largely unchanged even after school demographics underwent a drastic shift over the next few decades. After *Brown v. Board of Education* integrated public schools in 1954, white families fled to the suburbs and private schools in droves. The schools they left behind declined quickly without their property taxes and donations. Schools weathered another blow when the 1966 Child Nutrition Act conditioned federal lunch funding on the state of a school's kitchen. Poor urban schools could not afford to modernize and repair their cooking facilities and equipment, if they had any at all. For many, their founders had not foreseen the creation of school lunch programs—assuming that children would always go home for lunch—and had established the schools in buildings without kitchens. In many districts, adding kitchens was prohibitively expensive or architecturally unfeasible.

Even when schools had the capacity to offer meals, they often ran their programs inconsistently or haphazardly. A 1968 school commission report found that eligibility requirements for free or reduced-price lunches were not uniform across districts—local budgets and priorities shaped the meals more than student need. The areas with the greatest need had the least capacity to meet it.[9] Then in the same year, a CBS documentary, *Hunger in America*, shocked the nation with graphic footage of starving children,[10] and the Citizens' Board of

Inquiry into Hunger and Malnutrition in the United States released a popular report titled *Hunger U.S.A.*[11] The problem became too visible for politicians to ignore.

President Richard Nixon hosted a White House conference on Food, Nutrition, and Health in 1969 and increased the funding for school meals. He explained that "There can be no doubt that hunger and malnutrition exist in America, and that some millions may be affected. For them, there must be first sufficient food income. But this alone would only begin to address the problem, for what matters finally is what people buy with the money they have. People must be educated in the choosing of proper foods. All of us, poor and non-poor alike, must be reminded that a proper diet is a basic determinant of good health."[12] This response deflects much of the responsibility for the problem onto individuals instead of policies by emphasizing education over economics. Nixon's assumption that poor people choose their foods—and choose badly—ignored the reality of poverty.

To address the problem of nonexistent or inadequate kitchens, the USDA gave into pressure from the National Restaurant Association in 1970 and allowed schools to turn their programs over to the private, for-profit sector.[13] Schools began to outsource their meal schemes to corporations. Impoverished lunchrooms continued to make up for small budgets by leaning heavily on commodity foods until 1973, when the USDA informed Congress that it could no longer afford to make these products available to schools for free or at low cost.[14] This announcement triggered a shift in the nature of the commodities program, through amendments to the National School Lunch Act in 1974, from the agricultural sector providing free food to schools to schools supporting the industry by buying commodities.[15] A later amendment required schools to put at least 12 percent of their federal food assistance funds toward purchasing commodity foods.

In the 1980s, President Ronald Reagan's administration slashed the federal school lunch budget by 25 percent because he believed that families who could pay for meals should not receive any free food from the government, even if payments strained their budgets. His government also interfered with lunch menus, classifying ketchup as a vegetable. The media mocked this move, leading him to reverse course, but Reagan set a precedent for putting industry priorities over health.

In this climate, attitudes toward school lunchrooms changed. Very little local or school board money went to cafeterias because people did not consider them part of education. Districts began to expect school food service operations to sustain themselves, using the money families paid for lunch for labor, supplies, and any cost of free meals not covered by federal funds. In short, districts treated kitchens more like small businesses than government programs. Lunchrooms adjusted to budget cuts by switching from fresh to processed foods. Many schools turned their food operations over to private corporations like Sodexo, Aramark, and Chartwells.

This trend has continued, bringing with it a decline in labor standards because these companies cut costs by paying their employees less. It has also increased branded and prepackaged offerings. Schools that do not outsource their food service often try to coax more dollars out of students by selling foods that resemble or come from fast and junk food companies, like chicken nuggets and pizza. In some schools, corporations like McDonald's and Chick-fil-A sell their products as competitive foods outside the cafeteria, along with snack foods like Doritos in vending machines. At first, outside companies did not need to adhere to the nutritional guidelines for school meals. That changed with the 2010 Healthy, Hunger-Free Kids Act, but food corporations bounced back by reformulating products to create versions that meet the requirements.

TODAY, APPROXIMATELY 94 percent of U.S. public schools participate in the USDA's National School Lunch Program. Only public schools in rich areas, like New York's Voorheesville district, can afford to forgo federal funding and the supply of free commodity foods to offer students healthy lunches. Attendance at the country's wealthiest public schools is overwhelmingly white; only 8 percent of white students attend high-poverty schools, compared to 45 percent of Latine students, 44 percent of Black students, 38 percent of American Indian/

Alaska Native students, 24 percent of Pacific Islander students, and 14 percent of Asian students.

Students with families who have the time and resources to send them with home lunches can avoid cafeteria foods. They can also afford to buy alternative meals for sale at schools. Students who live in households with incomes under 185 percent of the poverty threshold are eligible for free or reduced-price lunch. (In 2021, the federal poverty level for a family of four was a yearly income of $26,500 or less.) Foster children, participants in the Head Start and Migrant Education programs, and students receiving services under the Runaway and Homeless Youth Act also get free lunches. Some districts, including New York City, the largest school district in the country, offer free lunch to all students. Of the more than 2.4 billion school breakfasts served in 2019, 80 percent were free, and another 5 percent were reduced price.[16] Poor students, who are disproportionately Black, Indigenous, and Latine, eat most of the meals served in school cafeterias.

Commodity foods are corn, soybeans, wheat, rice, dairy, sugar, peanuts, meat, and feed grains like sorghum. Meat and dairy make up two thirds of the commodities sent to schools. Commodities that go to schools must be processed and packaged to conform to federal food storage and transportation regulations. Schools that lack the capacity to process commodity foods in their kitchens often outsource the job to Big Food companies like Kraft Heinz, Del Monte, Conagra, and Tyson. Processing drains food of its nutrients. Fresh corn becomes corn syrup. Meat is ultra-processed into carcinogenic deli slices, corn dogs, chicken nuggets, or sausage links. Potatoes, the most popular vegetable, become french fries or tater tots. Fruit is served as part of muffins and pastries. And the packaging surrounding the foods adds harmful chemicals.

By 2009, school lunches had defeated their original purpose of building a strong army: obesity was the main medical reason for turning away military recruits. A letter signed by dozens of retired generals and admirals called these would-be soldiers "too fat to fight." But this time, the government did not adjust—it doubled down instead, opening school doors wide to welcome in food corporations.

Domino's began making Smart Slices for school cafeterias in

forty-seven states in 2011.[17] Doritos chips are the base for a popular chili and cheese school meal branded a Walking Taco. In 2023, Lunchables reworked their ingredients to create a school lunch product that meets the federal dietary guidelines. The USDA's stamp of approval means that millions of consumers will believe Lunchables are healthy or, at least, healthy enough. At Coral Reef Senior High School in Miami, Florida, Emily Sarasa remembers eating a two-dollar slice of pizza from Papa Johns, Domino's, or Pizza Hut and a one-dollar cookie for lunch every day. "I never even stepped into the lunchroom because this was served out of the theater concession stand." Little Caesars, Pop-Tarts, Funyuns, and Cheetos also have a strong public school presence.

Even when fast-food companies don't sell their products directly in schools, they are omnipresent. In elementary school, Emily earned coupons for Papa Johns and Chuck E. Cheese as a reward for her good grades. Fire safety guides come with fast-food coupons attached. Students and classes that raise the most money during PTO drives earn fast-food prizes, like pizza parties for their classes. Fast food is promoted on school buses, scoreboards, and school signs and at games and fundraisers.

Milk also has a strong presence on cafeteria trays and walls. Twitter user @innesmck was eating dinner in a California junior high school lunchroom plastered with milk promotion ads in 2019. They rated the posters in a series of viral tweets. One "Got Milk? bodybymilk" ad featured a milk-mustached girl lying on a tree branch at night holding a glass of milk. "1. ambiguous but inspirational. did she climb the tree in those boots? did milk equip her to do that? 5/10" One milk mustache poster boasting the slogan "NBA Cares" promises that "Nutrients Aren't The Only Things That Milk Can Help Replenish." "5. WHAT else can they replenish? author was CLEARLY winking after writing this. deeply uncomfortable and unsuitable for a school environment. 9/10."

The ads were reminiscent of GENYOUth, a collaboration between the USDA's Dairy Marketing Inc., the National Football League, and the National Dairy Council that is a dairy promotion scheme masquerading as a public school student health and wellness initiative. GENYOUth preys on students' passions for sports and celebrities. On GENYOUth's Fuel Up to Play 60 (FUTP60) app, kids accumulate points toward becoming a Student Zone Ambassador at a student summit where they can meet NFL players. To earn these points, students participate in activities at school and at home. The At Home projects include the Four Ingredient Challenge, which requires creating a recipe using milk, yogurt, a tortilla, and a banana in forty-five minutes or less. Students can also make cheese, strawberry sorbet, smoothies, milkshakes, or hot chocolate with two cups of whole milk and a quarter cup of refined sugar. Another At Home activity instructs students to collect coins in milk jugs and then donate them to food banks so that they can buy milk. The app also has videos of NFL players, interviews with dairy farmers, and a film showing children playing football interspersed with images of farmers milking cows to inspirational music. The FUTP60 student summit sponsors include Borden Cheese, Dairy MAX, Domino's, Frito-Lay, and PepsiCo.

As of 2019, over forty million school children, including 81 percent of those who are eligible for free and reduced meals, had participated in GENYOUth programs. Its participants are disproportionately Black and Latine students, despite their high rates of lactose intolerance, diabetes, and other dairy-related health conditions. The all-white board of directors included DMI CEO Thomas Gallagher, former Wall Street executive and Fox Business Network personality Alexis Glick, NFL commissioner Roger Goodell, NDC Chair Audrey Donahoe, and Domino's Chief Operating Officer Russell Weiner. A GENYOUth report written for dairy producers identifies schools as rife with profit opportunities for the industry. In a GENYOUth YouTube video, "The Importance of Dairy," Alexis Glick describes the program as "an extension of America's dairy farmers."[18]

Students seeking alternatives to milk at school run up against stringent USDA regulations. The agency dictates that schools "must offer" milk in school breakfasts and lunches. They "may not offer water in place of milk. Fluid milk is a required component of a reimbursable meal. Program operators must not promote or offer water, juice, or any other beverage as an alternative selection to fluid milk in a reimbursable meal throughout the food service area."[19]

At Honolulu's Waikiki Elementary School, which has a predominantly Asian student body, children are not allowed to leave the lunchroom until they have finished their milk. They can toss the food on their tray in the trash, but they must drink their milk under the watchful eyes of the lunchroom staff. If any public school student across the United States, including the approximately 80 percent of Black and Indigenous students who are lactose intolerant, wants to drink plant-based instead of cow's milk at school, they need to see a doctor to get a diagnosis that they have a disability.

In 2022, thirty million students ate school lunches. To pull off the feat of serving vast waves of students in short twenty-to-thirty-minute time windows, lunchrooms depend on prepackaged commodities and popular corporate food products. In their efforts to keep their kitchen operations streamlined, lunchroom staff have teamed up with the food industry to fight any changes to USDA guidelines that would hamper their ability to perform these daily miracles.

AT THE BEGINNING of "Art Teacher," the seventh episode of the Emmy Award–winning TV show about a Philadelphia public school, *Abbott Elementary*, teachers Barbara (Sheryl Lee Ralph) and Jacob (Chris Perfetti) are in the lunchroom "overseeing nutrition." Jacob points to a student struggling with an unidentifiable meat patty hanging off their fork and says, "I can't believe this is what they're serving the children." For once, Barbara, a veteran Black teacher, and Jacob, a white millennial, agree. They shake their heads in rhythm, murmuring, "Mm, mm, mm." "Budget cuts," Barbara explains. "And it gets worse every year."

Jacob asks Devin (Reggie Conquest), who runs the lunchroom, "Are there even any vegetables in these meals?" "Yeah,'" Devin replies sarcastically, "we've got sprouts flown in from Brussels every morning." "No use getting frustrated with him," Barbara advises Jacob. "They're just like us, doing the best with what they got." Jacob tells Barbara about some teachers in Kentucky who started a school garden. Barbara agrees to start one with him at Abbott.

The garden eventually produces a baby zucchini that Jacob and

Barbara proudly present to Devin. He unceremoniously drops it into the trash can. "What am I supposed to do with a twerp squash? Feed half a kid? Come on, man." Jacob promises that this is just the first of many and that soon the school will be "swimming in squash." "And then what?" Devin asks, "We prepare them? We do not have time. We're barely getting by as is. You all can make-believe on your own time." Discouraged, Barbara concedes, "He's right. We're being foolish. I can't believe I let myself get carried away. Projects like this, they do not work in public schools."

Determined to bring vegetables into the students' meals, Jacob arrives at school the next morning carrying several trays of zucchini that he bought from the farmers' market and then stayed up all night preparing. Barbara is delighted and impressed. The pair head to the lunchroom. Devin eyes them warily. "Just what I need, a man who wears used pants bringing me a tray of pickles." Jacob tries to win him over. "We realize how difficult your day must be. You work under stressful conditions, and you still provide for hundreds of kids a day." Barbara jumps in. "And I am sorry for insulting your food. I'm sure it is great." Devin nods. "I appreciate that. And it is great. You should try some." Barbara demurs. "Oh, I have." Devin insists. "Not with this new micro-wave we got. These things is piping hot."

Devin pushes a tray containing a few breaded lumps toward her. "Go ahead, give it a try." He winks at Jacob. Barbara uses a fork to pick one up and then puts the whole thing in her mouth. "Mmm, tater tots." "Oh, that's a chicken nugget," Devin corrects her. To distract Devin from Barbara's disgust, Jacob pushes the trays of zucchini toward him. "Any-way, here it is, all ready to serve." "Oh yeah," Devin says as he effortlessly slides the trays straight into the trash. "That's a health code violation. I can't be serving food you all made at home."

The episode vividly illustrates how scale and food safety regulations prevent schools from serving nutritious foods, even when they come directly from a school garden. Waikiki Elementary School has a gor-geous, bountiful garden, yet the produce does not make its way into its school lunch offerings. Instead, it goes to a high-end restaurant where servers boast that local students grew and harvested it. A produce stand lets wealthier parents purchase some of the fruits of their children's labor to eat at home. Some schools require food vendors to have liability insurance that would cover the cost of any potential lawsuits for foodborne illnesses, an expense that is out of reach for many small producers. Other schools insist on even distribution of foods among students—if one gets a fresh carrot, then they all must get a fresh carrot. Few, if any, school gardens will yield enough vegetables to feed an entire school in one sitting.

The USDA's Farm to School Program has made some headway in adding harvests into school meals through grants, research, technical assistance, and training. But the challenge of feeding hundreds or thousands of students each day requires extreme efficiency. It is difficult if not impossible to piece together large-scale meals from small local sources, and the USDA makes commodities available in bulk quantities packaged specifically for institutional kitchens.

The budgetary and logistical challenges of running a school lunchroom put the dream of healthier school lunches further and further out of reach. To bring it closer, federal funds would need to support fresh produce and whole ingredients, making them cheaper than processed meat, soy, and corn. But the Big Food industry is not going to loosen its hold on school meals any time soon. Whenever advocacy for healthier school meals has led to regulatory reform, corporate pushback has been swift and effective. The 2010 Healthy, Hunger-Free Kids Act (HHFKA), passed by President Barack Obama's administration, encouraged schools to include more fruits, vegetables, whole grains, and fat-free and low-fat milk in their cafeteria offerings. It reduced the acceptable levels of sodium, saturated fat, and trans fats in school meals. It even extended these requirements to competitive foods, creating challenges for the fast-food companies that sell these items on school grounds.

Previously, regulations imposed weekly limits on calorie counts and nutrition requirements, allowing lunchrooms some flexibility to play with the daily numbers—one day could be over the limit as long as others were under it. When the HHFKA replaced these rules with daily limits on meals and menu items, many competitive foods didn't cut it.

Popular items got downsized or removed altogether, triggering protests from disappointed students. Food companies resented the cost of reformulating their products, but found ways to stay in the game. Chick-fil-A converted its regular breaded chicken sandwich, which clocked out at 440 calories, to one that fit into federal strictures of 350 calories or less.

The HHFKA's attack on french fries took the form of a proposed reduction in the acceptable number of weekly servings of white potato. The potato and frozen-food lobbies rallied. Senator Susan Collins from Maine, a top potato-producing state, cried foul play. She crashed Secretary of Agriculture Tom Vilsack's senate budget hearing carrying a potato in one hand and a head of lettuce in the other, demanding to know, "What does the department have against potatoes?"

The potato lobby won the day, then took up arms again in 2023 when President Joe Biden's administration threatened changes similar to the Obama administration's. A National Potato Council press release warned that "certain activist voices will be extremely loud during this process and intend to place burdens on potatoes and/or attempt to reclassify America's favorite vegetable into another category entirely (grains). Such efforts have no basis in science, raise costs for consumers, and further burden already-expensive federal nutrition programs with huge new costs." The council implores, "Those costly, misleading and unscientific efforts should be rejected by the DGAs and all federal policymakers outright."

Cranberry growers won a battle to keep their product in cafeterias, despite its extremely high sugar content. Sweetened dried cranberries count as a fruit serving. Sugar-sweetened raisins rode the coattails of this victory and also remained on school menus, even though raisins, unlike cranberries, are naturally sweet. Even though the HHFKA increased the requirement of fresh and even canned and frozen fruits, cafeterias are still allowed to meet the minimum servings with fruit juices, which can also take the form of a dessert (think Minute Maid popsicle).

When the USDA had doubts about continuing to allow two

tablespoons of tomato paste on a pizza to count as eight tablespoons of whole tomatoes—that is, a full vegetable serving—the Coalition for Sustainable School Meal Programs, an industry group, spent $5 million to lobby for the standard to stay in place. One of the most beloved school foods, pizza, brings in over $450 million to school cafeterias yearly as a popular meal choice that students are willing to spend their lunch money on. USDA rules glorify it as a combination of grains, protein, and a full serving of vegetables. Leaving aside the debate about whether tomatoes are a fruit or a vegetable, the new rule would have equated the two tablespoons of tomato paste to just two tablespoons of vegetables, not a full serving, and pizza would have fallen short of the HHFKA requirements. Schwan Food Company, which manufactures 70 percent of school pizzas, ultimately persuaded Congress to insert an exception to the tomato rules into the federal budget, maintaining the reign of pizza in school lunchrooms.

Comedian Seth Meyers and Kermit the Frog mocked the absurdity of Congress' surrender to Big Food on *Saturday Night Live*. A cartoon by MacLeod introduced a new food pyramid with only three food groups: salt, fries, and pizza. A character from Babar explains the chart: "We can guarantee that our kids eat healthy food—by calling the food that they eat 'Healthy Food'!" But while adults laughed at these workarounds, students pushed back against Obama's healthy lunch guidelines, posting pics of meager, unappetizing portions with the hashtags #ThanksMichelleObama and #BrownBagginIt. They organized lunch strikes. A Kansas high school student's parody of the song "We Are Young," retitled "We Are Hungry," shows a USDA representative explaining the new MyPlate guide to students who are collapsing from hunger. Instead of the line "set the world on fire," the parody urges listeners to "set the policy on fire." Students in the video watch their wealthier friends with envy as they stock up on chips and other snacks.

Rejecting the new, often smaller, offerings that met the stricter guidelines, students ate less school food. With fewer students participating in the program, the number of federal reimbursements fell. Cafeteria workers who had to exclude incomplete meals from the lunch counts they provided to the USDA looked on helplessly as students chose to go hungry, bring lunch from home, or buy food elsewhere. Program participation decreased by a million students over the 2012–13 school year, the law's first year of implementation. Prices shot up when demand declined. Some schools decided to give up federal funding altogether and bank on creating their own school lunch programs that did not have to meet the new standards and would appeal to more students, generating more dollars from their families.

Part of Obama's school lunch reform was a nationwide order that flavored milk in school lunchrooms had to be fat-free. The Los Angeles Unified School District, the second largest in the U.S., went a step further, banning chocolate and strawberry milk altogether because of their high sugar and fat content. Chocolate milk champions protested, pointing to food waste and lost nutrients when students throw away or refuse plain milk. Brent Walmsley of SugarWatch, a nonprofit health organization, responded, "I can't think of anywhere else we would do this. We wouldn't serve caramel apples to increase apple consumption. We wouldn't glaze carrots with sugar to get increased carrot consumption. . . . Milk is getting this odd pass here."[20] Researchers found that, contrary to the propaganda that insisted that students would starve without chocolate milk, removing it from cafeterias did not lower their nutrient intake.

The ban lasted only as long as the Obama presidency. One of President Donald Trump's first actions in office was to ease up the lunchroom dietary requirements, signaling his support for the food industry and indifference to student health. After Trump reversed Obama's fat-free flavored milk rule, 80 percent of public school districts, including LAUSD, reinstated strawberry and chocolate milk—a move that disproportionately affected minority students. The LAUSD's student population is 73.6 percent Latine, 10.5 percent white, 7.6 percent Black, 5.9 percent Asian, 2 percent mixed race, .02 percent Pacific Islander or Native Hawaiian, and 0.1 percent Indigenous or Alaska Native.[21]

LAUSD school board members were divided about the benefits of chocolate milk. One thing they agreed on, though, was that federal funding should not depend on milk being a required part of school meals. When New York proposed a chocolate milk ban in 2019, dairy farmers begged the city not to implement it, even while acknowledging that it would have a positive impact on children's health.[22] Whole milk is the next frontier for the dairy industry. Banned from cafeterias in 2012 to reduce childhood obesity, it now has to compete in the real world with oat, almond, and soy milk. Milk lobbyists argue that, if children can't drink the tastier (whole-fat version) of their product, they will turn to soda and other unhealthy drinks instead.

No matter how many incremental changes alternating administrations make to school food requirements, there will be no significant reform until the USDA is divorced from Big Food and Ag. Meanwhile, instead of devoting resources to improving the health profiles of the thirty million students in the school lunch program, the USDA is studying the dietary guidelines' compatibility with the processed food industry. A 2023 USDA report celebrates the fact that a person following the 2020–25 guidelines can enjoy a diet made up of 91 percent processed foods.[23] This is our future.

ALONG WITH BEING treated as depositories for cheap commodity foods, students receiving school lunches often have to endure their peers' ridicule. At some schools, just eating in the lunchroom can make you a target. "The cafeteria was for the poor kids. The food there was gross. Kids who did not eat in the cafeteria were embarrassed to go into it during lunch for fear that others would think they were getting free or discount lunch."[24] At one school, "white kids ate upstairs and Mexicans ate downstairs." The National School Lunch Act directs schools not to identify students who get free lunch,[25] but their meal systems make it obvious. Up to one-third of public high schools have separate lines, stations, floors, or rooms for students who get free lunch, often for ease of service or accounting purposes. Others sell school lunches and competitive foods in different locations.

Sociologist Janet Poppendieck shares two of her UC Santa Cruz students' observations about their school lunchrooms: "There was the cafeteria line, mostly filled with Hispanic kids with lunch tickets. Then there was the food area adjacent and that sold cookies, bagels, sodas, brand name . . . expensive items." "Those who were provided with lunch . . . were the only ones who actually ate the school food. . . . There was also a separate door for them to go to, to receive their lunch, and they had to eat in the cafeteria because the school dishes and trays were not allowed outside."[26]

Seventy percent of Texas public school students receive free lunch. In *Free Lunch*, Rex Ogle's award-winning middle school memoir, he writes about the struggles he endured as a poor Latino boy in Texas trying to hide his free lunch status from his friends.

One time, I wrote down my name and "Free Lunch Program" on paper. I handed it to the cashier, hoping she would read it, and no one around me would hear. But she said, "Oh, honey. I forgot my glasses at home. Can you read it to me?" So that didn't work. Last week, I tried to wait to be the last student in line. No matter how many times, I said, "You can go ahead of me," there were more students. I ended up with only two minutes to eat my food before the bell rang.

Today, I have a new idea. When I get to the register, I point to the red folder and say, "Page 14. Rex Ogle." The cashier nods. Even though she's slow 'cause she's old, it's still faster than most days. She gets the red folder, finds the page, and puts the check next to my name. It takes a second to realize it worked. I did it. I feel awesome. I didn't have to say it—those words I hate, the ones that make me feel like a beggar: *free lunch*. My joy lasts maybe two seconds. As I walk away, the students behind me ask, "What's in the red folder?" I don't look back. Instead, I duck my head and run until Mr. Lopez shouts, "No running in the cafeteria, Ogle!"[27]

Students who get free lunch often suffer name-calling, humiliation on social media, and other forms of bullying. It can get so bad that they

would rather go hungry than stand in the lunch line. School administrators either don't see this behavior, ignore it, or are afraid to discipline
students. In *Mahanoy v. B.L.*, the Supreme Court held that schools cannot discipline students for social media posts made off school grounds
and outside of school hours.[28] This leaves students free to make online
attacks that can drive their peers out of the lunch line. @unc_jeff offers
#FreshmanAdvice: "Don't eat free lunch pictures will be taken of you."[29]

When the San Francisco school district removed competitive foods
from their schools for health reasons in 2009, it got an unexpected
result: a reduction in bullying and discrimination.[30] But most schools
cannot afford to help their students in this way.[31] Individual schools
rake in an average of $10,000–$15,000 a year from their percentage
of competitive food sales and another $1,000–$10,000 from vending
machines, with some schools bringing in more than $50,000 in one
year. Perpetually under-resourced public schools need every penny
they can get, whether it comes from fast-food corporations or struggling parents.

SOMETIMES, IT'S THE schools' employees who shame their students.
Tara Chavez had to calm her distraught son, a second grader at Phoenix, Arizona's Desert Cove Elementary, where a cafeteria worker had
stamped his wrist with the words "LUNCH MONEY." His account still
had enough in it to cover his lunch that day, with seventy-five cents
left over. Usually, the school sent children home with a reminder slip
when their accounts were running low. Another parent, Juan Forten-
berry, angry about the way Desert Cove treats their students, tweeted:
"Y'all couldn't think for two minutes about the numerous references of
branding someone as a stigma?"[32]

At a school near Birmingham, Alabama, the stamp on Jon Bivens's
son's arm taunted him with a smiley face under the words "I Need
Lunch Money." Bivens was not amused. He pulled his child out of Gar-
dendale Elementary School for the remaining few days of second grade,
leaving the $1.38 in his lunch account unused. Bivens condemned the

school's behavior as bullying, shaming, and branding. In response, Principal Laura Ware offered to allow the Bivens family to switch to receiving email alerts instead of stamps, but she kept the system in place for other students.[33] Cherry Creek School District in Colorado fired kitchen worker Della Curry for giving lunch to first graders who did not have the money to pay for them.[34]

Indiana's Kokomo High School followed a policy of giving students with lunch debt an "alternative tray" of two cold slices of processed cheese between two slices of white bread, and then blamed the school's wealthy families. Complaining about the list of 499 students with lunch debt, communications director David Barnes said, "Some of the people on the list, I'm sorry, are making $100,000 a year. Family of four, and have a debt of over $100. I'm sorry, those people need to pay their bills." But Barnes did not explain why it was necessary to stigmatize students with an alternative tray of unappetizing, inadequate food to collect the debt.[35]

In most cases, lunch debt is not the result of parents' negligence. Most indebted families simply cannot afford school meals. Families living on the edge of poverty must often juggle finances, forgoing payments some months to meet other pressing obligations. Lunch debt is one piece of an economic puzzle facing low-income families each month. Also, in some cases, families who are eligible for free lunch do not fill out the paperwork for a variety of reasons, including undocumented immigration status, language barriers, or houselessness.

Lunch shaming can involve throwing students' trays in the garbage, forcing them to clean tables or do other demeaning chores in exchange for food, and barring them from field trips, extracurricular activities, or prom. A cafeteria worker in Canonsburg, Pennsylvania, dumped Caitlin Dolan's lunch tray into the trash after finding out her family owed lunch money, wasting the food and reducing the seventh grader to tears.[36] At Salt Lake City's Uintah Elementary School, the child nutrition manager made cafeteria employees throw away forty hot meals in one sitting.[37] District regulations prohibit the meals going to other children, but the manager still wanted to stop students with lunch debt from eating them. The children got milk and fruit instead.

That night, one Uintah student went home and made forty lunches to bring in the next day, showing more empathy and resourcefulness than the school employees or the USDA.

In Pennsylvania's Wyoming Valley West School District, administrators made it clear that humiliation was the point of their lunch debt collection scheme. The district first sent letters to parents who owed ten dollars or more, threatening to put their children into foster care. Head of federal programs Joseph Muth wrote, "Your child has been sent to school every day without money and without a breakfast and/or lunch. . . . This is a failure to provide your child with proper nutrition and you can be sent to Dependency Court for neglecting your child's right to food. If you are taken to Dependency Court, the result may be your child being removed from your home and placed in foster care."[38] @stephanie_437 succinctly pointed out how ludicrous this move was. "First of all, school lunch is disgusting and ridiculously expensive. The fruits and vegetables are almost always rotten. Some of the foods aren't even cooked all the way. But you're telling me that lunch debt for low quality food can put us in foster care? Unacceptable."[39]

When Todd Carmichael, CEO of local La Colombe coffee company, said that he would pay off the district's entire $22,476 lunch bill, the school board refused his offer.[40] School board president Joseph Mazur thought the money should come from the indebted families instead of a generous benefactor.[41] More offers to pay the debt poured in. Ultimately, Mazur could not justify refusing them.

Cranston School District in Rhode Island hired a collection agency to harass families with outstanding lunch debt. In Warwick, Rhode Island, restaurant owner Angela Penta tried to pay off the school district's $4,000 lunch debt. She wanted Warwick to stop giving indebted students sunflower butter and jelly sandwiches instead of a hot lunch. Warwick turned down her money. Houston theater technician Kenny Thompson started a fundraiser after seeing a cafeteria worker hassle a fourth grader who couldn't pay because their mother was in the hospital. Thompson collected more than $30,000 for school lunch bills. Before donating it, he extracted a promise from administrators not to give inferior meals to students with lunch debt.

In 2017, GoFundMe had thirty active campaigns to raise money for school lunch debt. In 2016, writer Ashley C. Ford tweeted, "A cool thing you can do today is find out which of your local schools have kids with overdue lunch accounts and pay them off." The tweet generated hundreds of thousands of dollars in donations across the U.S.[42] The mother of Philando Castile, a Black man killed by police during a traffic stop in Minnesota in 2016, honored him by donating $8,000 to pay off student lunch debt. As a nutrition services supervisor in the St. Paul school district, Castile had often paid for lunches when students fell short. His mother's gesture inspired a crowdfunding campaign that raised $178,000.[43]

This generosity is a stunning substitute for institutional accountability. The USDA is responsible for feeding students who cannot afford lunch. Letting empathetic strangers pick up the tab falsely frames poverty, food insecurity, and discrimination as individual, not systemic, issues. Still, instead of stepping in to spare students indignities like cleaning tables or getting cold food, the USDA issued a guidance document in 2017, encouraging school districts to appeal to their communities for lunch money through "random acts of kindness" funding and school fundraisers.[44]

Seventy-five percent of school districts have unpaid lunch debt, but only some state and local laws prohibit lunch shaming. An Arkansas law allows schools to contact a parent or guardian to try to get lunch money or ask them to apply for benefits but not to prevent the student from eating.[45] This is a step in the right direction, but it is not nearly enough.[46] A 2019 federal Anti–Lunch Shaming Bill would have stopped schools from giving children with debt handstamps, wristbands, inferior meals, or extra chores. The bill did not pass. Regardless, there are protocols that schools should follow voluntarily. The first is not to segregate students according to their lunch status. Schools should use pin numbers or identical cards to track students' accounts so that only the person working the register knows whether the lunch is free or not.

Better yet, give everybody free school lunch, as in California, Maine, Massachusetts, New Mexico, Vermont, Michigan, Colorado, and Puerto Rico. Any school or district with 40 percent of students eligible for free lunch can give all its food away for free. In 2021, the Universal School Meals Program Act would have amended the National School Lunch Act to make this the norm in every public school district in the United States.[47] It did not pass.

Bathgate Elementary School in Mission Viejo, California, has "sharing stations" where students can turn in food they aren't going to eat, and other students can take it. Although this is a lovely idea, it seems hard to imagine how students taking advantage of it would avoid their peers' mockery. North Bronx teacher Adrian Brooks believes that lunch shaming has the power to alter students' tastes. "The stigma attached is that it is automatically not good to them—like, it doesn't taste good, because to them it's cheap."[48]

Even when students bring food from home, they might be bullied for having the wrong lunch. On the pilot episode of the critically acclaimed series *Fresh Off the Boat*, eleven-year-old Eddie Huang (Hudson Yang) moves with his mother Jessica (Constance Wu) and two younger brothers from DC to Orlando, Florida. On Eddie's first day at his new middle school, his teacher stumbles over his Chinese name. At lunchtime, Eddie reaches into a brown paper bag when a white boy at another table calls to him. "Yo, Chinese kid. What's your name again? Something Chinese?" After the two bond over their love for Biggie Smalls, the white boy invites Eddie to his table, where everyone is eating hamburgers. Eddie pulls a round Tupperware container filled with noodles out of his bag. When he screws the top off, the children at the table recoil. "Ugh. What is that?" "Gross!" "You gotta get it out of here." "Ying Ding's eating worms!"

When Jessica meets Eddie at the bus, he cuts her off before she can finish asking about his day. "They said my lunch smelled." She replied, "It smelled delicious." "No, they said it stank, Mom. I had to eat my lunch behind the gym where the janitor flies his kite."

The next morning at breakfast, Jessica announces that Eddie's younger brother Evan won't be going to school because a new friend gave him string cheese, which made him sick. "His body is rejecting white culture," she says, "which makes me kind of proud. Good job, Evan." Eddie sees her packing his lunch and yells for her to stop. "Mom, no! I don't want Chinese lunch. I want white people food." Jessica insists, "The kids at school will get used to it." Eddie walks off in a huff and then tosses his lunch into the nearest trash bin.

That evening at dinner, Eddie admits that he threw the lunch away. His parents are appalled at the waste, but Eddie fights back. "I need white people lunch. That gets me a seat at the table. And then, you get to change the rules. Represent. Like Nas says. I'm not trying to eat with the janitor for the rest of my life. I've got big plans."

Convinced by this logic, Jessica takes Eddie to a store to buy Lunchables. "Wow, everything fits perfectly inside a box, awesome," Eddie marvels. He returns to the school cafeteria with a swagger, pausing to compare his Pizza Lunchables to another kid's Turkey and Cheese. In the real world, Eddie's embrace of Lunchables would likely have a long-lasting impact on his health, and Evan might start to eat cheese, even though it made him sick. Illness is the price to pay for living up to the white, American dietary ideal.

In one study, more than two-thirds of Asian American participants reported embarrassing incidents related to their cultural food practices growing up.[49] White participants reported none. Asian students described complaining to their parents about the home-cooked lunches they took to school. Some parents voluntarily changed their children's diets. In 2020, @bunnygenders tweeted, "I had to eat disgusting school lunch every day bc my mom was scared ppl would bully me for bringing asian food."[50]

Statistics on obesity, diabetes, and food insecurity usually lump Asian students into one large group. They count Indian, Chinese, Japanese, Filipinx, and Samoan children as the same, when their histories, cultures, and health profiles are drastically different. California provides a good example of this confusion. A 2019 study of obesity in school children reports that 28 percent of white students are obese compared to 48 percent of Latine students, 42 percent of Black students, and 31 percent of Filipinx students. The study claims that only 24 percent of Asian children are obese, revealing what the researchers called a "reverse disparity" where students of color fare better than white students.[51] For the purposes of this study, Filipinx students do not count as

Asian. This confusion makes it difficult to assess the harms that Asian Americans experience from participating in school lunch programs.

Even though Asian American obesity rates are generally lower, they are growing. Between 2011 and 2015, Asian American girls' obesity rates almost doubled while the rate for white girls decreased by 2 percent.[52] The commonly held stereotype that some Asian American groups are a model minority, an example of immigrant success, makes it difficult to challenge or change the structures that lead to obesity and other food-related problems in their communities.

STUDENTS WHO RELY on free lunches often consume very few calories outside of school or get them through fast food or cheap, low-quality convenience foods. This means that the USDA has control over most of their food intake. When USDA food is not nutritious, food-related sickness is practically inevitable. Poor nutrition and food insecurity also affect test scores and information retention and can cause depression and anxiety. When schools discipline young people suffering from these conditions with suspensions, which they disproportionately dole out to Black and Latine students, hunger becomes part of the punishment if there is no food at home.

For corporations, their privileged position in school lunchrooms is a gift that keeps on giving. They profit first from their original sales and then many times over across the lifespan of students who form their dietary habits and preferences in childhood. School lunches, initially conceived as a way to level unequal access to food, have created separate nutritional tracks along race and class lines that lead to lifelong health disparities.

# 6

# Dee-licious!

As the guest host on the comedy show *Saturday Night Live* on November 7, 2020, when the Black Lives Matter movement had resurged and race was a hot topic, comedian Dave Chappelle broke some employment news.

While many Black people who had lost their jobs during the pandemic hoped to get them back some day, one woman who had devoted over a century to her craft faced permanent retirement. In a corporate building, three white executives deliver the news to Aunt Jemima, played by Maya Rudolph, that she is being let go. She has done nothing wrong, and the HR representative concedes that everyone loves her pancakes. The problem is how she makes white people feel about what they've done. Arguing that she makes the fluffiest and most mouthwatering pancakes, Aunt Jemima reveals her secret ingredient to the audience with a wink: her own breast milk. The executives profess their love and thank her for breastfeeding their children, but they stand firm: she has to go. Aunt Jemima cries sexism, demanding to know about Uncle Ben. If she's going down, he is too.

Uncle Ben, played by Kenan Thompson, suddenly appears at her side, berating Jemima for dragging him into her mess. Ben doubts he will be able to get another job—all he knows is rice. He also has a brood of nieces and nephews to care for, but the execs are cleaning house—even though Ben and Jemima know that white people never clean their own houses. Enraged, Ben calls for them to fire the Allstate Guy, too. Dave Chappelle, playing the Allstate Guy, using the bass tones of the real Allstate Guy (Dennis Haysbert), protests that he's not even a food product. He sells security, and his "deep black voice makes white people feel safe." And, unlike the others, he's a real person, not a character. He demands to know why they don't fire Count Chocula. Count Chocula pops up, played by Pete Davidson, arguing that he's not even Black, just made of chocolate. Aunt Jemima and Uncle Ben assert that they, too, are chocolate. Still, the executives refuse to budge. Everyone but the Allstate Guy is fired. Uncle Ben warns them that they have made a big mistake. Indifferent to his warning, the corporate executive played by Alec Baldwin tells his colleague to send in the next in line—the Land O'Lakes lady.

THE SKIT'S PUNCH LINE was corporations trying to win consumers over by getting rid of the racist brands that they never should have created in the first place. PepsiCo finally retired its pancake syrup mascot Aunt Jemima in 2020, when she was over a century old. The company had borrowed the character from a minstrel song popular in the late 1800s, which white men performed in drag and blackface. Their exaggerated features were supposed to justify the enslavement, exploitation, and abuse of Black people by making them appear ugly and stupid, subhuman. Aunt Jemima's generous figure embodies the stereotype of a mammy, an enslaved Black woman who loves taking care of white children while neglecting her own. She performs her domestic tasks happily, without the slightest hint of suffering family separation, long hours, grueling labor, or sexual harassment and assault.

Aunt Jemima's jolly nature helped assuage white people's fears about Black people's entry into society after emancipation by allowing them to possess what historian Maurice Manning calls a "slave in a box."[1] The brand persisted throughout the ages despite repeated protests.[2] Aunt Jemima was never popular among Black consumers.[3]

In the late nineteenth and early twentieth centuries, advertising regularly used racist images even when they had no connection to

the product for sale. Images of Indigenous leaders appeared on cigarette trading cards, romanticizing the United States' genocidal efforts
and suggesting that Indigenous people are historical characters, not
living people.[4] An advertisement from around 1900 for Nigger Head
Tobacco portrays a cartoonish painting of a Black man doing archery
with the caption "'Dis Nigger head am de crack shot! Yah! Yah! Yah!'"[5]
This broken speech pattern reinforced dehumanizing tropes about
Black people, as did brands like Mammy salted peanuts.[6]

When Black people appeared in early food ads, they were servers,
maids, or domestic workers, often offering advice to white mothers. A
1929 Hostess Cake ad in the *Ladies' Home Journal* showed a smiling
Black woman dressed as a maid holding out a cake on a tray.[7] Because
of Black domestic workers' expertise in food preparation, their presence signaled authority and authenticity.[8] Hires Root Beer drew on a
similar trope in a *Life* magazine ad featuring a Black porter reassuring
a white couple, "Yassuh . . . it's genu-wine Hires."

B&G Foods' Black mascot for its Cream of Wheat cereal first
appeared on its boxes in 1893 as Rastus, a derogatory word for Black
men. Rastus was a caricature of a happy-go-lucky illiterate servant.
One Cream of Wheat ad shows Rastus smiling at the camera while
holding a pan over one shoulder and a tray in the other hand, ready to
serve a tiny white girl. The caption reads: "Little Miss Muffet, sat on a
tuffet, winsome, charming and sweet, our fat darkey spied her and put
down beside her a luncheon of good Cream of Wheat."[9]

In another Cream of Wheat ad, Rastus smiles and holds up a sign
that reads: "Maybe Cream of Wheat ain't got no vitamines. I don't
know what them things is. If they's bugs they ain't none in Cream of
Wheat but she's sho' good to eat and cheap. Costs 'bout 1 cent fo' a great
big dish."[10] In *Ordinary Notes*, English literature and Black studies professor Christina Sharpe describes an encounter with this image "post-
er-sized and mounted for display" at an antique shop with her brother
when she was thirteen years old. "We were offended and we told the
owners so; afterwards, between us, the phrase 'if they's bugs' became
shorthand for some white people's *brutal imaginations*."[11]

In 1925, Rastus evolved into Chef Frank White. The name was

different, but the connotations were the same. Despite his elevated status, Chef White existed to serve white people. Although the chef no longer appears on the product's packaging, he was still on the B&G website as recently as 2023, smiling down at a white child spooning cereal into her mouth.[12]

Banana producers United Fruit Company introduced their mascot Miss Chiquita, a singing banana in a red skirt and wide-brimmed fruit-filled hat, in 1944. She later became an exoticized Latina woman wearing a blue dress, heels, and the same hat.[13] Mars created Uncle Ben, also a Black servant-mascot, in 1946, evoking the lost South, where Black people were often referred to as uncle or aunt, saving the more respectful forms of address of mister and missus for white people.[14] Mars later promoted Ben from uncle to chairman of the board, but he continued to symbolize Black servitude.

Stereotypical advertising also targeted poor white people. Mountain Dew, owned by PepsiCo, got its name from the moonshine (homemade alcohol) typically produced in the South. Its 1960s marketing campaigns relied on classist caricatures of Appalachians, embodied by brand mascot Willy the Hillbilly. Although Willy is no longer, the Mountain Dew name remains.[15]

Backlash against racist brands eventually led to some change. In the 1960s, Pillsbury changed its drink mix brands Chinese Cherry and Injun Orange to Choo Choo Cherry and Jolly Olly Orange. Around the same time, Conagra introduced Mrs. Butterworth's syrup in a voluptuous bottle, shaped to evoke the mammy stereotype. Ironically, Thelma Butterfly McQueen, who played Scarlett O'Hara's maid in *Gone with the Wind* and was likely the bottle's model, was a vocal opponent of Hollywood's racial stereotyping.[16] When critics petitioned Conagra to get rid of Mrs. Butterworth, the company slimmed down her figure and used a white woman's voice in television commercials.

Despite the legal advances of the civil rights movement in the 1950s and '60s, the only path to eliminating racist branding was through threats to corporations' reputations, although advocates increasingly turned to the courts with creative claims. PepsiCo's Lays introduced a new racist mascot, Frito Bandito, in 1967. The character was a Mexican thief

wearing a sombrero, speaking broken English, and carrying six shoot-
ers. The National Mexican American Anti-Defamation Committee first
responded by politely asking Frito-Lay to ditch it. After the company
ignored its request, the committee brought a lawsuit against the corporation alleging defamation of Chicanos as "lazy, thieving people."[17] The
class action suit against Frito-Lay and its advertising agency, Foote, Cone
& Belding, sought $10 million to finance anti-discrimination programs
and $100 in punitive damages for every Spanish-speaking person liv-
ing in the U.S., totaling $610 million. The bad publicity surrounding
the suit persuaded PepsiCo to lay the bandit to rest voluntarily in 1971.

Advocates also used the courts to fight a battle against Crazy Horse
Malt Liquor, rolled out to consumers in 1992. The brand invoked the
history of settlers' introduction of alcohol into Indigenous communities in efforts to subdue resistance. Crazy Horse Malt Liquor, produced
by Hornell Brewing Company and distributed by G. Heileman Brewing
Company, sought to capitalize on the association between Indigenous
people and alcoholism, despite its tragic legacy of fetal alcohol syndrome and substance dependency. Ironically, Crazy Horse, or Tasunke
Witko, the revered Oglala Lakota leader, had urged Indigenous people
not to drink alcohol.

Immediately after Hornell branded the beer with Witko's name and
image, the American Indian Movement called for a national boycott.
The U.S. surgeon general held a press conference in support of AIM,
condemning Hornell's "insensitive and malicious marketing." When
Hornell refused to make a change, U.S. senators Tom Daschle and Brock
Adams proposed a law making the use of the name Crazy Horse on alcoholic beverages illegal.

Hornell responded to the bill with a lawsuit arguing that banning
the brand violated the company's First Amendment free speech rights.[18]
Although the court sided with Hornell, it acknowledged that "the use
of the name of a revered Native American leader, who preached sobri-
ety and resisted exploitation under the hand of the United States government, is offensive and may be viewed as an exploitation of Native
Americans across this country."

After this loss in federal court, Witko's estate brought a new suit in the Rosebud Sioux Tribal Court. By the time it ended with a settlement in 2001, SBC Holdings (formerly Stroh Brewery) had acquired the brand from Heileman. John Stroh III made a public apology to Mr. Seth Big Crow, Witko's estate administrator, and presented him with thirty-two Pendleton blankets, thirty-two sweetgrass braids, thirty-two tobacco twists, and seven thoroughbred horses. No money changed hands.[19] Crazy Horse Malt Liquor became Crazy Stallion Malt Liquor. It took another two decades before Land O'Lakes agribusiness and food company ceased using the image of a kneeling Indigenous woman as a mascot to sell sticks of butter.

Rastus was resurrected to join the national conversation about racism in a special guest appearance on HBO's acclaimed 2020 horror science fiction drama *Lovecraft County*. In Episode 8, "Jig-a-Bobo," the 1921 Cream of Wheat ad appears on a poster in an alley where one of the main characters, Dee, a young Black girl, escapes from a threatening white man. The poster evokes the relationship between stereotyped characters and the violence at the heart of the episode: the open casket funeral of Emmett Till, the Black fourteen-year-old abducted, tortured, and murdered after a white woman falsely accused him of flirting with her in 1955. In Episode 1, "Sundown," the show's main characters stop at a gas station next to a billboard advertising Aunt Jemima pancakes. Aunt Jemima's face is in a broad smile next to the phrase "Dee-licious!"

Not all stereotypical branding has disappeared. The popular supermarket chain Trader Joe's sells a variety of products under its Trader José, Trader Ming, Trader Joe San, and Arabian Joe's labels. In response to consumer backlash, the corporation has asserted that these brands are not racist.[20] The 2016 animated comedy *Sausage Party*, starring food products who discover the fate that awaits them in the outside world, features characters drawn straight from the playbooks of Trader Joe's and Hornell. Although a character based on Uncle Ben did not survive the film's focus group screenings, white actor Bill Hader's impersonation of an Indigenous leader personifying an alcoholic beverage called

Firewater made the cut.[21] *Sausage Party* was a success, earning more than $120 million over its budget.

The ethnic aisles in supermarkets represent another holdout. Ethnic is an ambiguous term that stores apply loosely to any food not categorized as Black or white. These aisles carve out sections, often in the most neglected areas of the store, "dedicated to soy sauce, duck sauce, oyster sauce, rice vinegar, coconut milk, rice crackers, stir-fry sauces, yum yum sauce, curry paste, corn flours, adobo seasoning, bagged tortillas, refried beans, salsas and hundreds of other products connected, sometimes tenuously, to Asian and Latin American countries."[22]

This food segregation reinforces the idea that Asian and Latine food, no matter how common it has become among white people (think Taco Tuesday), is forever something separate and exotic. In ethnic aisles, the notion of the "perpetual foreigner" that hangs over Asian American and Latine consumers also haunts the foods associated with them. Economically, it forces these foods to compete against each other for scarce supermarket space. In many stores, the manufacturer, not the food, determines product placement. Frontera-brand tortilla chips live in the ethnic aisle while Tostitos reside in the much larger space for general snacks.

A satirical announcement on a Miami website, The Plantain, announced new ethnic aisles in local grocery chain Sedano's, making "Anglo" food easier to find. These shelves stocked "almond milk, brussels sprouts, goji berries, kombucha, gluten-free crackers, and assortments of artisanal jams sold in mason jars." "South Florida is a community of immigrants," said Carlos Perez-Santiago, a Sedano's spokesperson. 'We are proud to provide our newly arrived Anglo neighbors with food from their homeland.'"[23]

Former vice president of grocery at Whole Foods, Errol Schweizer, calls ethnic aisles "a legacy of white supremacy and colonialism." He views them as part of the systemic racism of the grocery business that includes low wages for hourly workers and the absence of workers of color in higher-paid positions, like buyers. His efforts to remove Whole Foods' ethnic aisles met significant resistance.[24] But where worker advocacy failed, social media may succeed. TikTok and Instagram attract millions of millennials to new cuisines that may shoot up demand for ingredients previously viewed as exotic or fringe.[25]

ALONG WITH SUPERMARKETS and select products, restaurants can be sites of racist branding. Restaurants featuring names, décor, or architecture romanticizing the time and practices of enslavement soared to the height of their popularity as the civil rights movement gained steam during the 1950s and 1960s. In *Burgers in Blackface*, social scientist Naa Oyo A. Kwate focuses on four of these: Coon Chicken Inn, Mammy's Cupboard, Richard's Restaurant and Slave Market, and Sambo's Restaurants.[26]

Coon Chicken Inn operated from 1925 until 1957. The patrons of its Salt Lake City, Seattle, and Portland branches entered the restaurants by walking through a Black man's caricatured mouth. His large face with its winking eye and exaggerated features, topped by a skewed porter's cap, appeared on restaurant advertisements and menus. Kwate describes the restaurants' interior as a "racism zone replete with racist kitsch." Head waiter Roy Hawkins, who was Black, told the *Salt Lake Tribune* that he often retaliated against insulting white patrons, like one woman whose mink he "'accidentally' spilled a coffee pot on."[27]

The grandson of Coon Chicken Inn's founders defends his grandparents as entrepreneurs interested in "preserving a part of history that should remind us all of the senselessness of racial prejudice."[28] His words ring hollow, considering that his family still profits from this prejudice by shipping Coon Chicken Inn menus, matchbooks, toothpick holders, and dishware around the world as collectors' items. Coon Chicken Inn is gone but not forgotten. On the 2022 final episode of the television series *Atlanta*, a Black sushi chef who keeps losing his customers to the Popeyes outlet visible from his restaurant window calls the fast-food chain a "modern Coon Chicken."[29] This poignant reference reminds the viewer that food oppression takes many forms. It is easy to see the harm that Coon Chicken Inn's ghoulish name and architecture did to Black people. It is harder to see how fast-food joints like Popeyes, which capitalizes on an association between Blackness and fried chicken, inflicts damage on the community through cheap and convenient foods that lead to diabetes and obesity.

Richard's Restaurant and Slave Market, operating in Berwyn, Illinois, during the 1960s and '70s, featured mannequins and cocktail waiters dressed as enslaved women. Kwate paints a dire picture of the restaurant's location. "Berwyn was a sundown town, a municipality in which local customs and/or laws forbade Black persons (and in some instances, members of other racial or ethnic groups) from remaining in town after dark, under threat of arrest, violent expulsion, or worse. When Richard's opened in 1952, not a single Black person resided in any of the town's census tracts. Forty years later, one family, the Campbells, bought a house in Berwyn. The family, parents and children alike, were greeted with arson and other threats of violence. City officials paid little mind, and the family soon moved out." Although the Richard's sign did not include the words "Slave Market," its newspaper advertisements did.

When restaurateurs Sam Battistone and Newell Bohnett launched Sambo's restaurant in Santa Barbara, California, they insisted that its name had nothing to do with the children's book, *The Story of Little Black Sambo*. Instead, they claimed that they arrived at the name Sambo's simply by combining Battistone's first name with the beginning of Bohnett's last name. Nonetheless, they chose to capitalize on this apparent coincidence with Little Black Sambo–inspired décor. In the late 1970s, the Sambo's chain had 1,200 locations in forty-seven states.[30] Some of them were in sundown towns—Medford, Eugene, and Salem, Oregon, and Eureka, California. Another California town with a Sambo's, Ukiah, had a heavy Ku Klux Klan presence.

When Sambo's tried to expand to the northeast in the 1970s, it met resistance. The Commission on Human Rights and Opportunities in Hartford, Connecticut, asked the franchise owners to operate their Hartford outlet under a different name. Brockton, Massachusetts's License Commission withheld Sambo's license to try to force a name change. In Ann Arbor, Michigan, in 1971, city council member Norris Thomas vowed to organize a boycott of Sambo's if the city permitted it to open under that name. Sambo's succumbed to the pressure, initially operating under the name Jolly Tiger. But after the franchise steadily lost money, its owner requested and obtained permits for two Sambo's signs in 1978. A year later, Ann Arbor reacted by revoking the sign permits. Sambo's responded by suing the city for violating its free speech rights. Sambo's won the right to keep its name, but Judge J. Keith wrote a scathing and insightful dissent.

In this dissent, Judge Keith described racist restaurants as a form of hate speech that, although legal, could cause serious harm. He evoked a finding by the Rhode Island Commission for Human Rights that the name Sambo's clearly signaled to Black consumers that "their patronage was unwelcome, objectionable, and not acceptable, desired, or solicited." Racist branding was an unofficial way to maintain Jim Crow segregation after the law formally prohibited it. A sign reading "Sambo's" is essentially the same as one declaring "Whites Only." Judge Keith noted that the name's "offensiveness and harm is not lessened simply because the word is contained in an advertisement or placed on a sign 30 feet in the air."

Eating, like sex, is an intimate act. Preventing intimacy was one of the main drivers of segregation, as white people feared that mixed-race children and families would blur the racial lines they wanted to maintain. Trying to stop interracial relationships was so important to the South that, even after the Supreme Court rendered state laws against Black-white marriages unconstitutional in 1963's *Loving v. Virginia*, some states continued to enforce these laws for decades. Alabama, the last holdout, got rid of its interracial marriage ban as late as 2000. Similarly, although the 1964 Civil Rights Act made segregation in public accommodations, including restaurants, illegal, racist restaurants allowed their owners to effectuate segregation informally.

Sambo's won its legal battles but eventually succumbed to bankruptcy. Denny's, a restaurant chain infamous for racist incidents against its customers, bought some of Sambo's former buildings. In June 2020, after the murder of George Floyd by police in Minneapolis, the last Sambo's restaurant changed its name to Chad's. Its Santa Barbara patrons railed against the new name.[31] But they managed to retain a vestige of old times: the restaurant, which sits on the city's well-traveled waterfront, has a plaque that marks it as Sambo's birthplace and proudly declares, "on this location June 17, 1957 the first of Sambo's nationwide chain of family restaurants opened its doors."

The entrance to Mammy's Cupboard, which still serves lunch daily in Natchez, Mississippi, is at the bottom of Mammy's giant skirt. Mammy's huge head, neck, blouse, and arms, which hold out a tray, sit atop the building. In addition to food, Mammy's Cupboard sells Mammy-shaped lamps and dolls balancing cotton bales on their heads.

Why do white consumers hold on to racist restaurants so tightly? Perhaps these spaces are a haven for people clinging to their social and economic capital in hard times. Inside these fantasylands, they can experience their whiteness as a tangible good that signals their superiority over at least one part of the population.[32] It is a feeling that may be harder and harder to come by as the white population continues to decrease. Marketing food through explicit racism may soon be a thing of the past.[33]


UNLIKE SAMBO'S, MODERN fast-food chains can be bastions against racial discrimination. They offer fixed and affordable prices. Everyone stands in line for service, so there is no need to worry about getting seated near the bathrooms or pushed aside for higher-priority customers. Fast-food outlets also give many Black and Latine youth their first jobs. In her Pulitzer Prize–winning book *Franchise*, Marcia Chatelain explores the complexities of McDonald's status in Black communities.[34] While providing a welcome economic boost by bringing jobs to Black neighborhoods, the corporation exploits its low-wage, fungible workforce. And although it uplifts the community by sponsoring local events, it pushes foods that contribute to rampant cases of diabetes and obesity. McDonald's also failed to keep its workers, who are disproportionately Black and brown, safe during Covid.[35] Naa Oyo A. Kwate's *White Burgers, Black Cash* chronicles fast food's fascinating path from initially excluding Black customers to eventually exploiting them.

Sit-down chain restaurants are still rife with opportunities for racism. Cracker Barrel and Denny's are two popular chains that have faced a slew of lawsuits for discrimination.[36] The allegations cover the full range of reprehensible behavior, with the complaints describing incidents where servers make Black customers wait for seating while white patrons sail right in; deny Black customers entry because of dress codes that white people flagrantly violate; seat Black customers in segregated sections, the smoking section, the back of the restaurant, or next to the bathroom, and, even then, refuse to serve their tables; ask Black customers to leave before they've finished eating so that white people can sit down; serve Black diners food from the trash; wear racist T-shirts; use code words to refer to Black diners, use racial slurs against them or ignore it when other customers do; charge Black customers for utensils or seating; insist on collecting payment upfront; impose mandatory tipping; call the police and accuse patrons of crimes they didn't commit; and hide pork in Muslim diners' meals. Takeout, which would be a partial solution to this problem, can be hard to access because restaurants often refuse to deliver to Black and Latine neighborhoods.

Other food companies, including McDonald's, Chick-fil-A, and Coca-Cola have also faced discrimination lawsuits from their executives, workers, and franchise owners.[37] While investing in local community events for marketing purposes, these companies face allegations that include McDonald's creating a hostile work environment by firing thirty Black executives at once[38] and steering Black franchise owners to subpar locations where the company fails to support their enterprises.[39]

MAJOR CORPORATIONS FIRST targeted their advertising exclusively toward white people. If they considered non-white consumers at all, they relied on a belief that white buyers' impulses and tastes would trickle down to them. In her comprehensive history of the Black consumer market, "Realizing Marketplace Opportunity: How Research on the Black Consumer Market Influenced Mainstream Marketers, 1920–1970," Judy Foster Davis reveals that Curtis Publishing Company, which put out the *Saturday Evening Post* and the *Ladies' Home Journal*, wrote that it consciously ignored Black readers and other "subnormal" consumer groups because "the colored peoples have fewer wants, lower standards of living, little material prosperity and are not generally responsive to the same influences as the whites."[40]

To counter this type of ignorance, journalist, publisher, and entrepreneur Claude A. Barnett founded the Associated Negro Press in 1919. The organization provided its members, 95 percent of which were Black media outlets, with national news items.[41] Barnett then went on to become a successful advertising executive who revolutionized the industry by using Black models in both mundane and luxury settings. Barnett's agency operated under the slogan "I reach the Negro." Before Barnett, the Black female models who appeared in advertising typically had medium brown skin and short curly hair. Barnett rejected this norm, favoring light-skinned Black women with long, straight hair. His fans celebrated this look as a glamorous step forward from the worn-out servant aesthetic. For others, it contributed to colorism.

Marketing directly to Black consumers was the only way for Black business owners to reach them because general trade associations and their publications were only open to white enterprises.[42] But large companies also began to recognize the Black consumer market's potential. Lifebuoy soap, White Owl cigars, and Chevrolet cars were the first major brands to advertise in Black newspapers, beginning in the 1920s. In Los Angeles, smaller businesses that sold coffee, cigarettes, medicine, and music records appealed to Mexican consumers by advertising in Spanish magazines and sponsoring Spanish radio shows.[43]

Determined to expand the reach of mainstream advertising, researchers began to collect data on Black purchasing patterns in the 1920s and 1930s. Black businesses also banded together during that time. In 1928, in Mobile, Alabama, when large grocery chains like A&P threatened to push out Black-owned grocery stores, they collaborated to create a collective advertising fund through the Colored Merchants Association. In 1929, Black-owned businesses appealed to their communities with the slogan "Don't Buy Where You Can't Work."[44] In the 1930s, Camel cigarettes, Seagram's liquor, Kellogg's Corn Flakes, and Pepsi-Cola ran ads in Black newspapers. Stores in Detroit, Atlanta, and Richmond reported selling more Kellogg's products as a result.[45]

White economics professor Paul K. Edwards published the first mainstream book about Black consumers, *The Southern Urban Negro as a Consumer*, in 1932. Black college students, teachers, and social workers collected data from 3,000 Black households in Washington, DC, Baltimore, and Philadelphia. Their studies, published in 1945, showed that Black consumers were "unusually brand loyal" and became increasingly "brand conscious" as their economic prospects improved.[46]

At 10 percent, the Black domestic market share for consumer goods was larger than the country's entire export market. *The National Negro Market* reported on a 1946 study of 5,000 Black consumers in twenty-seven cities that found that they had over $10 billion a year in disposable income and spent $2.5 billion a year on food, $2 billion on clothes, $1.1 billion on home and furniture, $350 million on personal care products, $200 million on tobacco products, $200 million on cars, and $500 million on soft drinks and liquor.[47]

Tristan Donovan's book *Fizz* contrasts soft drink competitors Coke and Pepsi's approaches to Black-targeted marketing. In 1940, Pepsi hired Herman T. Smith to oversee Pepsi's marketing efforts targeted at Black consumers.[48] The twenty-eight-year-old was one of very few Black people holding major positions in large corporations at the time. Pepsi also brought on two recent college graduates, Allen McKellar and Jeanette Maund. Although they were only interns, McKellar and Maund became responsible for Pepsi's national sales to Black consumers. In this role, they traveled to the South under hostile conditions.[49] Donovan recounts, "Train conductors would draw the curtains on their windows when coming into stations so that white passengers would not see them and cause trouble because there were black passengers—as opposed to railroad employees—on board. Some of the [white] Pepsi bottlers they came to help struggled to accept the idea of black people teaching them how to improve their sales and tried to get them to clean the plant or make deliveries."

Pepsi hired Black pianist and composer Duke Ellington as a spokesperson and offered discounts on its products to Black businesses.[50] Pepsi CEO Walter Mack ran integrated Pepsi-Cola Centers for Servicemen and Junior Clubs, offered scholarships to Black students, and hired a civil rights activist, Ed Boyd, to lead Pepsi's "Negro-Market" team. Boyd's office created an ad campaign featuring prominent Black scientists, bankers, and businesspeople titled "Leaders Within Their Own Fields," which some social studies teachers adopted for their classes. Black consumers showed their appreciation by switching to Pepsi. Another groundbreaking Pepsi campaign portrayed the first happy Black family in advertising. The boy featured in the ad, Ron Brown, later became the first Black secretary of commerce. A few years later, Pet Milk company followed suit, launching its "Happy Family" campaign to sell evaporated milk and formula to Black households.[51]

Coke rejected this approach, steadfastly focusing on white consumers until it became embarrassing and unprofitable to keep doing so. Coke executives likely harbored the common corporate fear that advertising in Black media would cost them valued white customers. But the company fundamentally misunderstood both white and Black consumers' mentalities. In 1946, Pepsi had 45 percent of the cola market compared to Coke's 36 percent and Royal Crown's 16 percent. Judy Foster Davis highlights how, early in the 1940s, *Tide* magazine reported on a market research interview with a white woman who revealed that "advertisers probably don't realize how often the choice of a brand for household work depends not on the lady of the house but on her Negro houseworker."[52] This simple statement, obvious in retrospect, was a game changer.[53] Still, Black children rarely appeared in food ads until the 1950s.

Companies' ability to reach the Black consumer market directly depended on the growth of Black media, which, in turn, needed corporate advertising dollars to survive. John H. Johnson published the first national edition of *Ebony*, a lifestyle magazine for Black readers, in November 1945. Chesterfield cigarettes and Kotex were the first companies to place ads in its pages in 1946, with Zenith Radio joining them the next year.[54] Riding the wave of *Ebony*'s success, Johnson published the first edition of *Jet*, which he labeled "The Weekly Negro News Magazine," in 1951.

Johnson sought to increase advertising to Black consumers by partnering with the Department of Commerce to produce a 1954 short film, *The Secret of Selling to the Negro*.[55] Describing Black consumers as a multibillion dollar "new," "fresh," and neglected market, the film introduces "the new Negro family. Their name is Wells or Wilson, Smith or Brown or Alexander or Breen. They live in Chicago, Atlanta, New York, Detroit, and St. Louis, enjoying new prosperity."

Shying away from any explicit mention of racism, the narrator gently refers to "mistaken out of date ideas about how [the Black consumer] lives and buys," which is actually "pretty much the same way as other folks." The narrator reveals that a third of Black families in cities own homes and make their payments more often than white families in the same income bracket do. They also buy higher-quality products. Cutting to the chase, the film asks, "Why let a lot of old-fashioned ideas hurt profits?" In the modern age, a product cannot be "number one" without Black consumers' dollars.

The film goes on to instruct white salespeople how to sell to Black consumers. "One word: recognition. People want to be recognized. That's basic in all of us. But perhaps because the Negro had so little of it, he needs more." Also, he "has been sold a lot of shoddy second class products" even though "good quality merchandise" is key to earning the "admiration of friends and relatives." Therefore, "when he specifically asks for something, don't try to sell him something else. He wants to be sold on quality not price." It is equally important to respect Black business owners. To that end, "a little friendliness and courtesy helps a lot. I usually call a man Mr. Brown or Mr. Smith until he tells me to call him by his first name." Avoid obsequious attempts to participate in Black culture: "Don't talk about Negro celebrities, prize fighters, and singers. Don't patronize. Stick to business."

Black-targeted advertising required Black sales and marketing people. Recognizing this, along with Pepsi, Philip Morris and Lever Brothers led the way in integrating their sales teams. By the early 1950s, there were over forty Black salespeople at major corporations tasked with promoting products to their communities.[56] Pabst Brewing Company and Pepsi created entire offices staffed with Black people dedicated to reaching Black consumers. These offices relied on their employees' personal connections. Their marketing efforts went beyond traditional advertising to engaging with communities by sponsoring sports teams, religious gatherings, fraternities, and conventions.

White supremacists took note of Pepsi's efforts. When Harvey Russell became the company's first Black vice president (of corporate planning) in 1965, Ku Klux Klan members encouraged white people to take action against Russell and his family. "Below, picture of Negro vice president of Pepsi-Cola, at left, and his white wife, in center; Let the Pepsi people know what you think of their vice president and his white wife." Pepsi doubled down, capitalizing on the organization's move by urging consumers to "Fight the Klan, Drink Pepsi."[57]

Pepsi's inclusive hiring, although far behind what it should have been, helped its bottom line and represented a small step toward nondiscriminatory employment practices. The company's early race-targeted marketing also produced positive images of Black people that were essential to counter the long-held stereotypes common in food advertising for over a century. But advertising is not a public good. It is a tool of corporate manipulation that can increase debt, decrease health, and leave its targets worse off. This makes its centrality in the civil rights movement surprising.

The 1967 Kerner report, commissioned by President Lyndon Johnson in response to racial violence across the country, identified lack of Black representation in media and marketing as a catalyst for protest and resistance. The report therefore recommended that Black "reporters and performers should appear more frequently—and at prime-time—in news broadcasts, on weather shows, in documentaries, and in advertisement."[58] Many Black activists fought for greater inclusion in product marketing to create equality between Black and white consumers. They also advocated for more jobs for Black people in the advertising industry.[59]

To achieve their first goal, activists pushed for a move away from companies placing some of their ads in Black media and a shift toward integrated advertising that would run in white media. To advance their second objective, advocates cautioned corporations that Black consumers would not support products made by companies that did not hire Black executives. Advertising professor and historian Jason Chambers recounts the warning of Clarence Holte, founder of Nubian Press Inc. and the first Black executive at a mainstream marketing firm, to a *Wall Street Journal* reporter, "'If an employer has an unfair employment policy, and it's known to Negroes, he can advertise, he can promote, he can do anything he wants to, and he won't sell merchandise.'"

Corporations like Jell-O and Coca-Cola tried to reach Black consumers in the 1970s by using what was known at the time as Ebonics and other speech patterns stereotypically associated with Black people.[60] McDonald's encouraged Black eaters to "Get Down With a Cheeseburger," assuring them that "You can relax and get down with good food that won't keep you waitin.'"[61] Other insulting ad type read, "On the real, kids can really dig gettin' down with McDonald's." "Every bite is happyfyin' light."[62] Burger King also interjected the phrase "have mercy" in some of its Black-targeted ads, presumably to appeal to Black churchgoers.

After cigarette giant Philip Morris acquired Kraft/General Foods in 1988, these food companies led the way in race-targeted food advertising.[63] General Foods infiltrated grocery stores to collect detailed information about customers, from their product choices to their lifestyle habits. The company used this data to create customer profiles that allowed it to narrow down purchase preferences by race and gender. The resulting database, called the African-American Targeted Lifestyle & Attitude Segments, revealed that Kool-Aid, Kraft BBQ sauce, Miracle Whip, and Menthol cigarettes were the company's most popular products among Black shoppers. General Foods also launched a Latine-focused database that amassed information on family size, children's ages, parents' educational levels, and responsiveness to product displays.

Using these databases, General Foods tailored its ads to Black and Latine values and culture. Harnessing Black vernacular, Stove Top stuffing became "dressing" in ads that featured Black models. After these ads ran, Black consumers bought more stuffing. After learning that Black and Latine households prefer sweeter foods than white households, Kool-Aid designed new ads to appeal to them. One Kool-Aid spot features a Black mother holding an empty pitcher out to her two smiling children with the captions, "Alright, who drank all the

Kool-Aid?" and "Don't worry, it's only a quarter the price of soda. So make another pitcher and keep them smiling!" Kool-Aid also created a new Mandarina Tangerine flavor packaged in boxes with Spanish labeling and marketed on Spanish-language networks. Sugar is a cheap way to boost spirits on limited budgets, but it is also extremely harmful. Among other ill effects, sugar greatly increases the risk of heart disease.[64] But corporations were not concerned with what happened after their products sold.

Philip Morris's Minority Business Development Office coordinated marketing across its tobacco, alcohol, and food branches. It donated money to the NAACP (National Association for the Advancement of Colored People). It sponsored community events with test kitchens, free samples, and hospitality suites. It funded wildly popular Black Family Reunion events in seven U.S. cities in partnership with the National Council of Negro Women and the Black newspaper the *Chicago Defender*. In 1993, a commemorative cookbook collected recipes from the events. Promoted in *Ebony*, on Black Entertainment Television, and in Black-owned businesses, the reunions attracted more than a million attendees in some cities. McDonald's and Coca-Cola paid to become reunion co-sponsors. Branded Advergames, which became popular in the 1990s, used Black models or Spanish versions to draw in Black and Latine children. Thanks to General Foods' innovative market segmentation, "ethnic" marketing became a thriving industry right in time for the digital age.[65]

For the consumer using basic technology, identity-based websites and initiatives like McDonald's Black & Positively Golden,[66] HACER scholarships for Latine students,[67] Asian Pacific American Next program,[68] and Share the Pride[69] woo Black, Latine, Asian, and queer consumers. Other technologies that allow corporations to identify and target smaller and smaller slices of the population dictate innovative marketing strategies. When television's Nielsen data revealed that the show *It's Me or the Dog* appealed to Latine bacon lovers, Taco Bell replaced the regularly scheduled advertising with an ad for its Bacon Club Chalupa.

Now, 95 percent of teens have access to a smartphone.[70] Forty-five percent of them report that they are "almost constantly" online. Food corporations are there to meet them. The top twenty-seven fast-food companies have Instagram, YouTube, Facebook, and Twitter accounts, and twenty-three are on TikTok.[71] These platforms help corporations evade the guidelines and restrictions imposed on more traditional forms of advertising such as television and radio. They profit from the law's inability to keep up with technological advances. Social media sites, influencers, celebrities, and gaming now dominate race-targeted marketing.

Food marketers fund a new generation of social media macro-influencers. They pay influencer dieticians to post content that contradicts medical knowledge. After the World Health Organization warned that aspartame, an artificial sweetener used in diet drinks, might be carcinogenic, the industry group American Beverage gave an undisclosed amount to a dozen health professionals to post videos touting the product's benefits.[72] The Canadian Sugar Institute paid registered dietitian Lindsay Pleskot for a post where she claimed, "What's actually worse than eating sugar is the guilt and stress we place upon ourselves when we do eat it." Her "dietician-approved" methods to cut sugar were "With a knife, With my hands, even with my teeth." For young people, YouTube "kidfluencers" promote junk food to their millions of followers. Even though 79 percent of food brands partner with Instagram influencers, most of them disguise product boosting as regular content and do not disclose their sponsorship relationships.

While children entertain themselves on apps, analytical software mines their data, studies their behavior patterns, and tracks their geographic locations. Marketers use this information to create detailed profiles that identify which children are most likely to prefer their products.[73] These sophisticated technologies enable food companies to expose Black and Latine youth to a disproportionate number of ads for unhealthy foods. This race-targeted marketing contributes directly to racial disparities in food-related conditions.[74]

Food corporations disproportionately target young Black and Latine consumers because they spend more money on fast food than white children their age. Companies see them as trendsetters, definers of cool. They are also more vulnerable to targeted marketing because they are in the unique position of developing their personal and racial identities at the same time.[75] Black and Latine youth have phones even when their families cannot afford computers or tablets at home. Fast-food companies track phones' locations and send coupons to customers who are within a few blocks of their outlets. The streets of many urban neighborhoods are an endless parade of fast-food places.

When young consumers visit a McDonald's outlet, the company encourages them to become brand ambassadors, doing free advertising for the company through Snapchats framed with the McDonald's logo. It encourages them to use branded emojis and colors. Fast-food and junk-food companies also rely on Black and Latine celebrities to attract their targeted audiences.[76] Young people who do not commonly see positive images of themselves in the media and have fewer role models are more susceptible to this type of marketing.[77] McDonald's partnered with rapper Travis Scott to create the Travis Scott Meal—a Quarter Pounder with cheese, bacon, onions, and lettuce, medium fries with BBQ sauce, and a Sprite. The meal had 1,195 calories, more than half the recommended daily intake for adults and three-quarters for kids, 50 grams of fat (65 percent of the recommended daily value) and 148 grams of carbs (54 percent RDV). The collaboration also led to Scott selling a full-body McNugget pillow as part of his celebrity merchandise collection.

Following the campaign's success, McDonald's teamed up with reggaeton artist J. Balvin in the fall of 2020 for a celebrity meal deal of a Big Mac without pickles, fries with ketchup, and an Oreo McFlurry (1,430 calories, 65 grams of fat [85 percent RDV)] and 172 grams of carbs [63 percent RDV]). Balvin's merchandise included two-finger brass knuckles with a McDonald's logo, a hot pink french fry bed-spread, and temporary tattoos of a Balvin celebrity meal deal receipt. Despite their popularity, these items never reached consumers due to flimsy manufacturing.[78]

Rapper Saweetie was McDonald's first female collaborator. Her meal was a Big Mac, four-piece Chicken McNuggets, medium fries, medium Sprite, Tangy BBQ Sauce, and a renamed Saweetie 'n Sour sauce. Saweetie's meal is 1,375 calories, 59 grams of fat (77 percent RDV) and 172 grams of carbs (63 percent RDV). Celebrity rapper couple Cardi B and Offset announced their celebrity meal at the 2022 Superbowl.

Food companies also pander to Black and Latine youth with songs, dance battles, and social justice initiatives.[79] Cheetos enlisted Puerto Rican singer Bad Bunny to promote its giveaway of $25,000 scholarships to twenty young Latine TikTokers who "leave their mark" (Deja tu Huella) on their communities. General Mills' Old El Paso brand challenged Black NBA players Andre Drummond and Andrew Wiggins to make slam dunks without spilling a tortilla bowl, inviting people to post videos of themselves attempting the same #messfreechallenge on Instagram. It then donated $15,000 to organizations fighting food insecurity. PepsiCo, Mountain Dew, and Ruffles started scholarships for Black and Latine youth and Ben & Jerry's and PepsiCo launched a diversity youth hiring initiative. LifeWtr sponsored a Black Art Rising initiative to "immortalize Black protest art."

Mimicking youth culture is another popular tactic, embraced in Sprite's release of its new Ginger drink in February 2020. Marketing Dive describes the scale of the marketing campaign: "By tapping hip-hop and streetwear influencers and releasing the beverage along with an apparel and accessories line—which the brand said is its first capsule collection—Coca-Cola is pitching Sprite Ginger as part of its lifestyle brand push. The social media and out-of-home rollout mirrors that of a hip-hop album or sneaker drop, where hints are released ahead of a release in order to build buzz."[80]

During the pandemic lockdown, without concerts, sporting events, and other activities, screen time skyrocketed. Food corporations scrambled to meet consumers where they were—at home. They infiltrated popular games, installing virtual vending machines and letting gamers order takeout from within the game.[81] No need to press pause and think about whether there might be something healthier in the fridge or cupboard. Mountain Dew created a can with a no-slip grip that mimics the feel of gaming hardware and accessories. Easy to open and drink with one hand, the drink's ingredients are carefully crafted to "improve accuracy and alertness" with caffeine, herbs, and sugar.

Twitch is a platform similar to YouTube and populated mostly by gamers. It boasts that 64 percent of its users buy products touted by Twitch influencers. Food giants like KFC, Hershey, Burger King, and

PepsiCo's Mountain Dew take advantage of Twitch's unskippable ads and cross-promotion opportunities. Coca-Cola inserted itself into the popular culinary game *Cooking Fever* and sends swag to Twitch influencers. Dr. Pepper put *Fortnite* players on its bottles. Food corporations also use gaming for data collection. Anzu's ad technology allows advertisers to follow gamers while they play or move from game to game, observing their brand preferences and adjusting ad content in real time.

In 2019, fast-food companies spent $5 billion on advertising. Their Spanish-language TV campaign spending increased 33 percent from 2012, reaching $318 million. They appealed to Latine youth with soccer themes and sponsored Latine soccer events.[82] Another $99 million went to Black-targeted TV shows. None of the companies' corporate responsibility initiatives that focus on racial justice, diversity, and inclusion make any mention of the damage done by targeting vulnerable young consumers with their marketing blitz.

THESE DAYS, COMPANIES believe they have a greater market share to gain by shunning instead of embracing racist practices and stereotypes. Through advertising spots and selective community investments, companies signal that they are on the side of the oppressed, which serves both to boost profits and to deflect attention away from their shortcomings. They invest millions in ad campaigns that declare their commitment to anti-racism while they lag in diversifying their executives, exploit workers in the U.S. and Global South, and coax young people into buying or begging their parents for food that makes them sick.[83]

The corporate cost-benefit analysis of social justice–oriented campaigns is clear. After firing Aunt Jemima, PepsiCo pledged to donate $5 million to support and engage with the Black community. It also promised to increase its workforce diversity and invest over $400 million in Black communities. That number is a drop in the bucket for PepsiCo, which in 2022 reported a net revenue of $86.392 billion and a core operating profit of $12.325 billion, allowing it to pay out $6.172 billion in dividends to shareholders.[84]

In "Woke-Washing: 'Intersectional' Femvertising and Branding

'Woke' Bravery," digital media studies scholar Dr. Francesca Sobande explains that woke washing "can range from subtle nods to 'wokeness' by using language and visual symbols associated with social justice movements but without naming or actively supporting them, to explicitly attempting to communicate the brand's alleged 'woke' credentials by declaring their support of specific social justice movements and activists, including in the form of financial contributions."[85] Woke washing can take the form of employing racial tropes like the white savior and Black excellence as shorthand to communicate corporations' progressive values.

In Pepsi's 2017 "Live for Now" ad, an example of woke washing gone wrong, model and TV personality Kendall Jenner, a member of the Kardashian family, stops a Black Lives Matter protest from getting out of hand by giving a police officer a Pepsi. The idea that a white woman could solve racism with a soft drink inspired outrage across communities, causing Pepsi to pull the ad.[86] *Saturday Night Live* spoofed the spot, showing the white male director on the phone moments before the shoot begins, realizing that his vision is not the racial epiphany he thought it was and trying, in vain, to stop production before his faux pas becomes public.[87]

Marketing that relies on the Black excellence trope appeals to consumers by highlighting exceptional Black people in contrast with everyday Black people.[88] Good Black people are educated, rich, and talented, implying that regular Black people are uneducated, poor, and useless or criminal. In this kind of marketing, the closer the Black figure comes to embodying white excellence, the more appealing they are. Gatorade's "Unmatched" spot, featuring tennis star Serena Williams, follows her career trajectory from a young girl training with her dad in Los Angeles's Compton neighborhood to becoming the top tennis player in the world. "Unmatched," Sobande argues, suggests that a Black person like Serena Williams can earn respectability only by outperforming white people, through sheer force of will or raw talent.

Woke washing is a form of corporate performance that seeks to boost companies' bottom line without engaging with real-world causes of racial justice. An industry study shows that up to 80 percent of consumers would stop buying a product if they disagreed with the company's political position. Black consumers, in particular, use their dollars to register approval or disapproval.[89] After the study came out in January 2021, Starbucks pledged to invest $100 million in small businesses and community development in BIPOC communities.[90] Mountain Dew promised a $1 million prize to a Black entrepreneur who wins its Real Change Ideas Pitch Competition, and Chipotle added Paul Quinn College, a historically Black college, to its employee tuition reimbursement program.

A flurry of food companies embraced woke washing after George Floyd's murder and the Black Lives Matter protests turned a global spotlight on racism in the United States. As anti-racist sentiments suddenly sprung up everywhere, some food corporations jumped on the bandwagon. Popeyes Chicken reacted to Floyd's murder by tweeting "Popeyes is nothing without Black lives." This empty statement would have been bad enough. The age-old trope associating Black people with fried chicken made it that much worse. Critics wondered why Popeyes didn't put its money where its mouth was and offer to pay protesters' bail or take any other kind of concrete action.[91] After a swift backlash, Popeyes deleted the tweet. Then after what must have been some very quick cultural sensitivity training, it tweeted, "There's no room for injustice. We commit to strengthening every facet of our culture and policies to foster an environment where equality for Black people is a priority. We'll use our platform to support this movement. #BlackLivesMatter." Those were Popeyes's last words on the racial justice movement.

Wendy's similarly tweeted that its "voice would be nothing without Black culture" and promised to "amplify Black voices." Gushers and Fruit by the Foot, two General Mills candy brands, also tweeted meaningless platitudes. "Gushers wouldn't be Gushers without the Black community and your voices." "We're working with @fruitbythefoot on creating space to amplify that. We see you. We stand with you."

Other corporations took their newfound wokeness a bit more seriously by canceling their racist brand mascots. Following on the heels of the retirement of Aunt Jemima, Chef Frank White, and Uncle Ben, Nestlé changed some of the names of candy sold in the South American market: Negrita became Chokita, and Beso de Negra became Beso de Amor.[92] In North America, Nestlé's Eskimo Pies became Edy's Pies.

Beyond these marketing stunts, food corporations could create systemic change by revising their hiring, employment, and production practices. They could stop targeting Black and Latine youth with products that destroy their health. But instead, race-targeted marketing has evolved. Despite a greater awareness of Black and Latine consumers' vulnerabilities and health inequities, these companies have invested in precision-targeted campaigns designed to capture every single one of their precious food dollars.

RACIALLY TARGETED MARKETING also includes selling certain products to white people, predominantly healthy foods. Pitching items such as soy milk, whole wheat bread, organic strawberries, and plant-based meat to white consumers reinforces the assumption that the good life, and good health, are white. The trope also minimizes the need for food equality by implying that poor health in Black, Indigenous, and Latine communities is the natural product of bad choices, ignorance, and weak will, instead of underlying structural causes. Even health and medical professionals subscribe to this false narrative and focus on dietary education or scolding instead of on increasing access to a range of foods and people's financial ability to buy them.[93]

Marketing professor Aarti Ivanic explains, "Psychologically, we tend to associate with people who look like us. So if you've got these ads for unhealthy foods marketed toward a particular group, and you're African American, you begin to think it's normal for African Americans to eat unhealthy foods. Obesity now spans across races, but minorities are more overweight and obese. I live in a food desert in San Diego, with no grocery store but several fast-food restaurants. You are going to get the $1 meal at Taco Bell. Sometimes I feel these companies deliberately do that. They know people in these neighborhoods are lower-income and can't afford better food; it keeps reinforcing social norms."[94]

Black consumers want healthier food. Eight percent of Black Americans are vegetarian or vegan compared to 3 percent of the U.S. population.[95] Black consumers prioritize organic food and prefer fresh to frozen foods. They are 8 to 15 percent more likely than diners in general to choose restaurants with healthy and fresh offerings. Yet food marketing has not caught up with these differences, which became starker after the Covid-19 pandemic.

IDEALLY, CONGRESS WOULD enact laws restricting race-targeted marketing. Short of that, the USDA could counter its harm by taking effective action even without regulating. When stopping young people from smoking was a public health priority, a "Truth" campaign directed at youth exposed how the tobacco companies were manipulating them for profit. Young people responded with outrage and reduced their smoking. Later, messages to teens about the food industry had a similar impact.

Toronto high schoolers started a campaign to boycott McDonald's and its cohorts. They called it Stick it to Fast Food, with the slogan "Eat Fast Die Young."[96] One of their ads cautions, "We are the first generation of kids expected to live shorter lives than their parents." Other creative messaging to young people includes an image of french fries in rows in a cigarette box that warns, "The Obesity Death Rate is Overtaking Smoking." Another photo shows a McDonald's french fry box filled with bullets. In another, a young girl stares down a menacing cheeseburger lodged in a giant red box with french fries for fangs.

These campaigns produce meaningful results. Eighth graders who perceived healthy eating as an act of social justice made better food choices. These students acted in defiance of corporations that market to impressionable children and engineer junk food to make it addictive. Appealing to their sense of autonomy and social consciousness was more effective than teaching them about long-term health consequences. One challenge of launching this kind of effort in the food context is that other, healthier food must be available, unlike smoking, where a person can simply not smoke.

The USDA is unlikely to fund this type of food truth campaign because it would directly oppose its interests. It stands to gain more from supporting food industry giants than from making consumers aware of the harms that they cause. Fast food contains most of the subsidized commodities that the USDA's mandate compels it to promote—milk, meat, wheat, soy, and corn. Powerful corporate lobbying ensures that a shift in subsidy priorities is not going to happen any time soon, if ever. In the indefinite future, the USDA will remain heavily invested in the growth and prosperity of fast food, junk food, and soft drinks.

Congress should resist corporate influence and clamp down on race-targeted marketing by making it unlawful in all its forms. It should impose reparations-style penalties on food corporations that violate these regulations, consisting of significant investment in health and medical services for the communities they harm. Schools should be free of fast food and junk food. Unhealthy foods should come with clear, prominent warnings. Nutrition facts and labels should use plain language. Individual agency is important but can only exist when people have true options. Until ties between the industry and politicians are severed, the U.S. will continue to be a nation of fast and ultra-processed food.

# 7

# What's Law Got to Do with It?

After large agricultural corporations took charge of the Farm Bill, their singular focus on subsidized, single (or mono) crops put many smaller farms out of business. Big Ag quickly gained an outsized influence over food policy, and corporate interests came to determine most of the food we eat. By 2023, corn and soy each represented 30 percent of all U.S. crops.

Corporations do not feel compassion. Sickness and loss do not move them. Appealing to their humanity is not an effective political strategy. Looking to the White House and its agencies for solutions has yielded only temporary results at best. The Obama era saw improvements in school lunches that Donald Trump swept away during his brief tenure. Joe Biden reinstated stricter guidelines, and the corporations stood ready to beat them back down again. In the face of near-complete capture of the legislative and executive branches, it is time to turn to the courts.

WHEN THE EMANCIPATION of enslaved people ushered in a new phase of U.S. history, Congress soon realized that a formal proclamation of freedom alone was not going to cut it. It passed the Reconstruction Amendments, made up of the Thirteenth, Fourteenth, and Fifteenth Amendments, to stop states from impeding the path to lasting freedom and to move society toward racial equality. The Thirteenth Amendment bans slavery and involuntary servitude, forbidding all badges, markers, incidents, and vestiges of slavery; the Fourteenth Amendment grants formerly enslaved people and others who have historically experienced discrimination political and civil equality; and the Fifteenth Amendment guarantees adult citizens the right to participate in democracy and enjoy the full benefits of citizenship.

This formal, legal equality is hollow when people still suffer from violence, poverty, poor education, housing and employment discrimination, and bad health. Food laws, policies, and programs that treat Black, Indigenous, and Latine people as second-class citizens belie the commitment to egalitarianism enshrined in these constitutional amendments. However, the Constitution has an override button that allows the courts to interfere when foundational rights are at stake. If a law, policy, or practice is unconstitutional, then the court can strike it down.

Although written vaguely as a general promise of equal protection, the Fourteenth Amendment's origins mean that it kicks in at its highest gear when the government treats people differently based on their race. That gear is called strict scrutiny. When a law discriminates based on race, the court will decide whether that law is necessary to achieve a compelling purpose or whether the government can achieve its purpose in another way that doesn't classify people according to their race. The court's analysis in these types of cases is complicated by its failure to come up with a working definition of race.

Although the strict scrutiny standard sounds like it will guard effectively against encroachments on equality, the way that the court's interpretation of the Fourteenth Amendment has evolved has made racially discriminatory laws and policies almost impossible to strike down. A person challenging a law based on their belief that it violates equal protection must prove that it was enacted with a racist intent. If the racially discriminatory effect is unintended or even secondary to the law's main purpose, the court will not analyze it under strict scrutiny and will adopt the much more lenient rational review instead. Under that standard, if the law is rationally related to any conceivable legitimate government purpose, the court will leave it alone. These days, it is almost impossible to find a statement from law or policy-makers that proves an intent to discriminate. Without that smoking gun, laws or policies that arise from structural or systemic racism, rather than explicit racial hatred, are deemed constitutional, resulting in unfair rulings that go against the spirit, meaning, and legislative intent of the Thirteenth, Fourteenth, and Fifteenth Amendments.

Instead of accepting this current judicial state of affairs, it is important to argue for the law to work as it should, not just as it probably will. Not only do judges need to understand that racially discriminatory food law and policies are unconstitutional—people need to know it, too. Social movements are key to making substantial legal changes. Armed with the knowledge and conviction that current food law and policy is unconstitutional, racial and food justice advocates can drive political reform. All the significant civil rights victories have come after years- or decades-long campaigns driven by activists. The fight for food justice will be no different.

The reach of the Reconstruction Amendments should extend to the racial stereotypes that still haunt food marketing. Public pressure to abandon food brands that play on these stereotypes is a step in the right direction. But there is still a long way to go. Racial stereotypes related to food are not just insulting and upsetting. They lead to sickness and even death for the benefit of the food corporations that mine them for profit. The Thirteenth and Fourteenth Amendments should empower Congress to restrict race-targeted marketing and to impose changes on USDA nutrition programs.

UNDER THE THIRTEENTH Amendment, "Neither slavery nor involuntary servitude, except as a punishment for crime whereof the party shall have been duly convicted, shall exist within the United States, or any place subject to their jurisdiction."[1] Section 2 of the amendment empowers Congress "to enforce this article by appropriate legislation."[2] In the 1883 *Civil Rights Cases*, the Court extended the Thirteenth Amendment's protection to badges and incidents of slavery.[3] Policies and practices used during chattel slavery to oppress Black people fall under that umbrella, including food laws and policies. *A Sketch of the Laws Relating to Slavery*, a survey of laws governing enslavement in twelve states published in 1856, includes laws involving enslavers' control over food,[4] which were central to maintaining control. The history laid out in Chapter 2 demonstrates how the use of food as a tool of oppression continued throughout U.S. history. This throughline establishes that modern food laws and policies that create racial health disparities are badges or vestiges of slavery.

Removing parents' ability to decide what to feed their infants is one of those vestiges. Enslavers forced Black women to stop nursing their newborn babies so that the mothers could return to work.[5] Sometimes, this work was nursing white women's babies instead of their own. In an 1846 case, *Lee v. Mathews*,[6] the Alabama Supreme Court listed the property rights of enslavers to enslaved mothers' children as one of the incidents of slavery. Later, during the debates leading up to the Thirteenth Amendment's ratification, Iowa senator James Harlan included enslavers' prohibition of the "parental relation" as one of the incidents of slavery that the amendment would allow Congress and the court to dismantle.[7]

Another Thirteenth Amendment supporter, Senator Henry Wilson of Massachusetts, claimed that "the sacred rights of human nature, the hallowed family relations of husband and wife, parent and child will be protected by the guardian spirit of" the amendment.[8] Discussing the 1866 Civil Rights Act, Representative M. Russell Thayer of Pennsylvania declared that the Thirteenth Amendment was meant to guarantee natural rights.[9] These natural rights encompass the ability to parent,[10] including providing children with food and safeguarding their health.[11]

Legal scholar Priscilla Ocen argues that these debates established that Congress understood reproductive subordination to be one of the "constitutive elements of slavery." That subordination encompassed control over what infants ate. Restrictions on enslaved infants' and children's food led to countless deaths from malnutrition. Few enslaved mothers could nurse their children, and the gruel their babies received instead of breastmilk was extremely low in nutrition. Modern policies

that make breastfeeding impossible, including welfare work requirements and the lack of parental leave or accommodations for pumping
milk at work, severely limit the choice of foods that parents can give
their children. This leads to racial disparities in rates of infant sickness
and death that echo the past.

Because of structural obstacles to breastfeeding, Black parents
have the lowest rates at birth, six months, and twelve months. In the
United States, Black infants die at more than twice the rate (10.6) of
white infants (4.4) from Sudden Infant Death Syndrome, a risk that
breastfeeding for at least two months cuts in half.[12] This disparity has
remained the same since chattel slavery. Research also links formula
feeding to increased risk of gastrointestinal diseases and respiratory
tract infections.[13]

AFTER THE *Civil Rights Cases*, the Supreme Court had no further
meaningful discussion about the definition of "badges and incidents of
slavery" until its 1968 decision in *Jones v. Alfred H. Mayer Co.*[14] In *Jones*,
the Court considered whether an apartment owner's refusal to sell
property to an interracial Black and white couple was constitutional.
The *Jones* court held that, because racial discrimination in housing is an
incident of slavery, Congress can rely on the Thirteenth Amendment to
make it illegal under Section 1982 of the Civil Rights Act.

To reach this result, the *Jones* court examined the 1866 Civil Rights
Act's legislative history. The act's main purpose was to stop the continued persecution of freed people through the Black Codes. The Court
explained that, during the course of writing the Civil Rights Act, its
supporters rejected a proposal that would limit Congress's power to
strike down discriminatory laws and instead gave it the authority to
make new ones to prevent discrimination before it happened.[15] The
law's advocates intended the Act to go beyond eliminating de jure discrimination, which was codified into the legal system, to uproot de
facto discrimination, which happened in practice but was not written
down.[16]

The Court cited Senator Lyman Trumbull's belief that the Civil

Rights Act was intended to enforce the Thirteenth Amendment's abolition of slavery by "secur[ing] to all persons within the United States practical freedom." As Trumbull explained, "There is very little importance in the general declaration of abstract truths and principles unless they can be carried into effect, unless the persons who are to be affected by them have some means of availing themselves of their benefits."

But instead of expanding Thirteenth Amendment protection after *Jones*'s recognition that housing segregation is an incident of slavery, the Court limited it. Three years after *Jones*, the Court heard *Palmer v. Thompson*.[17] The lead-up to *Palmer* was a series of laws that chipped away at segregation in public places after *Brown v. Board of Education* struck down school segregation in 1954. *Palmer*'s events took place in Jackson, Mississippi, a city with unbearably hot temperatures in the summer. Jackson had five public swimming pools, four of them for white swimmers and one for Black swimmers. After a court ordered Jackson to integrate its public pools, the city closed them instead. The closure imitated the actions of school districts that had closed their public schools instead of integrating them and then helped white parents fund private school education for their children.

To decide whether Jackson's pool closures were constitutional, the Court considered whether Jackson had a duty to provide its residents with public swimming pools. The Court held that it did not. Instead of focusing on this question of duty, the Court should have decided the issue using a Thirteenth Amendment lens, asking whether segregated swimming pools were a badge or incident of slavery. During chattel slavery, banishing Black people from public recreational spaces was a way to mark them as inferior and justify their enslavement. Swimming pools are intimate spaces. They provide a place for scantily clad people to socialize together, potentially breaking down social barriers and forming new relationships. Jackson's segregated swimming pools represented an attempt to maintain the social separation that was a marker of enslavement.

The *Palmer* Court's choice not to use the Thirteenth Amendment to mandate Jackson to open its pools had dire and lasting consequences. Sixty-four percent of Black children in the United States do not know how to swim. An eleven-year-old Black child is ten times more likely to drown than a white child of the same age. Its constitutional consequences are equally serious. *Palmer* makes it harder to convince the Court that it should use the Thirteenth Amendment, not just to recognize Congress's power to make anti-discrimination law, but to stop government actions and policies that have roots in the subordination of enslaved people.

Despite this setback, *Jones* provides a strong basis for finding programs that perpetuate health discrimination unconstitutional. Food oppression works similarly to housing discrimination. It functions to make the lives of people who have historically experienced subordination harder and shorter. It signals inferiority by framing some groups as deserving of nutritious food and good health and condemning others to junk food and its consequences. The laws and policies that enable this to happen, in school lunchrooms, on Indian reservations, and in food marketing, are vestiges of slavery. The Thirteenth Amendment should give Congress and the courts the ability to invalidate aspects of USDA programs that perpetuate food oppression.

THE WORK REQUIREMENTS attached to the SNAP program should be among the first to go. In 2022, SNAP was a $113 billion program that provided average monthly benefits of $230.01 per person and $438.56 per household, although some people only get $23 a month.[18] Nearly all households that get SNAP have a child, an elderly adult, or someone with a disability in them.[19] One-fifth of SNAP users have no other income available to spend on food.[20]

At first, the public saw government assistance as a helping hand to white families who had fallen on unfortunate times. Over time, politicians and the media began to represent it as a handout to undeserving, lazy Black and brown people. This false rhetoric changed the way people responded to benefits programs. Instead of a means for the government to fulfill its responsibility to care for its citizens, people started to view social assistance as an undeserved entitlement.[21]

This shift in public opinion drove support for the 1996 Personal

Responsibility and Work Opportunity Reconciliation Act, a law that made welfare harder to get. One of the ways that PRWORA did this was by adding work requirements to SNAP. These requirements force most people aged 16–59 to register for work, participate in SNAP Employment and Training or workfare, take a suitable job if offered, and not voluntarily quit a job or reduce their work hours below 30 hours a week without a good reason.[22] Able-bodied adults without dependents aged 18–59 have to work 80 hours a month to be eligible for more than three months of benefits in a three-year period.[23]

The official explanation for work requirements was that they would help SNAP recipients get good jobs and exit the program. But research shows that work requirements don't do this. Instead, they shut people out of the program, making them more food insecure.[24] In the rare instances when work requirements help individuals leave SNAP for good jobs, they do so in a racially disparate way: participants who have been able to lift themselves out of poverty through employment are disproportionately white.[25] People who have lost their benefits because they could not meet SNAP's stringent work requirements are disproportionately Black and Latine.[26] Leveraging hunger as a method to force people into unskilled work that will not advance their social or financial status is a practice dating back to enslavement.[27]

Another vestige of enslavers' control is ownership and command of the food supply. On land where every available space was devoted to growing cash crops, enslavers brought in food from outside to feed the people they enslaved. Organizer and activist Bekah Mandell argues that food-centered dependency came to represent and define both Blackness and whiteness during this time. "To be the fed, to be dependent on another for one's very sustenance took on a racialized meaning just as lasting as the meaning assigned to skin-color. To be the fed was to be enslaved, to be black, to be powerless."[28] That is one of the reasons why growing food was an act of resistance as well as self-preservation.

Not only did enslavers exercise control over diets by rationing insufficient amounts of food, primarily corn meal, they used supplemental food as rewards. The distribution of small portions of sweet potato, meat, or molasses showed some enslaved people favor.[29] Conversely,

starvation was a common form of punishment.[30] For it to be effective, enslavers had to restrict access to food sources and make acts like
sneaking leftovers into sleeping quarters subject to retribution.[31] Tar
fences guarded fruit trees, and a trace of tar discovered on a piece of
clothing would trigger harsh discipline.[32]

Food was a form of power that constantly loomed over interactions
with enslavers. They used it as a tool of humiliation, forcing enslaved
workers to fight animals for scraps. They also conducted experiments
with it, pushing human endurance to the limit. In one example, enslavers gave enslaved workers cotton seeds mixed with corn to see how their
bodies would react.[33] Frederick Douglass identified "Want of food" as
his "chief trouble" during his first summer living on Colonel Edward
Lloyd's land.[34] Appalled at enslavers' disingenuous claim that enslaved
people received better food than any peasants in the world, Douglass
described his monthly rations: "a bushel of third-rate corn, pickled
pork (which was 'often tainted') and 'poorest quality herrings.'"[35] Extra
food rations also served as a consolation offered to enslaved women
for enduring sexual assault intended to lead to pregnancy.[36]

Work requirements that condition access to adequate nutrition on
the performance of labor are a vestige of slavery. They require poor people to work in low-wage, dead-end, unskilled jobs to get food instead
of receiving high-skilled job training or education. They prevent people
from fulfilling their family responsibilities. This is a modern form of
control over labor and diet.

Attaching work requirements to government benefits reflects a
belief that social assistance is not a right of citizenship but a gift that its
recipients must earn. It insists that poverty is not an accident of birth
and social circumstances but a reflection of individuals' bad choices
or capabilities. Once the fallacy of these assumptions becomes clear,
the idea that poor people should work to earn government support is
absurd at best. In many countries, people consider providing a social
safety net to the poor and vulnerable one of the government's fundamental roles. In Canada and Norway, where governments largely live
up to these expectations, there is far less social and financial inequality
than in the United States.[37]

In contrast, U.S. leaders preach an ethic of pull-yourself-up-by-the-bootstraps, personal responsibility. When you frame prosperity as the result of hard work, benefits become an unearned windfall for the lazy, who are guaranteed to squander the generosity they receive. The idea that these requirements promote work over dependency and can weed out the idle from the truly needy relies on stereotypes. It is sexist to believe that social assistance is a disincentive to work because positioning work and domesticity as opposites assumes that labor takes place only outside the home. This misperception reflects the devaluation of work that is done inside the home, which has traditionally fallen on women to perform. Holding out work requirements as a measure to ensure that benefits recipients engage in "real" labor is therefore discriminatory. The practical effect of these requirements is to double or triple many SNAP recipients' workloads.[38] Yet failing to meet the requirements can trigger the reduction or loss of benefits essential to food security.

The portrayal of people who get SNAP as lazy is a lie that grows from and feeds into racial stereotypes. Some people get stuck in low-wage jobs because they lack access to education or training for higher-paying jobs. Many people work hard but still can't get by without Medicaid or food stamps because their employers don't pay a living wage.[39] Their state might have no minimum wage.[40] They might work for Walmart, which offers only part-time jobs to avoid paying employee benefits. The Walmarts of this world welcome SNAP beneficiaries on their staff and as consumers.[41] The government money their workers receive to keep from starving, even though they have a job, often goes right into the corporation's pockets when employees do their shopping at work.[42]

The association of Black people with laziness was a tool that justified enslavers' brutality and alleviated white guilt. It continues to serve that purpose in political rhetoric that claims Black people were "better off" enslaved because they received food and shelter.[43] The laziness myth later rationalized the criminalization of idleness and vagrancy in the Black Codes.[44] The 1965 Moynihan Report, *The Negro Family: The Case For National Action*, claimed that Black people had a "natural" tendency to avoid work along with other "anti-social" behaviors like having children out of marriage.[45] Conservative sociologist Charles

Murray argues that welfare took away Black people's motivation to work.[46]

Some supporters of work requirements argue that they help remove the stigma associated with receiving government assistance. These workfare proponents claim that people who work to earn their benefits will receive more respect from society.[47] This is a circular argument. If society recognized state assistance as a solution to systemic failures, not a symbol of personal inadequacy, there would be no stigma attached to it. Also, the forty-two million people who used SNAP in 2022 would have run the risks of extreme poverty, houselessness, hunger, illness, and death without it. The harm of stigma is minimal in comparison.

The federal government gives the states money for SNAP benefit payments. The only costs that states pay are for program administration, which the federal government also partially covers. States manage the work requirements and can apply for waivers to exempt their residents from having to fulfill them.[48] Without a waiver, the cost for states to administer the program are likely higher because it is expensive to verify employment, track the benefits received, and offer job training programs.[49] This means that states that decide not to apply for waivers are making an ideological, not an economic choice. Waivers increase SNAP participation, which is good for states' economies.[50]

Kansas and Maine qualified for waivers but chose not to apply for them. Maine governor Paul LePage explains, "People who are in need deserve a hand up, but we should not be giving able-bodied individuals a handout . . . We must protect our limited resources for those who are truly in need and who are doing all they can to be self-sufficient."[51]

States can also impose harsher terms on participants than the federal program dictates. They can choose to require a minimum of thirty work hours instead of twenty. They can take away benefits from people who do not comply. Some states force non-working SNAP participants to do job search and workfare activities, even though studies show that they don't lead to long-term employment or raise incomes.[52] Despite its *own findings* that they are ineffective, the USDA spent more than $700 million on work-oriented programs in 2016.[53] Studies of work requirements in other programs such as Medicaid, welfare, and housing assistance show that, while they rarely lead to long-term employment, they move thousands of people into deep poverty.[54] Most people who do not complete the requirements want to fulfill them but cannot due to reasons beyond their control.

Some SNAP users are unable to get jobs because they are on probation or parole. Or they might have a conviction for driving under the influence. Black, Indigenous, and Latine people disproportionately have some kind of criminal history, often due to racial profiling and racism in the criminal legal system.[55] They can also lose out to others for jobs because of lower educational levels, which often arise from discrimination, unequal funding, and the school-to-prison pipeline.[56] A history of drug use or being fired from previous jobs, for any reason, can also make it hard to secure work.[57]

Sometimes a recipient has a job but does not follow the right procedures for recording their employment. SNAP instructions, like all government forms, can be unclear and confusing. Some people suffer from chronic illnesses that prevent them from working but do not match the legal definition of a disability to meet the social security insurance requirements that entitle them to food assistance. Others are houseless.

The nature of low-wage work can also make it difficult to meet SNAP's work requirements. Many jobs pay little, do not provide benefits, offer unpredictable hours, and have high turnover rates.[58] Employers in the low-wage sector often see their workers as disposable and are quick to fire them for alleged transgressions, such as a missed bus, a broken-down car, a doctor's appointment, or a sick relative. Even though SNAP is essential for workers who are between jobs and to supplement low wages, in 2016, 500,000 people who were underemployed or searching for work lost their SNAP benefits.

In 2015, Wisconsin created a work training program called Food-Share Employment and Training (FSET) for SNAP users. The state gave the FSET contract to the Kentucky-based company ResCare, which turned out to be a big disappointment. Only a third of FSET program participants found jobs. ResCare overbilled and cost taxpayers more than double per month what a SNAP recipient receives. One ResCare client reported that the company coerced her into labor at a food service facility. ResCare bused her to the facility, which was several hours away from her home. Once she arrived, ResCare took away her cell phone and compelled her to stay in a workers' dorm for three months, peeling potatoes for twelve hours a day, six days a week. She had no access to transportation home. Her story matched other allegations made against the company. It is unclear why Wisconsin chose to contract with ResCare, a for-profit company with a history of violating civil rights, rather than with a competing technical college program with a 97 percent job placement success rate.[59] It appears that corporations benefit more from SNAP work requirements than the people that SNAP is supposed to help.

For every five SNAP users who lose their benefits because of work requirements, only one person finds employment through the program and the people who do are mostly older adults. Each dollar spent on SNAP yields $1.80 in economic activity.[60] That makes the program an economic multiplier that benefits the general economy in addition to its participants. Of 50 million food insecure people in the United States, 26.1 percent are Black, 23.7 percent are Latine, 23 percent are Indigenous, and 10.6 percent are white.[61] Indigenous and Black households have the lowest incomes, with poverty rates double that of the U.S. population. In 2016, SNAP lifted 2.1 million Black people and 2.5 Latine people out of poverty and kept 1.2 million Black people out of deep poverty, raising both groups' monthly income by 29 percent.[62] SNAP work requirements, which keep large groups of people from receiving this assistance, are a vestige of the laws that kept Black people poor and hungry during enslavement. They are also a literal violation of the Thirteenth Amendment's prohibition of involuntary servitude, as demonstrated by Wisconsin's ResCare contract. But the Supreme Court is not willing to interpret them this way.

THE FIRST OPPORTUNITY for the Court to define involuntary servitude came in the 1872 *Slaughter-House Cases*, where it grappled with how to interpret the Thirteenth Amendment. Louisiana gave New Orleans's Crescent slaughterhouse a monopoly, forcing anyone in the business of butchering meat to work for the company or not at all. When butchers filed a complaint against the monopoly, the Court held that the Thirteenth Amendment could not help them because although it restricted workers' choices, it was not literal enslavement.[63]

Eleven years later came the *Civil Rights Cases*, where the Court expanded the amendment's reach to ban slavery and involuntary servitude in any part of the United States along with "badges and incidents of slavery."[64] Yet it did not find that segregation in public places like restaurants and theaters was one of those badges or incidents.[65] The Court saw the segregation of private, as opposed to government, spaces as a social, not a civil, rights issue that the law could not touch.[66]

In 1896, in *Plessy v. Ferguson*, the Court upheld the segregation of railroad cars based on the farce that the race-assigned carriages were "separate but equal."[67] Considering whether the Court could insist on integrating railway cars under the Thirteenth Amendment, the Court said it could not because the meaning of slavery in the amendment was limited to "a state of bondage; the ownership of mankind as chattel, or at least, the control of the labor and services of one man for the benefit of another[.]" It did not consider whether segregation was a badge or incident of slavery, although there is a strong argument that it is.

In 1906, white sawmill workers and farmers in Arkansas who resented Black people working alongside or instead of them drove Black workers out of their jobs through threats of violence.[68] The white aggressors faced charges for this intimidation under a federal law prohibiting interference with the ability to make contracts.[69] In *Hodges v. United States*, the Court sided with the white workers and struck down the law because it did not involve "the entire subjection of one person to the will of another."[70] The Court reasoned that, instead of compelling the victims to work, their attackers had forced them to stop working. The case showed the Court's reluctance to expand its understanding of what the Thirteenth Amendment forbids to include violence intended to deprive Black people of the ability to sustain themselves.

In 1926's *Corrigan v. Buckley*, the Court decided that the Thirteenth Amendment could not stop racially restrictive covenants.[71] These covenants were promises made by white homeowners never to sell their property to a Black buyer. Almost twenty years later, in the next case to interpret the Thirteenth Amendment, 1944's *Pollock v. Williams*, the Court was more receptive to the idea that the Thirteenth Amendment can eliminate racial injustice related to modern forms of labor exploitation.[72] The case involved a Florida law that made it a crime of fraud to accept advance payment for labor that a person did not later perform.

This type of law was popular in the South, where employers tried to make farm laborers work under conditions that resembled enslavement. Black men made up the majority of farm workers because post-Reconstruction laws excluded them from other lines of work.[73] Under the Florida law, failure to pay back an advance without fulfilling the contract was intent to defraud and came with exorbitant penalties. A county sheriff took Pollock, a Black laborer, into custody for failing to pay back $5 and set his release bond at $500 (about $8,500 in 2023).

Pollock argued that Florida's law violated the 1867 Anti-Peonage Act, which said that no one had the power to force a person to work against their will even if that person was in debt to them. The Court agreed, saying that the Thirteenth Amendment gave Congress the power to pass the Anti-Peonage Act because the amendment's goal was "not merely to end slavery, but to maintain a system of completely free and voluntary labor throughout the United States."

. In 1988 the Court clarified the meaning of involuntary servitude in *United States v. Kozminski*.[74] The case involved two intellectually disabled men working against their will on a dairy farm in Michigan owned by Ike Kozminski, his wife, Margarethe, and their son John. The two men labored seventeen hours a day, every day, at first for $15 a week and then for free. The *Kozminski* Court analyzed two statutes enacted under the Thirteenth Amendment that criminalized involuntary servitude.[75]

Margarethe had found Robert Fulmer on the road near a farm where he was working. She left a note at the farm declaring that he was gone then took him to the Kozminski farm. Ike encountered Louis Moltinaris on the street in Ann Arbor. Moltinaris was homeless after a state mental institution discharged him. The Kozminskis housed the two men in isolated, squalid conditions. They subjected them to physical and verbal abuse, including threats of institutionalization. They denied Louis and Robert medical treatment after a bull gored one of them and the other lost his thumb. They told the men's relatives that they had no desire to see them and ripped the phone out of the wall when they tried to make a call.

The family also kept the men docile by failing to provide them with adequate nutrition. Robert and Louis, who had the intellectual capabilities of an eight- and ten-year-old, tried to leave the farm several times, but the Kozminskis always brought them back. Eventually, a herdsperson working on the farm contacted county officials, who came to rescue the men, moving them to an adult foster care home.

To decide whether the Thirteenth Amendment could support the laws banning involuntary servitude, the *Kozminski* Court first had to define the phrase. It observed that, "in every case in which this Court has found a condition of involuntary servitude, the victim had no available choice but to work or be subject to legal sanction."[76] The Court clarified that, "'involuntary servitude' necessarily means a condition of servitude in which the victim is forced to work for the defendant . . . by the use or threat of coercion through law or the legal process." And, "the vulnerabilities of the victim are relevant in determining whether the physical or legal coercion or threats thereof could plausibly have compelled the victim to serve." SNAP users are particularly vulnerable to the legal coercion of losing their benefits if they don't fulfill the program's work requirements.

There have been civil cases in the lower courts that have found work requirements constitutional. But the courts got those cases wrong because they failed to understand that SNAP recipients, although they might appear to have some choice about whether they work for their food, actually do not. In 1990's *Brogan v. San Mateo County*, William Brogan suffered a disabling heart attack at age sixty-one.[77] He said that the bad working conditions at the county's workfare program, in which he had to participate to get his food stamps, caused the attack. The Ninth Circuit dismissed his complaint and found that the program did not rise to the level of involuntary servitude because the county did not engage in "improper or wrongful conduct that is intended to cause, and does cause, the other person to believe" they have "no alternative but to perform the labor."

Realistically, people who need food assistance have no alternative but to work to get it. If they had another source of money or food, they would use it. Looking only at the county or state's intent ignored the structural racism built into the system over years of discriminatory laws and policies. The history of U.S. food politics is one of a long series of wrongful government conduct that has left many Black, Indigenous, and Latine people facing only two choices—perform tedious, grueling work or go hungry. These are not reasonable options. They are a form of involuntary servitude. The *Kozminski* concurrence explains, "In some minimalist sense the laborer always has a choice no matter what the threat: the laborer can choose to work, or take a beating; work, or go to jail. We can all agree that these choices are so illegitimate that any decision to work is 'involuntary.'"

ON THEIR FACE, the Fourteenth Amendment's Equal Protection and Due Process clauses seem to promise fair treatment by the state. Read in their best light, they do not allow the government to implement laws and policies that ruin Black and brown people's health and shorten their lives. But the Court's insistence that data showing disparate impact, the fact that a law or policy affects people of different races differently, is not enough to establish an intention to discriminate renders them empty shells.

Still, on very rare occasions, a court will find that discrimination is the only possible explanation for a government action. 1886's *Yick Wo v. Hopkins* set this precedent.[78] At the time, California law excluded Chinese people from almost every occupation. One thing it did allow them to do was to run laundries. With few other options, Chinese people owned 89 percent of the laundries in San Francisco, and 95 percent of San Francisco's laundries were in wooden buildings. The city passed an ordinance that required all laundries to be in either brick or stone buildings unless the owner got a waiver from the city. City officials denied over two hundred petitions for waivers from Chinese laundry owners and granted eighty waivers to white laundry owners.

Even though Yick Wo's laundry passed its fire inspection, the city imprisoned him for violating the ordinance. He fought his conviction by claiming that the ordinance violated equal protection because it was racially discriminatory. The Supreme Court sided with Yick Wo, finding that San Francisco's only possible motivation for the ordinance was to discriminate against Chinese people.

In another case, in 1960, the city of Tuskegee changed an electoral district from a simple rectangle into a twenty-eight-sided shape that excluded four hundred Black people from its borders but no white people. Unable to come up with any reasonable explanation for this change, the Court decided that the act itself was enough to prove discriminatory intent in *Gomillion v. Lightfoot*.[79]

Aside from these two promising cases, the Supreme Court has resisted findings of discriminatory intent, even when statistics speak for themselves. In *McCleskey v. Kemp*, the Court upheld the petitioner's death sentence despite data showing that, under the Georgia criminal legal system, a Black defendant convicted of killing a white victim was over four times more likely to receive a death sentence than if the victim were Black.[80]

Indifferent to the study's results and the state's sordid history of discriminatory laws, the Court decided that Georgia's death penalty system did not violate equal protection because McClesky could not provide evidence that the state used the system *because* it had this impact. That motivation would be impossible for McClesky to prove.

A far better approach would be to recognize discriminatory purpose when there is a discriminatory impact, without requiring proof of the intentions of the people who participate in or design the discriminatory system. No court would accept a claim that the USDA intentionally structured school lunchrooms or FDPIR commods to create a racial health gap.[81] But the simple fact that these programs have a discriminatory effect should be enough to allow a court to reform or dismantle them in favor of new approaches to poverty and hunger that would protect everyone equally.[82]

Health equality is foundational to all other forms of equality, which people cannot enjoy in the face of sickness or death. USDA food programs are unconstitutional because they perpetuate racial health disparities that, in turn, reinforce social stratification. There are many ways to try to eradicate food oppression. One is to take an incremental, methodical, strategic approach to transforming the food system. This book contains numerous policy and practical changes that would improve USDA programs, reduce race-targeted marketing, and chip away at racial health disparities. They should all be implemented. But they still won't be enough.

It is necessary to acknowledge the past and try to repair it. Instead of focusing on small, band-aid solutions like food banks that rely on the current food structure, activists should demand that food and agricultural corporations take the profits they have made from exploiting racism and pour them back into the communities they have harmed. These reparations could take the form of parks, recreation centers, bike paths, medical centers, and affordable housing. Instead of providing food to people who are desperate for it, the government should give everyone a basic income that eliminates food insecurity, allowing all people to live beyond hand to mouth.

Legal scholar Amna Akbar asserts, "Once we better understand the structural and historical nature of the problems we study, we cannot rest on old modes of conceiving reform."[83] To see this problem with fresh eyes, reparations and abolition provide useful frameworks. Abolitionists reject systems built to perpetuate racial capitalism and seek new ways to structure society free of the burdens of historical subordination. In the words of geographer Ruth Wilson Gilmore, "Abolition is deliberately everything-ist; it's about the entirety of human-environmental relations."[84] Abolishing the corporate-dominated food system and building something new is the way forward. Abolition, according to Christina Sharpe, "joins and elaborates and imagines other ways of being together and in relation, other ways of enacting care for human and nonhuman life. . . . Abolition is remaking our vocabularies. Abolition is another word for love."[85]

# ACKNOWLEDGMENTS

My agent, Ayesha Pande, championed this book from the start. Because of her, I got to work with my editor, Riva Hocherman, and the dream team at Henry Holt: Alex Foster, Arriel Vinson, Alyssa Weinberg, Carolyn O'Keefe, Hannah Campbell, Alex Camlin, and Carol Rutan.

This work began as a twinkle in my eye in Angela P. Harris's class on the suburbs. As it grew over the years, so has our friendship, which has brought mentorship, inspiration, joy, and amazing food into my life.

Brilliant curators Honor Beddard and Marianne Templeton gave me an extraordinary opportunity to work with them on the Milk and Power exhibit at Wellcome Collection. The hours we spent talking all things milk were unforgettable, and the exhibit was compelling, frightening, and magical.

I wrote some of this in a building in Barcelona, haunted by the ghost of Miguel de Cervantes, and some of it on London's South Bank (thanks to the Fulbright commission, Anouska, and Ben). Weekly drinks at the National Theatre with Glen Duncan brought me back to life after a long lockdown.

My deans at the University of Hawai'i at Mānoa Richardson School of Law, Camille Nelson and Avi Soifer, appreciated and supported my research, and Southwestern Law School Dean Darby Dickerson made sure I got to the finish line.

Collaborating with Yance Ford has been a wonderful adventure, and it's only the beginning.

I have been lucky to work with so many wonderful, smart students on this project: Fern Grether, Emily Walker, Lydia Grasso, Kalina Nguyen Le, Elyse Nakamoto, Erin Dung, Kristin Fujiyama, Rachel Murakami, Lindsay Lipp, Sarah Williams, Emily Sarasa, Mykie Ozoa-Aglugub, Rochelle Sugawa, Denielle Pedro, Joyce Chang, Ian Tapu, Anthony Gilmore, Raul Garcia, Rocco Basile, culinary and legal genius Jennifer Hee, and radical, fabulous leader Khara Jabola-Carolus. Super-librarian Louis Rosen and Marisa Masters generously jumped in at the last stretch.

I can't imagine how I would have made this journey without dance. Thank you for the choreo, community, and joy: Corey Action Harrison (and for the fashion, photos, and bringing me to all kinds of church), Mara L. Bacon Chang, Malik Robinson, Olga González, Lisa Engelken, Sami Akuna, Edgar Page, Momo LeBeau, Allan Frias, David Schrag, Micaya, Darnell, Karen Arceneaux, Isabelle Duffy (dance therapy!), Lindsey Dantes, Nadiah Beleza, Lisha Yates, Blair Madison, Talia Little, Samar Nassar, Raquel Horsford, Jerod Williams, Peiling Kao and Betsy Fisher.

I am eternally grateful to the people who keep me grounded, make me laugh, and let me know that I am not alone: Mitra, Glen, Russell, Angela, Dan, Priscilla, Sarah, Molly, César, Margaret, Osagie, D'Lonra, Celia, Darlene, Jennifer, Jonathan, Addie, Doron, Lauren, Bertrall, Joy, Cammie, Jodi, Kekoa, and Kinohi.

All my love and gratitude to my two breathtaking companions, Alia and Serafino; you are everything.

# NOTES

**INTRODUCTION**

1. "Statistics About Diabetes," American Diabetes Association, https://diabetes .org/about-us/statistics/about-diabetes.
2. "Obesity Rates for Adults in the United States in 2021, by Race/Ethnicity," Statista, https://www.statista.com/statistics/207436/overweight-and-obesity -rates-for-adults-by-ethnicity/.
3. "Heart Disease Facts," Centers for Disease Control and Prevention, https: //www.cdc.gov/heartdisease/facts.htm.
4. "Stroke and African Americans," U.S. Department of Health and Human Ser- vices, Office of Minority Health, https://minorityhealth.hhs.gov/stroke-and -african-americans.
5. "Facts About Hypertension," Centers for Disease Control and Prevention, https://www.cdc.gov/bloodpressure/facts.htm.
6. George Washington to Major General John Sullivan, May 31, 1779, *Found- ers Online*, National Archives, https://founders.archives.gov/documents /Washington/03-20-02-0661.
7. Martin Teitel and Kimberly A. Wilson, *Genetically Engineered Food: Changing the Nature of Nature* (Rochester, VT: Park Street Press 2001), 68, citing Gwynne Dyer, "Frankenstein Foods," *Toronto Globe and Mail*, February 20, 1999.
8. Michael Ollinger, Sang V. Nguyen, Donald Blayney, William Chambers, and Ken Nelson, *Structural Change in the Meat, Poultry, Dairy, and Grain Process- ing Industries* (Washington, DC: USDA, Economic Research Service, 2005), http://www.themarketworks.org/sites/default/files/uploads/studies/Structural -Changes-Meat-Poultry-Dairy-and-GrainProcessing-Industries-Economic -Research.pdf.

9. Daniel Imhoff and Christina Badaracco, *Farm Bill: A Citizen's Guide* (Washington, DC: Island Press, 2019), 38.

10. Imhoff and Badaracco, *Farm Bill*, 75, 78–79.

11. John Kelly, "Mega-Farms, Government Agencies and the Rich Get Bulk of Federal Farm Aid, AP Survey Shows," Institute for Agriculture and Trade Policy, September 21, 2001, https://www.iatp.org/news/mega-farms-government -agencies-and-the-rich-get-bulk-of-federal-farm-aid-ap-survey-shows.

12. Nancy Watzman, "Farm Bill Allows Congress to Keep Crop Subsidies Secret," Sunlight Foundation, February 7, 2014, https://sunlightfoundation.com/2014 /02/07/farm-bill-allows-congress-to-keep-crop-subsidies-secret/.

13. Frances Fleming-Milici et al., *Fast Food Facts: Food Advertising to Children and Teens* (Hartford: University of Connecticut Rudd Center for Food Policy & Obesity, 2021), https: //media.ruddcenter.uconn.edu/PDFs/SocialMedia2021.pdf.

14. Jen Miller, "Frybread," *Smithsonian Magazine*, July 2008, https://www.smith sonianmag.com/arts-culture/frybread-79191/.

15. Michael W. Twitty, *The Cooking Gene: A Journey Through African American Culinary History in the Old South* (New York: Amistad, 2017), xii

16. Jessica B. Harris, *High on the Hog: A Culinary Journey from Africa to America* (New York: Bloomsbury, 2011), 208.

17. Hannah Garth, "Blackness and Justice in the L.A. Food Justice Movement," in *Black Food Matters: Racial Justice in the Wake of Food Justice*, ed. Hanna Garth and Ashanté M. Reese (Minneapolis: University of Minnesota Press, 2020), 110.

18. Jeffrey Pilcher, *Planet Taco: A Global History of Mexican Food* (New York: Oxford University Press, 2012), xiii.

19. Paloma Martinez-Cruz, *Food Fight! Millennial Mestizaje Meets the Culinary Marketplace* (Tuscon: University of Arizona Press, 2019), 14.

20. David Brooks, "How We Are Ruining America," *New York Times*, July 11, 2017, https://www.nytimes.com/2017/07/11/opinion/how-we-are-ruining-america .html.

## 1. WEAPONS OF HEALTH DESTRUCTION

1. Cecily Hilleary, quoting A-dae Romero-Briones, "Native American Tribes Fighting High Prices, Poor Food Quality," *VOA*, March 24, 2017, https://www .voanews.com/a/tribes-fighting-high-prices-poor-food-quality-in-indian -country/3780303.html.

2. Leslie Linthicum, "American Indian Activist Raises Ruckus Over Fry Bread," *Arizona Daily Sun*, February 27, 2005, https://perma.cc/Y48F-ECNY.

3. Dana Vantrease, "Commod Bods and Frybread Power: Government Food Aid in American Indian Culture," *Journal of American Folklore* 126, no. 499 (Winter 2013): 55–69.

4. Liza F. Kay, "Fry Bread: Two Sides of a Powwow Staple," *Baltimore Sun*, August

23, 2006, https://statesymbolsusa.org/symbol-official-item/south-dakota/state
-food-agriculture-symbol/fry-bread.

5. Jen Miller, "Frybread," *Smithsonian Magazine*, July 2008, https://www
.smithsonianmag.com/arts-culture/frybread-79191/.

6. Miller, "Frybread."

7. Suzan Shown Harjo, "My New Year's Resolution: No More Fat 'Indian' Food,"
*Indian Country Today*, January 26, 2005, https://perma.cc/RQ3Z-NEAX.

8. David Treuer, *The Heartbeat of Wounded Knee* (New York: Riverhead Books,
2019), 430.

9. Devon A. Mihesuah, *Recovering Our Ancestors' Gardens* (Lincoln: University
of Nebraska Press, 2020), 39–40.

10. Winona LaDuke, foreword to *Indigenous Food Sovereignty in the United States*,
ed. Devon A. Mihesuah and Elizabeth Hoover (Norman: University of Oklahoma Press, 2019), xiii.

11. Jennifer Leigh Hughes, "Where Language Touches the Earth: Folklore and
Ecology in Tohono O'odham Plant Emergence Narratives" (master's thesis,
Utah State University, 1996), 18, 24–25, https://digitalcommons.usu.edu/cgi/
viewcontent.cgi?article=5547&context=etd.

12. Mihesuah, *Recovering Our Ancestors' Gardens*, 147.

13. See Cynthia Fowler and Evelyn Konopik, "The History of Fire in the Southern
United States," *Human Ecology Review* 14, no. 2 (2007): 168.

14. Roxanne Dunbar-Ortiz, *An Indigenous Peoples' History of the United States*
(Boston: Beacon Press, 2014), 60.

15. Library of Congress, "Virginia's Early Relations with Native Americans," U.S.
History Primary Source Timeline, https://www.loc.gov/classroom-materials
/united-states-history-primary-source-timeline/colonial-settlement-1600
-1763/virginia-relations-with-native-americans/.

16. Rhiannon Koehler, "Hostile Nations: Quantifying the Destruction of the
Sullivan-Clinton Genocide of 1779," *American Indian Quarterly* 42, no. 4 (Fall
2018): 427, 433, citing "From George Washington to Major General John Sullivan, 31 May 1779," *Founders Online*, National Archives, https://founders.
archives.gov/documents/Washington/03-20-02-0661.

17. Claudio Saunt, *Unworthy Republic: The Dispossession of Native Americans and
the Road to Indian Territory* (New York: W. W. Norton, 2020), 154.

18. Dunbar-Ortiz, *Indigenous Peoples' History of the United States*, citing Joint
Special Committee, 38th Cong., *Report on the Condition of the Indian Tribes*
(Washington, DC: Government Printing Office, 1865), 417.

19. Wilburn Hill, interview by Billie Byrd, March 28, 1938, Indian Pioneer Oral
History Project, Okemah, Oklahoma, https://digital.libraries.ou.edu/cdm/ref
/collection/indianpp/id/7841.

20. Gerald Thompson, *The Army and the Navajo: The Bosque Redondo Reservation Experiment, 1863–1868* (Tucson: University of Arizona Press, 1976), 140.

21. Dunbar-Ortiz, *Indigenous Peoples' History of the United States*, 164–65, quoting Struck by the Ree of the Yankton Sioux, Special Report No. 39 (1867), 371. "Before the soldiers came along we had good health; but once the soldiers come along they go to my squaws and want to sleep with them, and the squaws being hungry will sleep with them in order to get something to eat, and will get a bad disease, and then the squaws turn to their husbands and give them a bad disease."

22. William T. Sherman to Philip Henry Sheridan, May 10, 1868, Philip Henry Sheridan Papers: Autograph Letters, 1865–1887, box 39, reel 17, Manuscript Division, Library of Congress, Washington, DC.

23. Carolyn Merchant, *American Environmental History: An Introduction* (New York: Columbia University Press, 2007), 20.

24. Dennis Wiedman, "Native American Embodiment of the Chronicities of Modernity: Reservation Food, Diabetes, and the Metabolic Syndrome Among the Kiowa, Comanche, and Apache," *Medical Anthropology Quarterly* 26, no. 4 (2012): 595, 601.

25. U.S. Department of Interior, Office of Indian Affairs, Rules Governing the Court of Indian Offenses (1883), http://robert-clinton.com/wp-content/uploads/2018/09/code-of-indian-offenses.pdf.

26. Treuer, *Heartbeat of Wounded Knee*, 147.

27. Devon Mihesuah, "Sustenance and Health Among the Five Tribes in Indian Territory, Postremoval to Statehood," *Ethnohistory* 62, no. 2 (April 2015): 277.

28. Mihesuah, "Sustenance and Health," citing *Indian Citizen*, January 31, 1901.

29. Treuer, *Heartbeat of Wounded Knee*, 133.

30. Dunbar-Ortiz, *Indigenous Peoples' History of the United States*, 212.

31. Louise Erdrich, *The Night Watchman* (New York: Harper, 2020), 99. Erdrich's grandfather Patrick Gourneau attended government boarding schools at Fort Totten, Haskell, and Wahpeton.

32. Treuer, *Heartbeat of Wounded Knee*, 138–39.

33. J. Norman Leard, interview by Hazel B. Greene, field worker, June 2, 1937, Indian-Pioneer History Project for Oklahoma, Hugo, Oklahoma, https://digital.libraries.ou.edu/cdm/ref/collection/indianpp/id/5187.

34. Mihesuah, "Sustenance and Health," 263, 275. These seminaries began as schools operated by the Cherokee Nation in 1851. They were closed during the U.S. Civil War, reopened in 1879, when they became tuition free, and sold to the state of Oklahoma in 1909. Before 1879, some parents traded wild game and garden items for tuition. By 1893, the school's food order reflected its dietary priorities: 16,000 pounds of white flour and 8,000 pounds of beef.

35. Patty Talahongva, "No More 'Die Bread': How Boarding Schools Impacted Native Diet and the Resurgence of Indigenous Food Sovereignty," *Journal of American Indian Education* 57, no. 1 (Spring 2018): 145, 146–47.

36. Mihesuah, "Sustenance and Health," 263; "Sanitorium to Open," *Chickasha Daily Express* (Chickasha, Indian Terr.), April 28, 1903, 1, https://gateway.okhistory .org/ark:/67531/metadc732349/m1/1/?q=obesity; "If You Read This," *Cherokee Republican* (Cherokee, OK), September 27, 1907, 8, https://gateway.okhistory .org/ark:/67531/metadc1718903/m1/8/?q=stomach.

37. Lewis Meriam, *The Problem of Indian Administration* (Baltimore: Johns Hopkins Press, 1928), 327.

38. Bethany Bella, "It All Began with a Sheep Unit," *Medium* (blog), May 2, 2017, https://medium.com/@bethanynbella/it-all-began-with-a-sheep-unit -b92da9da7f77.

39. Marsha Weisiger, *Dreaming of Sheep in Navajo Country* (Seattle: University of Washington Press, 2009), 135.

40. S. Ryan Johansson, "The Demographic History of Native Peoples of North America: A Selective Bibliography," *Yearbook of Physical Anthropology* 25 (1982): 133, 145 (citations omitted).

41. Dunbar-Ortiz, *An Indigenous Peoples' History of the United States*, 144.

42. Sandra Faiman-Silva, *Choctaws at the Crossroads* (Lincoln: University of Nebraska Press, 2000), 166–67.

43. U.S. Department of Agriculture, Office of the Inspector General, *Food Distribution Program on Indian Reservations,* Audit Report 27601–0001–21, February 2020.

44. Neal D. Barnard and Derek M. Brown, "U.S. Dietary Guidelines Unfit for Native Americans," Longevity Professor, accessed August 16, 2021, https:// longevityprofessor.com/articles/10-u-s-dietary-guidelines-unfit-for-native -americans.

45. Megan Mucioki, Jennifer Sowerwine, and Daniel Sarna-Wojcicki, "Thinking Inside and Outside the Box: Local and National Considerations of the Food Distribution Program on Indian Reservations (FDPIR)," *Journal of Rural Studies* 57 (2018): 88, 192. Charles "Red" Gate was hired by the Standing Rock Sioux Tribe, but it is unclear which nation he belongs to. "Standing Rock Tribe," USDA, accessed August 16, 2021, https://www.fns.usda.gov/contact /north-dakota-standing-rock-sioux-tribe.

46. Margaret Moss, "Trauma Lives on in Native Americans by Making Us Sick— While the US Looks Away," *Guardian*, May 9, 2019, describing adverse health outcomes in Indigenous communities, https://www.theguardian.com /commentisfree/2019/may/09/trauma-lives-on-in-native-americans-while -the-us-looks-away, http://perma.cc/G2WS-P8GX; Carmen Byker Shanks et al., "Assessing Foods Offered in the Food Distribution Program on Indian Reservations (FDPIR) Using the Healthy Eating Index 2010," *Public Health Nutrition* 19, no. 7 (May 2016): 1315.

47. Dunbar-Ortiz, *Indigenous Peoples' History of the United States*, 208.

48. Samantha Artiga and Kendal Orgera, "COVID-19 Presents Significant Risks for

American Indian and Alaska Native People" (San Francisco: Kaiser Faimly Foundation [KFF], 2020), https://www.kff.org/coronavirus-covid-19/issue-brief/covid-19-presents-significant-risks-for-american-indian-and-alaska-native-people.

49. Mucioki, Sowerwine, and Sarna-Wojcicki, "Thinking Inside and Outside the Box," 88, 192.

50. Krista Scott-Dixon, "Springtime in the Ancestors' Gardens: Native Health and Finding Comfort," *Spezzatino* 4 (2008): 40. See Mihesuah, "Sustenance and Health," 278n106.

51. D. S. Jones, "The Persistence of American Indian Health Disparities," *American Journal of Public Health* 96, no. 12 (December 2006): 2122–34, https://doi.org/10.2105/AJPH.2004.054262.

52. Michèle Companion, "Obesogenic Cultural Drift and Nutritional Transition: Identifying Barriers to Healthier Food Consumption in Urban Native American Populations," *Journal of Applied Social Science* 7, no. 1 (March 2013): 90.

## 2. SURVIVAL PENDING REVOLUTION

1. Booker T. Washington, *The Booker T. Washington Papers*: vol. 1: *The Autobiographical Writings*, ed. Louis R. Harlan and John W. Blassingame (Urbana: University of Illinois Press, 1972), 420.

2. Frederick Douglass, *My Bondage and My Freedom* (New York: Miller, Orton, and Mulligan, 1855), 58, https://www.gutenberg.org/files/202/202-h/202-h.htm.

3. Patrick Minges Blair, ed., *Far More Terrible for Women: Personal Accounts of Women in Slavery* (2013, e-book), citing interview by Pearl Randolph with Louisa Everett, Virginia, 1937. Louisa was known as Norfolk or Nor until she was freed and gave herself the name Louisa.

4. Harriet Jacobs, *Incidents in the Life of a Slave Girl* (Boston, 1861), 106.

5. Harriet A. Washington, *Medical Apartheid: The Dark History of Medical Experimentation on Black Americans from Colonial Times to the Present* (New York: Doubleday, 2006).

6. Richard H. Steckel, "A Dreadful Childhood: The Excess Mortality of American Slaves," *Social Science History* 10, no. 4 (Winter 1986): 427–28.

7. Michelle B. Pass and Sharon K. Bullock, "Black Health and Wellness: Past and Present Implications of the 'Slave Diet' for African Americans," *Black History Bulletin* 84, no. 12 (Fall 2021): 12–15.

8. Herbert C. Covey and Dwight Eisnach, *What the Slaves Ate: Recollections of African American Foods and Foodways from the Slave Narratives* (Santa Barbara: Greenwood, 2009), 15.

9. Clint Smith, *How the Word Is Passed: A Reckoning with the History of Slavery Across America* (New York: Little, Brown, 2021), 12.

10. "Art. X—Agricultural Improvement and Progress," *Debow's Review, Agricultural, Commercial, Industrial Progress and Resources* 14, no. 1 (January 1853): 175, 177–78, https://quod.lib.umich.edu/m/moajrnl/acg1336.1–14.002/185:10?rgn=full+text;view=image.

11. Covey and Eisnach, *What the Slaves Ate*, 15; see "United States African Americans," Food in Every Country, http://www.foodbycountry.com/Spain-to-Zimbabwe-Cumulative-Index/United-States-African-Americans.html, https://perma.cc/TD2D-G76J.

12. Minges, ed., *Far More Terrible for Women*, citing interview with Mary Reynolds by Heloise Foreman, Black River, Louisiana, 1937.

13. In *The 1619 Project*, Nikole Hannah-Jones makes excellent arguments for replacing the word "plantation" with "forced labor-camp." I agree with her but have occasionally used "plantation" here for clarity's sake. Nikole Hannah-Jones et al., eds., *The 1619 Project: A New Origin Story* (New York: New York Times, 2021).

14. Ralph Betts Flanders, *Plantation Slavery in Georgia* (1933; Cos Cob, CT: John E. Edwards, 1967); James Mellon, ed., *Bullwhip Days: The Slaves Remember, An Oral History* (New York: Grove Press, 2002), 38.

15. Minges, ed., *Far More Terrible for Women*, citing interview with Rose Williams by Sheldon Gauthier, Bell County, Texas, 1937.

16. Jacobs, *Incidents in the Life of a Slave Girl*, 25.

17. See, e.g., Minges, ed., *Far More Terrible for Women*, citing interview with Parthena Rollins by Anna Pritchett, Scott County, Kentucky, 1937.

18. Minges, ed., *Far More Terrible for Women*, citing interview with Ethel Daugherty by Grace Monroe, Indiana.

19. Booker T. Washington, *Up from Slavery* (Garden City, NY: Doubleday, Page, 1907), 10.

20. Minges, ed., *Far More Terrible for Women*, citing interview with Aunty Betty Cofer by Mary E. Hicks, Wachovia, North Carolina, 1937.

21. Nina Martyris, "Frederick Douglass on How Slave Owners Used Food as a Weapon of Control," NPR, February 10, 2017, https://www.npr.org/sections/thesalt/2017/02/10/514385071/frederick-douglass-on-how-slave-owners-used-food-as-a-weapon-of-control.

22. Leah Penniman, *Farming While Black: Soul Fire Farm's Practical Guide to Liberation on the Land* (White River Junction, VT: Chelsea Green Publishing, 2018).

23. Jacobs, *Incidents in the Life of a Slave Girl*, 22.

24. Wilma A. Dunaway, *The African-American Family in Slavery and Emancipation* (New York: Cambridge University Press, 2003), 132.

25. Covey and Eisnach, *What the Slaves Ate*, 18.

26. Annie Campbell, ed., "Excerpts from South Carolina Slave Code of 1740 No. 670 (1740)," U.S. History Scene, https://ushistoryscene.com/article/excerpts-south-carolina-slave-code-1740-no-670-1740/.

27. State v. Bowen, 34 S.C.L. 573 (1849).

28. "South Carolina Passes Negro Act of 1740, Codifying White Supremacy," Equal Justice Initiative, accessed June 25, 2022, https://calendar.eji.org/racial-injustice /may/10.

29. Thomas D. Morris, *Southern Slavery and the Law, 1619–1860* (Chapel Hill: University of North Carolina Press, 1996), 195. The states that followed South Carolina's lead were Alabama, Louisiana, Florida, North Carolina, Texas, and Georgia.

30. H. M. Henry, "The Slave Laws of Tennessee," *Tennessee Historical Magazine* 2, no. 3 (September 1916): 175, 186.

31. Tex. Const. of 1845, art. VIII, § 1, https://tarltonapps.law.utexas.edu/constitutions /texas1845/a8, https://perma.cc/4PHM-2S94.

32. William Goodell, *The American Slave Code in Theory and Practice* (New York: American and Foreign Anti-Slavery Society, 1853), 135; George McDowell Stroud, *A Sketch of the Laws Relating to Slavery in the Several States of the United States of America*, 2nd ed. (Philadelphia: Henry Longstreth, 1856), 48; see also Donald L. Grant, *The Way It Was in the South: The Black Experience in Georgia* (Athens: University of Georgia Press, 2001), 54.

33. Cheek v. State, 38 Ala. 227, 228 (1861).

34. Ala. Code, art. VII § 3297 (1852).

35. See, e.g., Mellon, ed., *Bullwhip Days*; Anne Yentsch, "Excavating the South's African American Food History," *African Diaspora Archaeology Newsletter* 11, no. 2 (June 2008): 1, 10.

36. Yentsch, "Excavating the South's African American Food History," 34n21, citing Charles Ball, *Slavery in the United States: A Narrative of the Life and Adventures of Charles Ball, a Black Man, who Lived Forty Years in Maryland, South Carolina and Georgia, as a Slave* (New York: J. S. Taylor, 1837).

37. *Federal Writers' Project: Slave Narrative Project, Vol. 4, Georgia, Part 4, Telfair-Young with combined interviews of others*, 1936, Library of Congress, accessed June 23, 2022, https://www.loc.gov/resource/mesn.044/?sp=185&st=text.

38. Washington, *Up from Slavery*, 4–5.

39. Psyche A. Williams-Forson, *Building Houses out of Chicken Legs: Black Women, Food, and Power* (Chapel Hill: University of North Carolina Press, 2006), 28.

40. Martyris, "Frederick Douglass on How Slave Owners Used Food as a Weapon of Control."

41. *Federal Writers' Project: Slave Narrative Project, Vol. 10, Missouri, Abbot-Younger*, 1936, Library of Congress, accessed June 23, 2022, https://www.loc .gov/resource/mesn.100/?sp=9&st=list.

42. Gardiner v. Thibodeau, La. Ann. 14, 732 (1859).

43. McCutcheon v. Angelo, La. Ann. 14, 34 (1859).

44. Jacobs, *Incidents in the Life of a Slave Girl*, 7.

45. Amanda Gibson, "The Economy of the Enslaved in Virginia," Encyclopedia Virginia, accessed September 8, 2021, https://encyclopediavirginia.org/entries/the-economy-of-the-enslaved-in-virginia/.

46. This power is not a thing of the past. In 2021, the state of Texas allowed private citizens to bring suits against anyone helping a person obtain an abortion, avoiding the constitutional implications of the state blocking access to a constitutional right.

47. "Slave Narrative of Martha Allen," Access Genealogy, accessed June 25, 2022, https://accessgenealogy.com/north-carolina/slave-narrative-of-martha-allen.htm.

48. "Sharecropping, Black Land Acquisition, and White Supremacy (1868–1900)," World Food Policy Center, accessed June 25, 2022, https://wfpc.sanford.duke.edu/north-carolina/durham-food-history/sharecropping-black-land-acquisition-and-white-supremacy-1868-1900/.

49. Jim Downs, *Sick from Freedom: African-American Illness and Suffering During the Civil War and Reconstruction* (New York: Oxford University Press, 2012), 2.

50. Downs, *Sick from Freedom*, 40.

51. Jeff Cannon, "The Bureau of Refugees, Freedmen, and Abandoned Lands 'The Freedmen's Bureau,'" last revised December 23, 2006, http://www.fivay.org/freedmen.html.

52. Ira C. Colby, "The Freedmen's Bureau: From Social Welfare to Segregation," *Phylon* 46, no. 3 (1985): 219, 226.

53. Senate Executive Doc. No. 6, 39th Congress, 2nd Sess. (1867).

54. Downs, *Sick from Freedom*, 89.

55. "The Freedmen's Bureau," EH.net (Economic History Association), accessed June 25, 2022, https://eh.net/encyclopedia/the-freedmens-bureau/.

56. Nikole Hannah-Jones et al., eds., *The 1619 Project: A New Origin Story* (New York: New York Times, 2021), 464.

57. Andrew Ward, *The Slaves' War: The Civil War in the Words of Former Slaves* (New York: Mariner Books, 2009), 252.

58. "Excerpt from Mississippi Black Codes (1865)," Facing History & Ourselves, accessed June 25, 2022, https://www.facinghistory.org/reconstruction-era/mississippi-black-codes-1865.

59. Ruth Delaney, Ram Subramanian, Alison Shames, and Nicholas Turner, "American History, Race, and Prison," in *Reimagining Prison Web Report* (New York: Vera Institute of Justice, 2018), https://www.vera.org/reimagining-prison-web-report/american-history-race-and-prison.

60. Douglas A. Blackmon, *Slavery by Another Name: The Re-Enslavement of Black Americans from the Civil War to World War II* (New York: Doubleday, 2008), 57.

61. Blackmon, *Slavery by Another Name*.

62. Christopher R. Adamson, "Punishment after Slavery: Southern State Penal Systems, 1865–1890," *Social Problems* 30 (1983): 555, 562.

63. Blackmon, *Slavery by Another Name*, 72.

64. Hannah-Jones et al., eds., *1619 Project*, 280, citing "Prison Abuses in Mississippi," *Chicago Daily Tribune*, July 11, 1887.

65. Blackmon, *Slavery by Another Name*, 109–10.

66. Anne L. Bower, ed., *African American Foodways: Explorations of History and Culture* (Urbana: University of Illinois Press, 2008), 76.

67. Yentsch, "Excavating the South's African American Food History," 24, citing Mason Crum, *Gullah: Negro Life in the Carolina Sea Islands* (Durham, NC: Duke University Press, 1940), 15–17.

68. Bower, ed., *African American Foodways*, 78

69. Denise M. Watson and Amy Poulter, "The Saga of Sharecropping: Reflecting on Its Tolls and the Tenacity of Family that Helped Build Virginia and the South," *Daily Press*, May 5, 2019, https://www.dailypress.com/history/dp-nws-sharecroppers-south-history-0506-story.html.

70. Robert T. Dirks and Nancy Duran, "African American Dietary Patterns at the Beginning of the 20th Century," *Journal of Nutrition* 131, no. 7 (July 2001): 1881, interview with Georgia Ford, https://www.academia.edu/226742/African_American_Dietary_Patterns_at_the_Beginning_of_the_20th_Century.

71. Dirks and Duran, "African American Dietary Patterns," interview with Dora Strong Dennis.

72. Dirks and Duran, "African American Dietary Patterns," interview with Annie Floyd.

73. Susan A. Mann, "Slavery, Sharecropping, and Sexual Inequality," *Signs: Journal of Women in Culture and Society* 14 (1989): 774, https://www-jstor-org.eres.library.manoa.hawaii.edu/stable/3174684?seq=1; Jacqueline Jones, *Labor of Love, Labor of Sorrow: Black Women, Work, and the Family, from Slavery to the Present* (New York: Basic Books, 2009), https://ebookcentral.proquest.com/lib/uhm/reader.action?docID=481165; Susan L. Smith, *Sick and Tired of Being Sick and Tired: Black Women's Health Activism in America, 1890–1950* (Philadelphia: University of Pennsylvania Press, 1995).

74. Watson and Poulter, "The Saga of Sharecropping."

75. Hughsey Childs, interview by Charles Hardy III, October 23, 1984, Goin' North: Tales of the Great Migration, Louie B. Nunn Center for Oral History, University of Kentucky Libraries, https://kentuckyoralhistory.org/ark:/16417/xt7cjs9h6w9w.

76. *Slavery by Another Name*, directed by Sam Pollard (Alexandria, VA: PBS, 2012), https://www.pbs.org/tpt/slavery-by-another-name/themes/sharecropping/. The PBS documentary was based on the book of the same title.

77. Britannica, s.v. "debt slavery," by Gerald D. Jaynes, accessed June 27, 2022, https://www.britannica.com/topic/debt-slavery; see, generally, Missouri

Digital Heritage, "Laws Concerning Slavery in Missouri," accessed June 27, 2022, https://www.sos.mo.gov/archives/education/aahi/earlyslavelaws /slavelaws.asp; Constitutional Rights Foundation, "The Southern 'Black Codes' of 1865–66," accessed June 27, 2022, https://www.crf-usa.org/brown -v-board-50th-anniversary/southern-black-codes.html.

78. Alferdteen Harrison, ed., *Black Exodus: The Great Migration from the American South* (Jackson: University Press of Mississippi, 1991), 21, citing Gunnar Myrdal, *An American Dilemma: The Negro Problem and Modern Democracy* (1944; New York: Harper & Row, 1994), 189–206.

79. Sarah Schmitz and Eve J. Lowenstein, "The Unwavering Doctor Who Unraveled a Medical Mystery," *International Journal of Women's Dermatology* 5, no. 2 (June 2019): 137.

80. Idelle Truitt Elsey, interview, June 29, 1984, Goin' North: Tales of the Great Migration, Louie B. Nunn Center for Oral History, University of Kentucky Libraries, https://goinnorth.org/items/show/1077.

81. Isabel Wilkerson, "The Long-Lasting Legacy of the Great Migration," *Smithsonian Magazine*, September 2016, https://www.smithsonianmag.com/history /long-lasting-legacy-great-migration-180960118/.

82. Minnie S. Whitney, interview, March 6, 1984, Goin' North: Tales of the Great Migration, Louie B. Nunn Center for Oral History, University of Kentucky Libraries, https://goinnorth.org/items/show/1073.

83. Beulah Collins, interview, August 1, 1983, Goin' North: Tales of the Great Migration, Louie B. Nunn Center for Oral History, University of Kentucky Libraries, https://goinnorth.org/items/show/1047.

84. Fannie Hutchinson, interview, June 25, 1984, Goin' North: Tales of the Great Migration, Louie B. Nunn Center for Oral History, University of Kentucky Libraries, https://goinnorth.org/items/show/1057.

85. Charles Vance, interview, March 4, 1984, Goin' North: Tales of the Great Migration, Louie B. Nunn Center for Oral History, University of Kentucky Libraries, https://goinnorth.org/items/show/1070.

86. Winn-Dixie started in Florida in 1925 and spread to Alabama, Mississippi, Georgia, and Louisiana. The supermarket is still open.

87. Piggly Wiggly opened in Memphis in 1916 as the first self-service grocery store—customers selected their own items instead of a clerk getting them.

88. Emily C. Sousa and Manish N. Raizada, "Contributions of African Crops to American Culture and Beyond: The Slave Trade and Other Journeys of Resilient Peoples and Crops," *Frontiers in Sustainable Food Systems* 4 (December 2020): 1, 17–18; Aravinda Berggreen-Clausen et al., "Food Environment Interactions After Migration: A Scoping Review on Low- and Middle-Income Country Immigrants in High-Income Countries," *Public Health Nutrition* 25, no. 1 (January 2022): 136.

89. Adrian Miller, *Soul Food: The Surprising Story of an American Cuisine* (Chapel Hill: The University of North Carolina Press, 2013). In segregated sections of cities, Black people were early adopters of their Chinese, Italian, and Mexican neighbors' foods.

90. Miller, *Soul Food*, 141.

91. Rev. Harvey E. Leggett, interview, August 1, 1981, A. P. Marshall African American Oral History Archive, Ypsilanti District Library, http://history.ypsilibrary .org/oral-histories/rev-harvey-e-leggett/.

92. Formed in 1904 as the Trustee Helpers of Brown Chapel African Methodist Episcopal Church, the group changed its name to the Palm Leaf Club in the 1930s when it officially separated from the church and became its own civic and social African American women's organization. It is the oldest organization of its kind in Ypsilanti and is affiliated with the Ypsilanti Association of Women's Clubs, Michigan State Association of Colored Women's Clubs, and the National Association of Colored Women's Clubs. "Ypsilanti's Palm Leaf Club," episode 5, *Ypsi Stories* (podcast), March 3, 2021, Ypsilanti District Library, https://www.ypsilibrary.org/2021/03/ys -ep5/.

93. Louise Bass, interview, December 13, 1980, A. P. Marshall African American Oral History Archive, Ypsilanti District Library, http://history.ypsilibrary.org /oral-histories/louise-bass/.

94. Ben worked as a dry cleaner at Trojan Laundry for over thirty years. In the 1930s, he joined the Amalgamated Clothing Workers, a trade union of mostly white and about ten Black members, where he organized laundry workers and led protests.

95. Benjamin Neely, interview, n.d., A. P. Marshall African American Oral History Archive, Ypsilanti District Library, accessed June 28, 2022, http://history .ypsilibrary.org/oral-histories/ben-neely/.

96. Charles Vance, interview, March 4, 1984, Goin' North: Tales of the Great Migration, Louie B. Nunn Center for Oral History, University of Kentucky Libraries, https://goinnorth.org/items/show/1070.

97. Commonwealth v. Moore, 32 Pa. D. & C. 630 (1937).

98. Milo Manly, interview, September 11, 1984, Goin' North: Tales of the Great Migration, Louie B. Nunn Center for Oral History, University of Kentucky Libraries, https://goinnorth.org/items/show/1060.

99. Marguerite Eaglin, interview by A. P. Marshall, n.d., A. P. Marshall African American Oral History Archive, Ypsilanti District Library, accessed June 28, 2022, http://history.ypsilibrary.org/oral-histories/marguerite-eaglin/.

100. Isadore M. Martin Jr., interview, August 30, 1984, Goin' North: Tales of the Great Migration, Louie B. Nunn Center for Oral History, University of Kentucky Libraries, https://goinnorth.org/items/show/1061.

101. Edgar Campbell, interview, September 26, 1984, Goin' North: Tales of the

Great Migration, Louie B. Nunn Center for Oral History, University of Kentucky Libraries, https://goinnorth.org/items/show/1045.

102. Arthur Dingle, interview, July 11, 1983, Goin' North: Tales of the Great Migration, Louie B. Nunn Center for Oral History, University of Kentucky Libraries, https://goinnorth.org/items/show/1049.

103. Horn & Hardart opened its first automat—or waiterless restaurant—in 1902 on Chestnut Avenue in Philadelphia. Its first coffee shop opened in 1888. The chain later expanded to New York, including a spot in Times Square, and the last one closed in 1991.

104. John (Jack) Jones, interview, June 1, 1982, Goin' North: Tales of the Great Migration, Louie B. Nunn Center for Oral History, University of Kentucky Libraries, https://goinnorth.org/items/show/1081; see, generally, *The Automat,* directed by Lisa Hurwitz (Slice of Pie Productions, 2021).

105. Leo Adam Biga, "Great Migration Stories," *Reader,* March 12, 2019, https://thereader.com/news/great-migration-stories.

106. Kenneth Mashatt and Helen Mashatt Palmer, interview, n.d., A. P. Marshall African American Oral History Archive, Ypsilanti District Library, accessed June 28, 2022, http://history.ypsilibrary.org/oral-histories/ken-mashatt-and-helen-mashatt-palmer/. Some veterans experienced worse. "Hundreds of Black veterans were beaten, maimed, shot, and lynched." Hannah-Jones et al., eds., *1619 Project,* 32.

107. Jackie Mansky, "How One Woman Helped End Lunch Counter Segregation in the Nation's Capital," *Smithsonian Magazine,* June 8, 2016, https://www.smithsonianmag.com/history/how-one-woman-helped-end-lunch-counter-segregation-nations-capital-180959345/.

108. Frederick Douglass Opie, *Southern Food and Civil Rights: Feeding the Revolution* (Charleston, SC: American Palate, 2017), 51.

109. Bobby J. Smith II, *Food Power Politics: The Food Story of the Mississippi Civil Rights Movement* (Chapel Hill: University of North Carolina Press, 2023), 20–43.

110. Elizabeth Hinton, *America on Fire: The Untold History of Police Violence and Black Rebellion Since the 1960s* (New York: Liveright, 2021), 13.

111. Safiya Bukhari, interview, September 27, 1992, Arm the Spirit, http://whgbetc.com/mind/bpp-safiya-bio.html.

112. Raj Patel, "Survival Pending Revolution: What the Black Panthers Can Teach the US Food Movement," *Food First Backgrounder* 18, no. 2 (Summer 2012): 1, 2.

113. Erin Blakemore, "How the Black Panthers' Breakfast Program Both Inspired and Threatened the Government," History, last updated January 29, 2021, https://www.history.com/news/free-school-breakfast-black-panther-party.

114. Diane Pien, "Black Panther Party's Free Breakfast Program (1969–1980)," BlackPast.org, February 11, 2010, https://www.blackpast.org/african-american-history/black-panther-partys-free-breakfast-program-1969–1980/.

115. Blakemore, "Black Panthers' Breakfast Program."

116. Chinese American activists organized the Red Guard Party in San Francisco in 1969, inspired by the Black Panthers, and created a Free Breakfast Program for children in Chinatown and a free Sunday brunch program for elders. Daryl J. Maeda, "Black Panthers, Red Guards, and Chinamen: Constructing Asian American Identity through Performing Blackness, 1969-1972," *American Quarterly* 57, no. 4 (2005): 1079–91. I Wor Kuen, a revolutionary group that merged with the Red Guard in 1971, rose up against government efforts to close down Chinese stores by branding their products health code violations. Yellow Brotherhood ran an Asian food cooperative in Los Angeles and the Asian American Political Alliance gave out free food in San Francisco's Chinatown.

117. Analena Hope Hassberg, "Nurturing the Revolution," in *Black Food Matters*, 91.

118. "The Black Panther Party," Mutual Aid, October 2, 1996, https://www.mutualaid.coop/historic-event/black-panther-party/.

119. "For the Poor: More Hunger," *Time*, July 1, 1974.

120. "From Hunger," *Time*, January 23, 1984.

121. Allison Y. Zhu, "Impact of Neighborhood Sociodemographic Characteristics on Food Store Accessibility in the United States Based on the 2020 US Census Data," *Delaware Journal of Public Health* 8, no. 3 (August 2022): 94–101, https://www.ncbi.nlm.nih.gov/pmc/articles/PMC9495479/.

122. Zhu, "Impact of Neighborhood Sociodemographic Characteristics"; Siegel et al., "Association of Higher Consumption of Foods Derived from Subsidized Commodities with Adverse Cardiometabolic Risk Among US Adults," *JAMA Internal Medicine* 175, no. 8 (2016): 1125–26.

## 3. AMERICANIZATION THROUGH HOMEMAKING

1. Pearl Idelia Ellis, *Americanization Through Homemaking* (Los Angeles: Wetzel, 1929), 26.

2. Alison Krögel, "Food, Power, and Discursive Resistance in Tahuantinsuyu and the Colonial Andes," in *Food Studies in Latin American Literature: Perspectives on the Gastronarrative*, ed. Rocío Del Aguila and Vanesa Miseres (Fayetteville: University of Arkansas Press, 2021), 21; Heather Trigg, "Food Choice and Social Identity in Early Colonial New Mexico," *Journal of the Southwest* 46, no. 2 (Summer 2004): 223; Rebecca Earle, "'If You Eat Their Food . . .': Diets and Bodies in Early Colonial Spanish America," *American Historical Review* 115, no. 3 (June 2010): 688; Damon B. Akins and William J. Bauer Jr., *We Are the Land: A History of Native California* (Oakland: University of California Press, 2021), 64.

3. Gustavo Arellano, *Taco USA: How Mexican Food Conquered America* (New York: Scribner, 2013); Jeffrey M. Pilcher, "Industrial Tortillas and Folkloric Pepsi: The Nutritional Consequences of Hybrid Cuisines in Mexico," in *Food*

*Nations: Selling Taste in Consumer Societies*, ed. Warren Belasco and Philip Scranton (New York: Routledge, 2002), 235–41.

4. Alexandra H. Ibarra, "Eating Real Mexican: Identity, Authenticity, Americanization, Health, and Food Culture in the United States after 1900" (master's thesis, Portland State University, 2022), 13, citing John Harvey Kellogg and International Health and Temperance Association, *The Medical Missionary*, (Battle Creek, MI: International Health and Temperance Association, 1852–1943), 106–7, https://pdxscholar.library.pdx.edu/cgi/viewcontent.cgi?article=6989&context=open_access_etds.

5. "Mexican Diet: Not Conducive to American Energy," *New York Times*, October 6, 1908, https://timesmachine.nytimes.com/timesmachine/1908/10/06/105013112.html?pageNumber=20.

6. Abigail Carroll, *Three Squares: The Invention of the American Meal* (New York: Basic Books, 2013); Susan Kalčik, *Ethnic Foodways in America: Symbol and the Performance of Identity in Ethnic and Regional Foodways in the United States: The Performance of Group Identity*, ed. Linda Kay Brown and Kay Mussell (Knoxville: University of Tennessee Press, 1983), 37; Harvey Levenstein, *Revolution at the Table: The Transformation of the American Diet* (Oakland: University of California Press, 2003), 157.

7. George J. Sanchez, "'Go After the Women': Americanization and the Mexican Immigrant Woman, 1915–1929," in *Mothers & Motherhood: Readings in American History*, ed. Rima D. Apple and Janet Golden (Columbus: Ohio State University Press, 1997), 475, quoted in Alfred E. White, "The Apperceptive Mass of Foreigners as Applied to Americanization: The Mexican Group" (master's thesis, University of California Berkeley, 1923), 34–35.

8. East Coast programs targeted Irish, Slavic, Italian, and Portuguese immigrants. Detroit developed programs for Jews.

9. Magdalena L. Barrera, "'Doing the Impossible': Tracing Mexican Women's Experiences in Americanization Manuals, 1915–1920," *California History* 93, no. 4 (Winter 2016): 20, 22–25.

10. Vickie L. Ruiz, *From Out of the Shadows: Mexican Women in Twentieth-Century America*, 10th ed. (New York: Oxford University Press, 2008), 35.

11. Sanchez, "'Go After the Women,'" 479, citing Kenneth L. Roberts, "The Docile Mexican," *Saturday Evening Post*, March 10, 1928, 3.

12. Amanda Matthews Chase, *The Home Teacher: The Act, with a Working Plan and Forty Lessons in English* (San Francisco: Commission of Immigration and Housing of California, University of California Press, 1915).

13. Chase, *Home Teacher*, 5.

14. Over a century later, white parents still dominate parent teacher organizations in California's Alameda County.

15. Chase, *Home Teacher*, 5. All quotes in this section are from Chase's *Home Teacher*.

16. Amanda Matthews Chase, *Primer for Foreign-speaking Women*, part 2 (Sacramento: Commission of Immigration and Housing of California, 1918), 3.

17. Chase, *Primer for Foreign-speaking Women*, part 1, 20.

18. Chase, *Home Teacher*, 43.

19. Bertha M. Wood, *Foods of the Foreign-Born in Relation to Health* (Boston: Whitcomb & Barrows, 1922), 8–9, https://babel.hathitrust.org/cgi/pt?id=nnc2.ark:/13960/t0100m14x&seq=1.

20. Ellis, *Americanization Through Homemaking*, 30–31.

21. Sanchez, "'Go After the Women,'" 475, quoting White, "Apperceptive Mass of Foreigners," 34–35.

22. Ellis, *Americanization Through Homemaking*, 8.

23. Wood, *Foods of the Foreign-Born*, 6.

24. Ellis, *Americanization Through Homemaking*, 19.

25. Wood, *Foods of the Foreign-Born*, 9. The quotes in the following paragraphs are from *Foods of the Foreign-Born*.

26. Ellis, *Americanization Through Homemaking*, 19–20.

27. Office of the Commission of Immigration and Housing of California, *First Annual Report of the Commission of Immigration and Housing of California* (Sacramento: California State Printing Office, 1915), 71–96, https://babel.hathitrust.org/cgi/pt?id=uiug.30112062953705&seq=11.

28. Ellis, *Americanization Through Homemaking*, 34.

29. Gerardo Torres, "Constructing Citizenship: Americanization Efforts in the Southwest U.S. (1910–1931)" (master's thesis, University of Texas at El Paso, 2018).

30. Alice M. Guernsey, *Home Missions on the Border* (New York: Woman's Home Missionary Society, 1915), https://catalog.hathitrust.org/Record/101790694.

31. Alexandra H. Ibarra, "Eating Real Mexican: Identity, Authenticity, Americanization, Health, and Food Culture in the United States After 1900," (master's thesis, Portland State University, 2022), 45–46, https://pdxscholar.library.pdx.edu/open_access_etds/5917/.

32. Guernsey, *Home Missions on the Border*, 488–89.

33. Home Teacher Act, 37 Cal. Pol. Code. § 1617(b) (1915).

34. Annie McGlynn-Wright, "Farm Bill to Table: Pregnancy and the Politics of Food Assistance," (PhD diss., University of Washington 2019), 72, quoting *Malnutrition and Federal Food Service Programs: Hearing on H.R. 17144, H.R.17145, H.R. 17146, H.R. 17872, H.R. 17873, and Various Bills to Establish a Commission on Hunger*, Before the Comm. on Education and Labor, 90th Cong. 503 (1968) (statement of Mrs. Manuel Salinas Jr.).

35. See, e.g., *California WIC Authorized Food List Shopping Guide* (April 2, 2019), https://m.wic.ca.gov/WAFL/WAFL.aspx; see also *Ohio WIC Authorized Foods List*, effective 11/9/2020 through 03/31/2021, Ohio Department of Health (December 23, 2020), https://odh.ohio.gov/wps/portal/gov/odh/know-our-programs/women-infants-children/media/wic-authorized-foods-list; see

also *Massachusetts WIC Approved Food Guide*, Mass.Gov (January 2021), https://www.mass.gov/doc/wic-food-guide/download.

36. "WIC Eligibility Requirements," USDA, Food and Nutrition Service, accessed July 11, 2022, https://www.fns.usda.gov/wic/wic-eligibility-requirements. "Nutrition Risk Requirement: Applicants must be seen by a health professional such as a physician, nurse, or nutritionist who must determine whether the individual is at nutrition risk. In many cases, this is done in the WIC clinic at no cost to the applicant. However, this information can be obtained from another health professional such as the applicant's physician.

    'Nutrition risk' means that an individual has medical-based or dietary-based conditions. Examples of medical-based conditions include anemia (low blood levels), underweight, or history of poor pregnancy outcome. A dietary-based condition includes, for example, a poor diet.

    At a minimum, the applicant's height and weight must be measured and bloodwork taken to check for anemia. An applicant must have at least one of the medical or dietary conditions on the state's list of WIC nutrition risk criteria."

37. "QuickFacts," U.S. Census Bureau, accessed July 11, 2022, https://www.census .gov/quickfacts/fact/table/US/RHI725220. This may be an undercount due to some people's reluctance to participate in the census because of their immigration status.

38. See, e.g., *Hawaii WIC Approved Food List*, (Hawaii State Department of Health, August 2019), https://health.hawaii.gov/wic/files/2019/10/WIC-FoodList-2019 -Final-Spread-R1version.pdf; see also *South Carolina Food Guide*, (South Carolina Department of Health and Environmental Control, August 2020), https: //scdhec.gov/sites/default/files/Library/ML-025486.pdf; see also *Washington Shopping Guide* (Washington State Department of Health, 2017), https://www .doh.wa.gov/portals/1/Documents/Pubs/960-278-ShoppingGuide.pdf; see also *Wisconsin Women, Infants, & Children Nutrition Program Shopping Guide*, November 1, 2022 to October 31, 2025 (Wisconsin Department of Health Services), https://www.dhs.wisconsin.gov/publications/p4/p44578.pdf.

39. "Facts About Latinos in the Food Stamp Program," Center on Budget and Policy Priorities, April 19, 2007, https://www.cbpp.org/research/facts-about -latinos-in-the-food-stamp-program.

40. "What Can SNAP Buy?," USDA, Food and Nutrition Service, accessed April 14, 2022, https://www.fns.usda.gov/snap/eligible-food-items; "Is My Store Eligible?," USDA, Food and Nutrition Service, accessed March 3, 2022, https://www.fns.usda.gov/snap/retailer/eligible; "Farmer/Producer," USDA, Food and Nutrition Service, accessed August 6, 2021, https://www.fns.usda. gov/snap/farmer-producer; "Supplemental Nutrition Assistance Program (SNAP)," Farmers Market Coalition, accessed April 17, 2019, https://farm-ersmarketcoalition.org/advocacy/snap/; "Farmers Markets Increase Access to Fresh, Nutritious Food," Farmers Market Coalition, June 22, 2018, https://

farmersmarketcoalition.org/education/increase-access-to-fresh-nutritious -food/.

41. Chelsea R. Singleton et al., "Examining Disparities in Diet Quality between SNAP Participants and Non-Participants Using Oaxaca-Blinder Decomposition Analysis," *Preventive Medicine Reports* 19 (September 2020): 1.

42. Rudolfo A. Anaya, *Bless Me, Ultima* (1972; New York: Warner Books, 1994), 58.

43. Melissa L. Salazar, "Public Schools, Private Foods: Mexicano Memories of Culture and Conflict in American School Cafeterias," *Food and Foodways* 15, nos. 3–4 (October 2007): 153, 159.

44. Virginia B. Gray et al., "Dietary Acculturation of Hispanic Immigrants in Mississippi," *Salud Pública de México* 47, no. 5 (Sept.–Oct. 2005): 351, 357.

45. Sharon E. Taverno Ross et al., "Latino Parents' Perceptions of Physical Activity and Healthy Eating: At the Intersection of Culture, Family, and Health," *Journal of Nutrition Education and Behavior* 50, no. 10 (Nov.–Dec. 2018): 968, 973.

46. David Himmelgreen et. al., "'I Don't Make the Soups Anymore': Pre- to Post-Migration Dietary and Lifestyle Changes Among Latinos Living in West-Central Florida," *Ecology Food and Nutrition* 46, no. 5–6 (2007): 427, 439.

47. Valerie Rawlinson, "Diet and Nutritional Concerns of Hispanic Americans (bachelor's thesis, Utah State University, May 2006), on file with Utah State University Libraries.

48. Laura H. McArthur, Ruben P. Viramontez Anguiano, and Deigo Nocetti, "Maintenance and Change in the Diet of Hispanic Immigrants in Eastern North Carolina," *Family and Consumer Sciences Research Journal* 29, no. 4 (July 2009): 309, 318.

49. Pilcher, "Industrial Tortillas and Folkloric Pepsi," 235. In January 1999, the neoliberal Mexican government stopped subsidizing corn tortillas, opening the door to less-nutritious, cheaper, prepackaged flour tortillas.

50. North American Free Trade Agreement, Can.-Mex.-U.S., December 17, 1992, 32 I.L.M. 289; Alana D. Siegel, "NAFTA Largely Responsible for the Obesity Epidemic in Mexico," *Washington University Journal of Law and Policy* 50, no. 1 (2016): 195.

51. Dharma E. Cortés et al., "Food Purchasing Selection Among Low-Income, Spanish-Speaking Latinos," *American Journal of Preventive Medicine* 44, no. 3 (March 2013): 267, 269.

52. Gray et al., "Dietary Acculturation of Hispanic Immigrants in Mississippi," 352.

53. Jennifer Van Hook et al., "Healthy Eating Among Mexican Immigrants: Migration in Childhood and Time in the United States," *Journal of Health and Social Behavior* 59, no. 3 (September 2018): 391, 402. "Migration during sensitive periods of childhood—when the effects of being a societal outsider may be amplified—appears to raise immigrants' health risks."

54. McArthur, Anguiano, and Nocetti, "Maintenance and Change in the Diet of Hispanic Immigrants in Eastern North Carolina," 324.

55. Himmelgreen et al., "'I Don't Make the Soups Anymore,'" 436.

56. Gray et al., "Dietary Acculturation of Hispanic Immigrants in Mississippi," 357.

57. McArthur, Anguiano, and Nocetti, "Maintenance and Change in the Diet of Hispanic Immigrants in Eastern North Carolina," 319.

58. Francine Overcash and Marla Reicks, "Diet Quality and Eating Practices Among Hispanic/Latino Men and Women: NHANES 2011–2016," *International Journal of Environmental Research and Public Health* 18, no. 3 (2021): 1302–10. Women had higher mean intakes of total vegetables, vegetable subgroups (dark green, red/orange, starchy), and total dairy, and lower intakes of total protein than men. Mexican-origin Hispanic males have the highest prevalence of age-adjusted (>20 years) overweight and obesity compared with all other race/ethnicity groups. A majority of the men (n=10) cited that they often have difficulty shopping for, preparing, and consuming healthy meals due to lack of knowledge of convenient, accessible, and affordable recipes and time to prepare them. They believe that exposure to fast-food advertisements is detrimental to their and their families' health. For many Mexican men, eating convenient foods is not a matter of choice, but of being able to eat something between multiple jobs and long shifts or simply lacking access to healthier options. Spouses plan, shop for, and prepare all meals without their input. They may not show interest in the foods they consume because diet plans, weight loss, and healthy figures have been primarily marketed to a feminine audience and are therefore in conflict with their conceptualizations of masculinity.

59. Luis A. Valdez et al., "Mexican-Origin Male Perspectives of Diet-Related Behaviors Associated with Weight Management," *International Journal of Obesity* 41 (2017): 1824, 1827–28.

60. Restrained eating is a marker of status in the contemporary United States, particularly among white women. See John Cawley, "The Impact of Obesity on Wages," *Journal of Human Resources* 39, no. 2 (Spring 2004): 451; Katherine M. Flegal et al., "Prevalence and Trends in Obesity Among US Adults, 1999–2008," *JAMA* 303, no. 3 (2010): 235; Lindsay McLaren et al., "The Relationship Between Body Mass Index and Mental Health: A Population-Based Study of the Effects of the Definition of Mental Health," *Social Psychiatry and Psychiatric Epidemiology* 43, no. 1 (January 2008): 63; Jeffery Sobal and Albert J. Stunkard, "Socioeconomic Status and Obesity: A Review of the Literature," *Psychological Bulletin* 105, no. 2 (1989): 260; see also Melissa Mortazavi, "Consuming Identities: Law, School Lunches, and What It Means to Be American," *Cornell Journal of Law and Public Policy* 24, no. 1 (2014): 25. "At one time obesity was a sign of wealth, but today the inverse is true. Thinness now holds particular social capital and has a powerful impact in solidifying class

differentiation. Wealthier people are, on average, thinner than poorer people in the United States. As such, weight loss is about more than health, it is often about affirming or claiming a superior place in society: 'By trying to control eating and body size, [white women] can differentiate themselves from lower status ethnic and racial minorities and—perhaps unwittingly—uphold U.S. racial hierarchy.'"

61. Elizabeth Baier, "For Latino Immigrants, Good Health Hard to Maintain," MPR News, November 14, 2011, https://www.mprnews.org/story/2011/11/14/latino-immigrant-health.

62. Patricia Engel, *Infinite Country* (New York: Avid Reader Press, 2021), 109.

63. Gray et al., "Dietary Acculturation of Hispanic Immigrants in Mississippi," 357.

64. McArthur, Anguiano, and Nocetti, "Maintenance and Change in the Diet of Hispanic Immigrants in Eastern North Carolina," 324.

65. Elizabeth Villegas et al., "Continued Barriers Affecting Hispanic Families' Dietary Patterns," *Family and Consumer Sciences Research Journal* 46, no. 4 (June 2018): 363, 373.

66. Gray et al., "Dietary Acculturation of Hispanic Immigrants in Mississippi," 357.

67. Villegas et al., "Continued Barriers Affecting Hispanic Families' Dietary Patterns," 371.

68. McArthur, Anguiano, and Nocetti, "Maintenance and Change in the Diet of Hispanic Immigrants in Eastern North Carolina," 317.

69. Luisyana De Amor Gamboa, "The Perceptions, Knowledge, Benefits and Barriers of Hispanics Regarding the Dietary Guidelines for Americans" (master's thesis, University of Kentucky, 2015), on file with Dietetics and Human Nutrition at University of Kentucky UKnowledge.

70. Villegas et al., "Continued Barriers Affecting Hispanic Families' Dietary Patterns," 371.

71. Gray et al., "Dietary Acculturation of Hispanic Immigrants in Mississippi," 357.

72. Kristen M. J. Azar et al., "Festival Foods in the Immigrant Diet," *Journal of Immigrant and Minority Health* 15 (2013): 953.

73. McArthur, Anguiano, and Nocetti, "Maintenance and Change in the Diet of Hispanic Immigrants in Eastern North Carolina," 327.

74. Villegas et al., "Continued Barriers Affecting Hispanic Families' Dietary Patterns," 372.

75. Taverno Ross et al., "Latino Parents' Perceptions of Physical Activity and Healthy Eating," 968, 973.

76. Gamboa, "The Perceptions, Knowledge, Benefits and Barriers of Hispanics Regarding the Dietary Guidelines for Americans," 26.

77. Taverno Ross et al., "Latino Parents' Perceptions of Physical Activity and Healthy Eating," 973.

78. There are some exceptions and some cross subsidization of markets.

79. Gamboa, "The Perceptions, Knowledge, Benefits and Barriers of Hispanics Regarding the Dietary Guidelines for Americans," 20.

80. Nayeli Y. Chavez-Dueñas et al., "Skin-Color Prejudice and Within-Group Racial Discrimination: Historical and Current Impact on Latino/a Populations," *Hispanic Journal of Behavioral Sciences* 36, no. 1 (2014): 3.

81. Luz Calvo and Catriona Rueda Esquibel, *Decolonize Your Diet: Plant-Based Mexican-American Recipes for Health and Healing* (Vancouver, BC: Arsenal Pulp Press, 2015).

82. Marisol Medina-Cadena, "La Cultura Cura: How Latinos Are Reclaiming Their Ancestral Diets," *Folklife*, August 7, 2017, https://folklife.si.edu /talkstory/la-cultura-cura-how-latinos-are-reclaiming-their-ancestral -diets.

83. Alyshia Gálvez, *Eating NAFTA: Trade, Food Policies, and the Destruction of Mexico* (Berkeley: University of California Press, 2018); Andrew Jacobs and Matt Richtel, "A Nasty, Nafta-Related Surprise: Mexico's Soaring Obesity," *New York Times*, December 11, 2017, https://www.nytimes.com/2017/12/11 /health/obesity-mexico-nafta.html.

84. "Mexico's Junk Food Bans," NCD Alliance, accessed July 11, 2022, https:// ncdalliance.org/why-ncds/video-stories-of-change/mexicos-junk-food-bans #:~:text=Mexico%20has%20one%20of%20the,the%20adult%20popula- tion%20in%201996.

85. James Fredrick, "'We Had to Take Action': States in Mexico Move to Ban Junk Food Sales to Minors," NPR, September 14, 2020, https://www.npr.org/2020 /09/14/912029399/we-had-to-take-action-states-in-mexico-move-to-ban -junk-food-sales-to-minors.

86. Anthony Esposito, "Mexico's New Warning Labels on Junk Food Meet Super- sized Opposition from U.S., EU," Reuters, August 11, 2020, https://www .reuters.com/article/us-mexico-health/mexicos-new-warning-labels-on-junk -food-meet-supersized-opposition-from-u-s-eu-idUSKCN25802B.

87. Sharon Anglin Treat, "The Bully in the Lunchroom: The U.S. Moves to Weaken Mexico's New Junk Food Labeling Law," *Institute for Agriculture & Trade Policy* (blog), January 29, 2020, https://www.iatp.org/blog/202001/bully -lunchroom-us-moves-weaken-mexicos-new-junk-food-labeling-law; Fred- rick, "'We Had to Take Action.'"

88. Esposito, "Mexico's New Warning Labels on Junk Food Meet Supersized Opposition from U.S., EU."

## 4. THE UNBEARABLE WHITENESS OF MILK

1. Andrew Curry, "Humans Were Drinking Milk Before They Could Digest It," *Science*, January 27, 2021, https://www.science.org/content/article/humans -were-drinking-milk-they-could-digest-it.

2. Catherine Le Come, "Safeguarding Pastoralists and Their Food Systems," SNV Netherlands, https://snv.org/update/safeguarding-pastoralists-food-systems.

3. Mathilde Cohen, "Animal Colonialism: The Case of Milk," *AJIL Unbound* 111 (2017).

4. Jessica Eisen, Xiaoqian Hu, and Erum Sattar, "Dairy Tales: Global Portraits of Milk and Law," *Journal of Food Law & Policy* 16, no. 1 (2020), citing Kenneth Kiple and Virginia Kiple, "Slave Child Mortality: Some Nutritional Answers to a Perennial Puzzle," *Journal of Social History* 10, no. 3 (spring 1977): 284, 302n31.

5. Eisen et al., "Dairy Tales," citing Nicholas Scott Cardell and Mark Myron Hopkins, "The Effect of Milk Intolerance on the Consumption of Milk by Slaves in 1860," *Journal of Interdisciplinary History* 8, no. 3 (winter 1978): 507, 512–13.

6. Laura S. M. Humayun, "Is Milk a Form of Colonialism?," *Bright*, February 28, 2022, https://brightzine.co/news/milk-colonialism-racism-white-supremacy.

7. Juliet Larkin-Gilmore, "Cows on the Colorado: The History of Dairy Colonialism and Mohave Health," Environmental History Now, March 6, 2020, citing O. Babcock, Annual Narrative 1912, Reel 23, M1011, *Superintendents Narratives and Statistical Reports*, RG 75, NARA-DC, https://envhistnow.com/2020/03/06/cows-on-the-colorado-the-history-of-dairy-colonialism-and-mohave-health/.

8. Office of Indian Affairs, *Rules for the Indian School Service* (Washington, DC: U.S. Government Printing Office, 1898).

9. Melanie Dupuis, *Nature's Perfect Food: How Milk Became America's Drink* (New York: New York University Press, 2002), 5.

10. Harry G. Day, *Elmer Verner McCollum, 1879–1967* (Washington, DC: National Academy of Sciences, 1974), http://www.nasonline.org/publications/biographical-memoirs/memoir-pdfs/mccollum-elmer.pdf.

11. U.S. Food Administration and U.S. Department of Agriculture, *United States Food Leaflet* (Washington, DC: U.S. Government Printing Office, 1917), 36, https://archive.org/details/unitedstatesfood00unit/page/n17/mode/2up.

12. Elmer Verner McCollum, *The Newer Knowledge of Nutrition: The Use of Food for the Preservation of Vitality and Health* (New York: Macmillan, 1919), https://archive.org/details/cu31924104225937/page/n31/mode/2up.

13. It is interesting that, without influential advocates like Hoover, the promotion of leafy vegetables, which McCollum equated with milk, fell by the wayside.

14. National Dairy Council pamphlet, quoted in Dupuis, *Nature's Perfect Food*, 117.

15. Franklin C. Bing and Harry J. Prebluda, "E. V. McCollum: Pathfinder in Nutrition Investigations and World Agriculture," *Agricultural History* 54, no. 1 (January 1980): 162.

16. Elizabeth Deane March, "Drink Milk Campaign Across America—1920s," *Farmer's Wife Magazine*, February 1922, accessed October 21, 2022, https://

farmerswifemagazine.com/2022/05/31/drink-milk-campaign-across-america
-1920s/.

17. Ulysses Prentiss Hedrick, *A History of Agriculture in the State of New York* (Albany: New York State Agriculture Society, 1933), 117–18.

18. Eisen et al., "Dairy Tales"; See Andrea Wiley, *Re-Imagining Milk: Cultural and Biological Perspectives*, 2nd ed. (New York: Routledge, 2016), 34; Ann Folino White, "Performing the Promise of Plenty in the USDA's 1933–34 World's Fair Exhibits," *Text and Performance Quarterly* 29, no. 1 (January 2009): 22.

19. Dana Vantrease, "Commod Bods and Frybread Power: Government Food Aid in American Indian Culture," *Journal of American Folklore* 126, no. 499 (Winter 2013): 55–69.

20. Kenny Malone, "Government Cheese: Well-Intentioned Program Goes Off the Rails," NPR, September 7, 2018, https://www.northernpublicradio.org/post /government-cheese-well-intentioned-program-goes-rails.

21. Ward Sinclair, "Cheese Giveaway Churning," *Washington Post*, December 5, 1981, https://www.washingtonpost.com/archive/politics/1981/12/05/cheese -giveaway-churning/4f3aa750-cf4b-494d-b87a-5a02c94336f5/?utm_term =.825983768258.

22. Myles Karp, "WTF Happened to Government Cheese," *Vice*, February 19, 2018, https://www.vice.com/en/article/wn7mgq/wtf-happened-to-government -cheese.

23. Bobbi Dempsey, "The Tyranny and the Comfort of Government Cheese," ChangeWire, August 23, 2018, https://changewire.org/the-tyranny-and-the -comfort-of-government-cheese/.

24. "Actor, Restaurateur and Former New Kid on the Block Donnie Wahlberg Embraces His 'Cheesy' Past," *Daily News*, October 18, 2014, https://www .nydailynews.com/2014/10/18/actor-restaurateur-and-former-new-kid-on -the-block-donnie-wahlberg-embraces-his-cheesy-past/.

25. @Wahlburgers, Twitter, February 12, 2014, 9:42 a.m., https://twitter.com /wahlburgers/status/433687563681812481?lang=en.

26. Frank Bruni, "Life in the Fast-Food Lane," *New York Times*, May 24, 2006, https://www.nytimes.com/2006/05/24/dining/24note.html?pagewanted=all.

27. "Playboy Visited El Paso, and the Political Fall Out that Followed," *El Paso Times*, October 20, 2009, https://www.elpasotimes.com/story/news/local/blogs /media-buzz/2009/10/20/playboy-visited-el-paso-and-the-political-fall-out -that-followed/31494939/.

28. Luis Alberto Urrea, "A Weird Calm at the Edge of the Abyss," *Playboy*, October 2009, https://refusethejuice.typepad.com/files/playboy-article.pdf.

29. Eduardo Cepeda, "An Ode to the Soupy, Sloppy Chico's Tacos, El Paso's Most Divisive Restaurant," Remezcla, June 19, 2019, https://remezcla.com/features /food/el-paso-most-divisive-restaurant-chicos-tacos/.

30. Mark C. "We Want the Government Cheese Back!! #Chicostacos," Avazz.org,

July 31, 2020, https://secure.avaaz.org/community_petitions/en/mark_clary
_we_want_the_government_cheese_back_chicostacos/

31. El Paso History Alliance, Facebook, September 29, 2018, https://www.facebook
    .com/elpasohistoryalliance/posts/chicos-tacos-established-july-4-1953-at
    -4230-alameda-avenue-by-joe-morachicos-ta/2676653589026799/.

32. Karp, "WTF Happened to Government Cheese."

33. Kelsey Gee, "America's Dairy Farmers Dump 43 Million Gallons of Excess Milk,"
    *Wall Street Journal*, October 12, 2016, https://www.wsj.com/articles/americas
    -dairy-farmers-dump-43-million-gallons-of-excess-milk-1476284353.

34. "USDA Announces Plans to Purchase Surplus Cheese, Releases New Report
    Showing Trans-Pacific Partnership Would Create Growth for Dairy Indus-
    try," USDA, press release, October 11, 2016, https://www.usda.gov/media
    /press-releases/2016/10/11/usda-announces-plans-purchase-surplus-cheese
    -releases-new-report.

35. U.S. Department of Health and Human Services, Milk Matters campaign,
    "Lactose Intolerance: Information for Health Care Providers," January 2006,
    https://www.nichd.nih.gov/sites/default/files/publications/pubs/documents
    /NICHD_MM_Lactose_FS_rev.pdf.

36. "Health Concerns About Dairy," Physicians Committee for Responsible Med-
    icine, accessed May 8, 2020, https://www.pcrm.org/good-nutrition/nutrition
    -information/health-concerns-about-dairy#:~:text=Milk%20and%20
    other%20dairy%20products,%2C%20ovarian%2C%20and%20prostate%20
    cancers.

37. Jessie A. Satia, "Diet-Related Disparities: Understanding the Problem and
    Accelerating the Solutions," *Journal of the Academy of Nutrition and Dietet-
    ics* 109, no. 4 (April 2009): 610, 613–15, https://www.ncbi.nlm.nih.gov/pmc
    /articles/PMC2729116/pdf/nihms106651.pdf.

38. Prethibha George et al., "Diagnosis and Surgical Delays in African Ameri-
    can Women with Early-Stage Breast Cancer," *Journal of Women's Health* 24,
    no. 3 (March 2015): 209–11, https://www.ncbi.nlm.nih.gov/pmc/articles
    /PMC4442576/; Beth Virnig et al., "A Matter of Race: Early-Versus Late-
    Stage Cancer Diagnosis," *Health Affairs* 28, no. 1 (January/February 2009),
    https://www.ncbi.nlm.nih.gov/pmc/articles/PMC2766845/pdf/nihms78588
    .pdf.

39. Kimberley Mangun and Lisa M. Parcell, "The Pet Milk 'Happy Family' Adver-
    tising Campaign," *Journalism History* 40, no. 2 (Summer 2014): 72–73.

40. "Got Apology? Milk Board Cans 'Sexist' Campaign," msnbc.com, July 22,
    2011, https://www.nbcnews.com/id/wbna43854582.

41. Eva Smith, "I'm a Positivity Ambassador for the California Milk Processor
    Board," Tech Food Life, September 26, 2011, http://techfoodlife.com/2011/09
    /26/im-a-positivity-ambassador-for-the-milk-processors-board/.

42. Michael Moss, "While Warning About Fat, U.S. Pushes Cheese Sales," *New*

*York Times*, November 6, 2010, https://www.nytimes.com/2010/11/07/us/07fat
.html.

43. "Grilled Cheese Burrito," Taco Bell, accessed May 7, 2021, https://www.tacobell
.com/food/burritos/grilled-cheese-burrito.

44. The dairy industry also causes serious environmental harms. But even though
dairy production is responsible for high greenhouse gas emissions that contribute significantly to climate change, the dietary guidelines make no mention of environmental impact. They treat climate science the same way they
do medical and nutritional science, prioritizing corporate greed over survival
and well-being. "Dietary Guidelines for Americans 2020 Released," Nutrition
Source, January 12, 2021, https://www.hsph.harvard.edu/nutritionsource
/2021/01/12/2020-dietary-guidelines/.

45. Associated Press, "Docs Happy: Lose-Weight-With-Milk Ads to Cease," *Los
Angeles Daily News*, May 11, 2007, https://www.dailynews.com/2007/05/11
/docs-happy-lose-weight-with-milk-ads-to-cease/.

46. Walter C. Willett and David S. Ludwig, "Milk and Health," *New England Journal of Medicine* 382, no. 7 (February 2020): 647.

47. "Nutrition Labelling: Front-of-Package Nutrition Symbol," Health Canada,
Government of Canada, 2022, last modified June 9, 2023, https://www.canada
.ca/en/health-canada/services/food-labelling-changes/front-package.html.

48. Willett and Ludwig, "Milk and Health," 645.

49. Wiley, *Re-Imagining Milk*, 30

50. U.S. Department of Agriculture and U.S. Department of Health and Human
Services, *Dietary Guidelines for America 2020–2025*, 9th ed. (Washington, DC:
USDA, December 2020), https://www.dietaryguidelines.gov/sites/default/files
/2020-12/Dietary_Guidelines_for_Americans_2020-2025.pdf.

51. "Doctors Call on Dietary Guidelines to Ditch Dairy to Fight Racial Health
Disparities," Physicians Committee for Responsible Medicine, July 9, 2020,
https://www.pcrm.org/news/news-releases/doctors-call-dietary-guidelines
-ditch-dairy-fight-racial-health-disparities.

52. "California Physicians Sue USDA Over Conflicts of Interest Related to the
Dietary Guidelines for Americans," Physicians Committee for Responsible Medicine, April 29, 2021, https://www.pcrm.org/news/news-releases
/california-physicians-sue-usda-over-conflicts-interest-related-dietary.

53. "2020–2025 Dietary Guidelines Not Applicable for a Majority of Americans;
Not Scoped for 60% of U.S. With at Least One Diet-Related Chronic Disease,"
Nutrition Coalition, December 29, 2020, https://www.nutritioncoalition.us
/news/2020-2025-dietary-guidelines-final-release.

54. Letter from Laurie Fischer, CEO, American Dairy Coalition, to Alex Azar,
Secretary of Health and Human Services, July 13, 2020, https://files.constant-
contact.com/a653daa8501/e2601369-a5ca-41d4-8263-0efa7f9164b5.pdf.

55. Andy Coyne, "The Dairy Companies Also Present in Dairy Alternatives,"

JustFood, https://www.just-food.com/features/plant-based-priorities-dairy-companies-also-in-dairy-free/.

56. Nathan Clay et al., "Palatable Disruption: The Politics of Plant Milk," *Agriculture and Human Values* 37 (January 2020): 945.

57. Wiley, *Re-Imagining Milk*, 29, citing "Special supplemental nutrition program for Women, Infants and Children (WIC): revisions in the WIC food packages; final rule," *Federal Register* 79, no. 42 (March 4, 2014): 12273–12300.

58. Jack Smith IV, "Milk Is The New, Creamy Symbol of White Racial Purity in Donald Trump's America," Mic, February 10, 2017, https://www.mic.com/articles/168188/milk-nazis-white-supremacists-creamy-pseudo-science-trump-shia-labeouf#.oJvzWRvct.

59. Ashitha Nagesh, "Secret Nazi Code Kept Hidden by 'Milk' and 'Vegan Agenda,'" *Metro*, February 21, 2017, https://metro.co.uk/2017/02/21/secret-nazi-code-kept-hidden-by-milk-and-vegan-agenda-6463079/.

60. Alex Swerdloff, "Got Milk? Neo-Nazi Trolls Sure as Hell Do," *Vice*, February 21, 2017, https://www.vice.com/en/article/kbka39/got-milk-neo-nazi-trolls-sure-as-hell-do.

61. Emma Grey Ellis, "The Alt-Right's Newest Ploy? Trolling With False Symbols," *Wired*, May 10, 2017, https://www.wired.com/2017/05/alt-rights-newest-ploy-trolling-false-symbols/.

62. Katie Canales, "Police Stopped a McDonald's in Scotland from Selling Milkshakes near a Nigel Farage Rally to Avoid Further Instances of Far-Right Activists Being Doused in Them," *Business Insider*, May 18, 2019, https://www.businessinsider.com/mcdonalds-scotland-milkshakes-nigel-farage-rally-brexit-2019-5

63. Jennifer Hassan, "Milkshake-Wielding Protesters Trap Nigel Farage on His Brexit Bus," *Washington Post*, May 22, 2019, https://www.washingtonpost.com/world/2019/05/20/what-is-milkshaking-ask-brits-hurling-drinks-right-wing-candidates/.

64. Iliana Magra, "Why Are Milkshakes Being Thrown at Right-Wing Politicians Like Nigel Farage?," May 21, 2019, https://www.nytimes.com/2019/05/21/world/europe/milkshake-nigel-farage.html.

## 5. SCHOOL FOOD FAILURE

1. Michelle Gant, "Parents Outraged by Viral Photo of Student's 'Pathetic' School Lunch," *Today*, September 24, 2019, https://www.today.com/food/parents-outraged-viral-photo-student-s-pathetic-school-lunch-t163234.

2. Gordon W. Gunderson, *The National School Lunch Program* (Washington, DC: U.S. Government Printing Office, 1971), https://fns-prod.azureedge.us/sites/default/files/resource-files/NSLP-program-history.pdf.

3. Robert Hunter, *Poverty: Social Conscience in the Progressive Era* (1904; Harper & Row: New York, 1965), 217.

4. John Spargo, *The Bitter Cry of the Children* (1906; Chicago: Quadrangle Books, 1968), 117.

5. These programs employed 7,442 female kitchen employees in thirty-nine states.

6. Act to Amend the Agricultural Adjustment Act, Pub. L. no. 74-320, 49 Stat. 750 (1935).

7. Nicholas Confessore, "How School Lunch Became the Latest Political Battleground," *New York Times*, October 7, 2014, https://www.nytimes.com/2014/10/12/magazine/how-school-lunch-became-the-latest-political-battleground.html.

8. National School Lunch Act Section 2, Pub. L. 79-3396, 60 Stat. 231 (1946).

9. Jean Fairfax, chairman of the Committee on School Lunch Participation, in *Their Daily Bread*, ed. Florence Robin (Atlanta: McNelley-Rudd Printing Service, 1968), 17.

10. *CBS Reports*, "Hunger in America," written by Martin Carr and Peter Davis, aired May 21, 1968, CBS News, https://www.cbsnews.com/video/hunger-in-america-the-1968-cbs-documentary-that-shocked-america/.

11. Citizens' Board of Inquiry into Hunger and Malnutrition in the United States, *Hunger U.S.A* (Boston: Beacon Press, 1968).

12. "1969: The Goal to End Hunger in the US," Growing a Nation, https://growinganation.org/content/show-content/3/105/159/.

13. Jennifer E. Gaddis, "The Big Business of School Meals," *Kappan*, September 21, 2020, https://kappanonline.org/big-business-school-meals-food-service-gaddis/.

14. Cora Peterson, "Evaluating the Success of the School Commodity Food Program," *Choices* 24, no. 3 (2009), https://www.choicesmagazine.org/magazine/article.php?article=84.

15. National School Lunch and Child Nutrition Act of 1974, Pub. L. 93-326, 88 Stat. 286 (1974).

16. "Participation in USDA's School Breakfast Program Doubled Between 1999 and 2019," USDA, Economic Research Service, last updated March 10, 2021, https://www.ers.usda.gov/data-products/chart-gallery/gallery/chart-detail/?chartId=100651#:~:text=Participation%20in%20USDA's%20School%20Breakfast,14.7%20million%20in%20FY%202019, https://perma.cc/LX42-HY3F.

17. Bettina Elias Siegel, *Kid Food: The Challenge of Feeding Children in a Highly Processed World* (New York: Oxford University Press, 2019).

18. Otter, "GENYOUth: The Importance of Dairy," YouTube video, February 19, 2018, https://www.youtube.com/watch?v=s-1ELHRZgAA.

19. Tina Namian, "Meal Requirements Under the National School Lunch Program

and School Breakfast Program: Questions and Answers for Program Operators Updated to Support the Transitional Standards for Milk, Whole Grains, and Sodium Effective July 1, 2022" (official memorandum, Washington, DC: USDA, Food and Nutrition Service, March 2, 2022), 27, https://fns-prod.azureedge.us/sites/default/files/resource-files/SP05-2022os.pdf.

20. Anna M. Phillips, "The Drought is Over at L.A. Schools. For Chocolate Milk, Anyway," *Los Angeles Times*, October 18, 2016, https://www.latimes.com/local/education/la-me-edu-chocolate-milk-20161018-snap-story.html.

21. "Overview of Los Angeles Unified School District," U.S. News and World Report, https://www.usnews.com/education/k12/california/districts/los-angeles-unified-106440.

22. Erica Chayes Wida, "New York City Proposal to Ban Chocolate Milk from Schools Sparks Debate," *Today*, September 18, 2019, https://www.today.com/food/new-york-city-proposal-ban-chocolate-milk-schools-sparks-debate-; Selim Algar, "New York City Schools Want to Ban Chocolate Milk," *New York Post*, September 15, 2019, https://nypost.com/2019/09/15/new-york-city-schools-want-to-ban-chocolate-milk/.

23. Maribel Alonso (contact), "Scientists Build a Healthy Dietary Pattern Using Ultra-processed Foods," USDA, Agricultural Research Service, July 11, 2023, https://www.ars.usda.gov/news-events/news/research-news/2023/scientists-build-a-healthy-dietary-pattern-using-ultra-processed-foods.

24. Anna Karnaze, "You Are Where You Eat: Discrimination in the National School Lunch Program," *Northwestern University Law Review* 113, no. 3 (2018): 629.

25. Cynthia Long, "Preventing Overt Identification of Children Certified for Free or Reduced Price School Meals" (official memorandum, Washington, DC: USDA, Food and Nutrition Service, 2012), https://www.fns.usda.gov/cn/preventing-overt-identification-children-certified-free-or-reduced-price-school-meals.

26. Janet Poppendieck, *Free For All: Fixing School Food in America* (Berkeley: University of California Press, 2010), 195.

27. Rex Ogle, *Free Lunch* (New York: W. W. Norton, 2019), 53.

28. Mahanoy Area Sch. Dist. v. B. L., 141 S. Ct. 2038 (2021).

29. @unc_jeff, Twitter, June 3, 2015, 10:43 a.m. https://twitter.com/unc_jeff/status/606199521568133121.

30. Rajiv Bhatia et al., "Competitive Foods, Discrimination, and Participation in the National School Lunch Program," *American Journal of Public Health* 101 (2011): 1380.

31. Ashlesha Datar and Nancy Nicosia, "Junk Food in Schools and Childhood Obesity," *Journal of Policy Analysis and Management* 31, no. 2 (Spring 2012): 312. "Middle and high schools earned an average of $10,850 and $15,233, respectively, from a la carte sales alone. . . . In addition, nearly a third of high schools and middle schools earned between $1,000–$9,999 . . . from vending

machines, another ten percent earned between \$10,000–\$50,000, and a small number earned in excess of \$50,000 per year."

32. Tamerra Griffin, "This Mom Says Her Son Was Stamped on the Wrist Because He Ran Out of Lunch Money," BuzzFeed News, April 1, 2017, https://www .buzzfeednews.com/article/tamerragriffin/lunch-money-stamp#.pbK0x13Klz.

33. Ivana Hrynkiw, "'I Need Lunch Money,' Alabama School Stamps on Child's Arm," AL.com, June 13, 2016, https://www.al.com/news/birmingham/2016 /06/gardendale_elementary_student.html.

34. Alex Heigl, "Colorado School District Fires Cafeteria Worker for Buying Student Lunch," People, December 20, 2020, https://people.com/celebrity/della -curry-kitchen-worker-fired-for-buying-students-lunch/.

35. Eun Kyung Kim, "Is This a 'Sandwich of Shame'? School Policy Calls Out Students Carrying Lunch Debt," Today, January 8, 2016, https://www.today.com /parents/sandwich-shame-school-policy-calls-out-students-carrying-lunch -debt-t65931.

36. Bettina Elias Siegal, "Shaming Children So Parents Will Pay the School Lunch Bill," New York Times, April 30, 2017, https://www.nytimes.com/2017/04/30 /well/family/lunch-shaming-children-parents-school-bills.html.

37. Lise Schencker, "Lunches Seized from Kids in Debt at Salt Lake Elementary School," Salt Lake Tribune, January 30, 2014, https://archive.sltrib.com/article .php?id=57468293&itype=CMSID.

38. Derrick Bryson Taylor, "Children Face Foster Care Over School Meal Debt, District Warns," New York Times, July 20, 2019, https://www.nytimes.com /2019/07/20/us/school-lunch-bills-overdue-payment.html.

39. @stephanie_437, Twitter, July 20, 2019, 8:12 p.m., https://twitter.com/stephanie _437/status/1152823767866867713.

40. David Williams, "A CEO Says a School District Turned Down His Offer to Pay Lunch Bills for Families Threatened with Foster Care," CNN, July 24, 2019, https://www.cnn.com/2019/07/24/us/pennsylvania-lunch-debt-offer-trnd /index.html.

41. Sophie Lewis, "A School District Threatened Parents Over Lunch Debt. Now, a CEO Says It Refused His Offer to Pay," CBS News, July 23, 2019, https:// www.cbsnews.com/news/pennsylvania-school-district-threatened-parents -children-could-be-put-in-foster-care-over-lunch-debt-refuses-ceo.

42. Eun Kyung Kim, "A Single Tweet Has Inspired Thousands of Donations to Pay Off School Lunch Debt," Today, February 2, 2017, https://www.today.com /parents/tweet-inspires-thousands-pay-school-lunch-debt-t107730.

43. Antonia Noori Farzan, "'It's Embarrassing to the Kids': Students Who Owe Lunch Money Will Get Only a Jelly Sandwich, District Says," Washington Post, May 8, 2019, https://www.washingtonpost.com/nation/2019/05/08/its -embarrassing-kids-students-who-owe-lunch-money-will-only-get-cold -jelly-sandwich-district-says/.

44. Angela Kline, "Overcoming the Unpaid Meal Challenge: Proven Strategies from Our Nation's Schools" (official memorandum, Washington, DC: USDA, Food and Nutrition Service, 2017), 45.

45. Ark. Code Ann. § 6–18–715(c)(2) (2021) (*Id.* § 6–18–715(d).

46. S.B. 374, 53 Leg., 1st Sess. (N.M. 2017).

47. Universal School Meals Program Act of 2021, S. 1530, 117th Congress (2021).

48. Erica Sweeney, "The Problem with School Lunch: How the Wealth Gap Is Shaming Students," HuffPost, August 20, 2018, https://www.huffpost.com /entry/school-lunches-wealth-gap_n_5b72ee42e4b0bdd0620d0b43.

49. Maya D. Guendelman, Sapna Cheryan, and Benoit Monin, "Fitting In but Getting Fat: Identity Threat and Dietary Choices Among U.S. Immigrant Groups," *Psychological Science* 22 (2011): 959, 960.

50. @bunnygenders, Twitter, Sep. 25, 2020, 8:43 a.m., https://twitter.com /bunnygenders/status/1309564183030181894.

51. Nuha Mahmood et al., "Racial/Ethnic Disparities in Childhood Obesity: The Role of School Segregation," *Obesity* 30 (2022): 1116, 1119; Alisha Farris et al., "Nutritional Comparison of Packed and School Lunches in Pre-Kindergarten and Kindergarten Children Following the Implementation of the 2012–2013 National School Lunch Program Standards," *Journal of Nutrition Education and Behavior* 46, no. 6 (2014): 621, 623–25.

52. Asheley Cockrell Skinner et al., "Prevalence of Obesity and Severe Obesity in US Children, 1999–2016," *Pediatrics* 141, no. 3 (March 2018), https://www .ncbi.nlm.nih.gov/pmc/articles/PMC6109602/ (table 3). Girls in every racial group but white saw an increase in obesity diagnoses.

## 6. DEE-LICIOUS!

1. Maurice M. Manning, *Slave in A Box: The Strange Career of Aunt Jemima* (Charlottesville: University of Virginia Press, 1998), 18–22.

2. Judy Foster Davis, "'Aunt Jemima is Alive and Cookin'?': An Advertiser's Dilemma of Competing Collective Memory," *Journal of Macromarketing* 27, no. 1 (2007): 92; Marilyn Kern-Foxworth, *Aunt Jemima, Uncle Ben, and Rastus: Blacks in Advertising, Yesterday, Today, and Tomorrow* (Westport, CT: Praeger, 1994); Diane Roberts, *The Myth of Aunt Jemima: Representations of Race and Region* (New York: Routledge, 1994); James Baldwin, *Notes of a Native Son* (Boston: Beacon Press, 1955); Katherine Nagasawa, "The Fight to Commemorate Nancy Green, the Woman Who Played the Original 'Aunt Jemima,'" NPR, June 19, 2020, https://www.npr.org/local/309/2020/06/19/880918717/the-fight -to-commemorate-nancy-green-the-woman-who-played-the-original-aunt -jemima; Maris Fessenden, "In 2014, Descendants of Woman Who Played Aunt Jemima Sued Quaker Oats," *Smithsonian Magazine*, October 7, 2014, https://www.smithsonianmag.com/smart-news/descendants-real-aunt

-jemima-are-suing-brand-bearing-her-name-180952964/; Kelly Tyko, "'It is Our History': Families of Aunt Jemima Former Models Oppose Quaker Oats' Planned Brand Changes," *MetroWest Daily News*, June 22, 2020, https://www .metrowestdailynews.com/news/20200622/it-is-our-history-families-of-aunt -jemima-former-models-oppose-quaker-oats-planned-brand-changes.

3. Judy Foster Davis, "Realizing Marketplace Opportunity: How Research on the Black Consumer Market Influenced Mainstream Marketers, 1920–1970," *Journal of Historical Research in Marketing* 5, no. 4 (November 2013): 471, 477. "Comments by a black female research subject explained these concerns ([5] BBDO, 1962): 'I have never used Aunt Jemima Pancake Mix [ . . . ] although I expect it's a very good product. I don't use it because I think it's insulting to Negroes. The picture of the lady with a rag on her head is definitely insulting.'"

4. William M. O'Barr, "A Brief History of Advertising in America," *Advertising & Society Review* 6, no. 3 (2005), https://muse.jhu.edu/article/377516.

5. "Racist Advertising Poster for Nigger Head Tobacco, c. 1900" (illustration), Granger Historical Picture Archive, https://www.granger.com/results.asp ?searchtxtkeys=nigger%20head%20tobacco.

6. "Popular and Pervasive Stereotypes of African Americans," National Museum of African American History & Culture, https://nmaahc.si.edu/explore/stories /popular-and-pervasive-stereotypes-african-americans.

7. Alice Adams Proctor, "This Month We Offer Virginia's Most Famous Cake," *Ladies' Home Journal*, September 1929, https://www.monmouth.edu/department -of-history-and-anthropology/wp-content/uploads/sites/525/2018/06/1920s -HostessCake1.pdf.

8. Jason Chambers, associate professor of advertising, University of Illinois, interview by Craig Chamberlain, February 26, 2008; Janine Danielle Beahm, "A Mother's Love: A Narrative Analysis of Food Advertisements in an African American Targeted Women's Magazine" (master's thesis, University of South Florida, July 3, 2012), on file with the Digital Commons @ University of South Florida, https://digitalcommons.usf.edu/cgi/viewcontent.cgi?article =5167&context=etd.

9. Cream of Wheat Advertisement (illustration), Monmouth.edu, https: //www.monmouth.edu/wp-content/uploads/sites/525/2018/06/1900s -CreamofWheat2.pdf.

10. Kirsten Delegard, "Cream of Wheat: Race and the Birth of the Packaged Food Industry in Minneapolis," Historyapolis Project, December 17, 2013, http:// historyapolis.com/blog/2013/12/17/cream-of-wheat-race-and-the-birth-of -the-packaged-food-industry-in-minneapolis/.

11. Christina Sharpe, *Ordinary Notes* (New York: Farrar, Straus and Giroux, 2023), 190.

12. Cream of Wheat, https://creamofwheat.com/, accessed December 6, 2022.

13. Maria Iqbal, "Bodies, Brands and Bananas; Gender and Race in the Marketing

of Chiquita Bananas," *Journal of Historical Studies* 4, no. 1 (2015): 2; Peter Chapman, *Bananas: How the United Fruit Company Shaped the World*, (New York: Canongate, 2014). In addition to exploiting racist imagery of Latinas to sell products, the company supported repressive regimes, participated in the overthrow of the Guatemalan government, and helped fund Colombian death squads.

14. Stuart Elliot, "Uncle Ben, Board Chairman," *New York Times*, March 30, 2007, https://www.nytimes.com/2007/03/30/business/media/30adco.html; Kern-Foxworth, *Aunt Jemima, Uncle Ben, and Rastus*.

15. Amy McRary, "Knoxville Museum Exhibit Reveals Mountain Dew's Roots in Hillbillies and Bourbon," Knox News, June 27, 2019, https://www.knoxnews .com/story/life/2019/06/27/mountain-dew-roots-go-back-to-hillbillies -bourbon-knoxville/1500652001/; Adam Clark Estes, "A Brief History of Racist Soft Drinks," *Atlantic*, January 28, 2013, https://www.theatlantic.com /national/archive/2013/01/brief-history-racist-soft-drinks/318929/.

16. Joey Morona, "Mrs. Butterworth's Syrup Is Considering Changing Up Its Branding and Famous Bottles," cleveland.com, June 17, 2020, https://www.cleveland .com/entertainment/2020/06/mrs-butterworths-syrup-is-consdering-changing -its-branding-and-packaging-too.html.

17. "Damage Suit Scores 'Frito Bandito' Ads," *New York Times*, January 1, 1971, https://timesmachine.nytimes.com/timesmachine/1971/01/01/83443867 .html?pageNumber=31.

18. Hornell Brewing Co., Inc. v. Nicholas Brady, 819 F. Supp. 1227 (1993).

19. Frank Pommersheim, "The Crazy Horse Malt Liquor Case: From Tradition to Modernity and Halfway Back," *South Dakota Law Review* 57 (2012).

20. Allyson Waller, "Trader Joe's Defends Product Labels Criticized as Racist," *New York Times*, August 1, 2020, https://www.nytimes.com/2020/08/01/us/trader -joes-jose-ming-joe-san.html#:~:text=After%20an%20online%20petition%20 denounced,felt%20still%20resonated%20with%20customers.

21. Nico Lang, "Sausage Party's Race Problem: This 'Equal Opportunity Offender' Is Just Plain Offensive," *Salon,* August 15, 2016, https://www.salon.com/2016 /08/15/sausage-partys-race-problem-this-equal-opportunity-offender-is-just -plain-offensive/.

22. Tim Carman, "To David Chang, the 'Ethnic' Food Aisle is Racist. Others Say it's Convenient; Chang Says Dedicating a Particular Supermarket Aisle to International Foods is Segregation," *Washington Post*, September 30, 2019, https://www.washingtonpost.com/news/voraciously/wp/2019/09/30/to -david-chang-the-international-food-aisle-is-a-last-bastion-of-racism-others -see-it-differently/.

23. Sam Worley, "The End of the Ethnic Food Aisle," Epicurious, May 17, 2017, https://www.epicurious.com/expert-advice/history-and-future-of-the-ethnic -food-aisle-in-grocery-stores-article.

24. Priya Krishna, "Why Do American Grocery Stores Still Have an Ethnic Aisle?,"

*New York Times*, August 10, 2021, https://www.nytimes.com/2021/08/10/dining/american-grocery-stores-ethnic-aisle.html.

25. Mark Hamstra, "Consumers Want Multicultural Products. And the Sales Reflect That," Supermarket News, January 18, 2023, https://www.supermarketnews.com/center-store/consumers-want-multicultural-products-and-sales-reflect.

26. Naa Oyo A. Kwate, *Burgers in Blackface: Anti-Black Restaurants Then and Now* (Minneapolis: University of Minnesota Press, 2019), 2–3.

27. Psyche A. Williams-Forson, *Building Houses out of Chicken Legs* (Chapel Hill: University of North Carolina Press, 2006), 68.

28. Max Lester Graham Family, "The History of Coon Chicken Inn," Jim Crow Museum, Ferris State University, https://www.ferris.edu/HTMLS/news/jimcrow/links/essays/chicken.htm.

29. *Atlanta*, season 4, episode 10, "It Was All a Dream," written by Donald Glover, directed by Hiro Murai, aired November 10, 2022, on FX.

30. David Segal, "Uncle Ben, CEO?," *Slate,* April 20, 2007, https://slate.com/culture/2007/04/uncle-ben-ceo-the-strange-history-of-racist-spokescharacters.html.

31. John Palminteri, "It's Official—Chad's Replaces Sambo's After 63 Years in Santa Barbara," keyt.com, July 15, 2020, https://keyt.com/news/money-and-business/2020/07/15/its-official-chads-replaces-sambos-after-63-years-in-santa-barbara/.

32. Cheryl I. Harris, "Whiteness as Property," *Harvard Law Review* 106, no. 8 (June 1993): 1701; Addie C. Rolnick, "Defending White Space," *Cardozo Law Review* 40 (2019): 1639.

33. Anthony Paul Farley, "The Black Body as Fetish Object," *Oregon Law Review* 76, no. 3 (1997): 457; Anthony Paul Farley, "The Poetics of Colorlined Space," *Law and Literature* 15 (Fall 2003): 421; Neil Gotanda, "Beyond Supreme Court Anti-Discrimination: An Essay on Racial Subordinations, Racial Pleasures and Commodified Race," *Columbia Journal of Race and Law* 1, no. 3 (2011): 273. "If one accepts Farley's description of racial pleasure, then a vast array of cultural activities, especially in American popular culture, are open to re-interpretation. Participation in music, sports, and dance include racial pleasures. Commercial activities such as cinema, theater, popular music, and professional sports are significant locales for the consumption of racial pleasures."

34. Marcia Chatelain, *Franchise: The Golden Arches in Black America* (New York: Liveright, 2020), 11–12, 16–18.

35. Rebekah Barber, "McDonald's Workers Strike Over Low Wages, Lack of COVID-19 Protections," Facing South, December 15, 2020, https://www.facingsouth.org/2020/12/mcdonalds-workers-strike-over-low-wages-lack-covid-19-protections.

36. Denny's outlets have refused to seat large groups of Black customers while

seating parties of the same size that were white: Stephen Laboton, "Denny's Restaurants to Pay $54 Million in Race Bias Suits," *New York Times*, May 25, 1994, https://www.nytimes.com/1994/05/25/us/denny-s-restaurants-to-pay -54-million-in-race-bias-suits.html. They asked Black customers to pre-pay for their food while white customers pay after their meal: Tanya A. Christian, "Waitress at Denny's Tries to Make Black Customers Pay Their Bill Before Being Served," *Essence*, October 26, 2020, https://www.essence.com/news /dennys-black-customers-racism/. They denied a Black child a free birthday meal: Cynthia Anaya, "The Denny's Racism Scandal You May Not Be Aware Of," Daily Meal, October 26, 2022, https://www.thedailymeal.com/1072802 /the-dennys-racism-scandal-you-may-not-be-aware-of/. They used code words to indicate that there were too many Black diners in the restaurant: Zachary W. Brewster and Sarah Nell Rusche, "Quantitative Evidence of the Continuing Significance of Race: Tableside Racism in Full-Service Restaurants," *Journal of Black Studies* 43, no. 4 (May 2012): 359. They made Black diners pay a sitting fee and wait hours for their meals to be served.

37.  Minyvonne Burke, "Black Execs Sue McDonald's, Claim Systematic Racial Discrimination against Workers, Customers," NBC News, January 9, 2020, https://www.nbcnews.com/news/us-news/black-execs-sue-mcdonald-s -claim-systematic-racial-discrimination-against-n1112931; Heather Haddon, "McDonald's Sued by Black Ex-Franchise Owners for Racial Discrimination," *Wall Street Journal*, September 1, 2020, https://www.wsj.com/articles/former -black-franchisees-sue-mcdonalds-alleging-discrimination-11598963169. The lawsuit alleges McDonald's set former franchisees up for poor results. Avi Wolfman-Arent, "Fast Food Fight: The Story of a Protest You Never Saw, and the Black Employees Who Made It Happen," Whyy, July 17, 2020, https://whyy .org/articles/fast-food-fight-the-story-of-a-protest-you-never-saw-and-the -black-employees-who-made-it-happen/; Greg Winter, "Coca-Cola Settles Racial Bias Case," *New York Times*, November 17, 2000, https://www.nytimes .com/2000/11/17/business/coca-cola-settles-racial-bias-case.html.

38.  Burke, "Black Execs Sue McDonald's."

39.  Haddon, "McDonald's Sued by Black Ex-Franchise Owners."

40.  Davis, "Realizing Marketplace Opportunity," citing Janice Ward Moss, *The History and Advancement of African Americans in Advertising Industry, 1895-1999* (New York: Edwin Mellen Press, 2003), https://www.proquest.com/docview /2217494034/fulltextPDF/3C069A612D974487PQ/2?accountid=27140.

41.  Sophie Lefebvre and Natalie Burclaff, "Consumer Advertising During the Great Depression: A Resource Guide," Library of Congress, last updated September 14, 2020, https://guides.loc.gov/consumer-advertising-great-depression.

42.  Robert E. Weems Jr., *Desegregating the Dollar: African American Consumerism in the Twentieth Century* (New York: New York University Press, 1998), 7–20.

43. George J. Sánchez, *Becoming Mexican American: Ethnicity, Culture, and Identity in Chicano Los Angeles, 1900–1945* (New York: Oxford University Press, 1993), 174.

44. Christopher Klein, "Last Hired, First Fired: How the Great Depression Affected African Americans," History, April 18, 2018, last updated August 31, 2018, https://www.history.com/news/last-hired-first-fired-how-the-great-depression-affected-african-americans.

45. Paul K. Edwards, *Southern Urban Negro as a Consumer* (New York: Prentice-Hall, 1936), 95–96.

46. Marcus Alexis, "Some Negro-White Differences in Consumption," *American Journal of Economics and Sociology* 21, no. 1 (January 1962): 11.

47. Susannah Walker, *Style and Status: Selling Beauty to African American Women, 1920–1975* (Lexington: University Press of Kentucky, 2007), 87.

48. Tristan Donovan, *Fizz: How Soda Shook Up the World* (Chicago: Chicago Review Press, 2013), 161.

49. Stephanie Capparell also tells their story in *The Real Pepsi Challenge: How One Pioneering Company Broke Color Barriers in 1940s American Business* (New York: Free Press, 2008), 20–30.

50. Estes, "A Brief History of Racist Soft Drinks"; Grace Elizabeth Hale, "When Jim Crow Drank Coke," *New York Times*, January 28, 2013, https://www.nytimes.com/2013/01/29/opinion/when-jim-crow-drank-coke.html.

51. Andrea Freeman, *Skimmed: Breastfeeding, Race, and Injustice* (Redwood City, CA: Stanford University Press, 2019). The campaign and other Black-targeted marketing by Pet Milk is documented in *Skimmed*.

52. Jason Chambers, *Madison Avenue and the Color Line: African Americans in the Advertising Industry* (Philadelphia: University of Pennsylvania Press, 2008), 32.

53. O'Barr, "A Brief History of Advertising in America." "Eighty percent or more of consumer purchases—except for big ticket items like appliances, automobiles, and homes—were made by women. Most key employees of advertising agencies until about 1950 were (white, protestant) men while women held jobs like receptionists and secretaries. Today, more than half the employees in American advertising agencies are women.

    In these early years of stricter gender roles, men were *advertisers*, and women were *consumers*. Thus, when advertising spoke to consumers, it usually did so with the voice of male authority. . . . It was not until the rebirth of feminism in the 1970s that advertising began to let women speak for themselves, use women as authority figures, and employ women in decision-making and creative roles in the advertising industry."

54. Jason P. Chambers, "Equal in Every Way: African Americans, Consumption and Materialism from Reconstruction to the Civil Rights Movement," *Advertising & Society Review* 7, no. 1 (2006).

55. Black Junction, "The Secret of Selling to the Negro (1954)," YouTube video, June 25, 2017, https://www.youtube.com/watch?v=lALQs1Hv9ww.

56. Chambers, *Madison Avenue and the Color Line*, 61.

57. Donovan, *Fizz*, 166.

58. National Advisory Commission on Civil Disorders, *Report of the National Advisory Commission on Civil Disorders* (Washington, DC: U.S. Government Printing Office, 1968), 212.

59. Chambers, *Madison Avenue and the Color Line*, 118.

60. Elena Gooray, "A Brief History of Companies Courting African-American Dollars," Public Standard, October 16, 2017, https://psmag.com/news/you -done-bad-dove.

61. Lenika Cruz, "'Dinnertimin' and 'No Tipping': How Advertisers Targeted Black Consumers in the 1970s," *Atlantic*, June 7, 2015, theatlantic.com/entertainment /archive/2015/06/casual-racism-and-greater-diversity-in-70s-advertising /394958/.

62. In "'Dinnertimin' and 'No Tipping,'" Cruz describes Obama's stylistic use of "g-dropping" (a layperson's term for the tendency to pronounce the -ing suffix with an alveolar nasal instead of a velar nasal) in a political speech. The Associated Press transcriber of this speech reflected this stylistic choice in his transcription ("Stop complainin'. Stop grumblin'. Stop cryin'.") Commentators for MSNBC claimed the AP's choice was racist.

63. Kim H. Nguyen et al., "Transferring Racial/Ethnic Marketing Strategies from Tobacco to Food Corporations: Philip Morris and Kraft General Foods," *American Journal of Public Health* 110, no. 3 (March 2020): 329.

64. Harvard Health Publishing, "The Sweet Danger of Sugar," January 6, 2022, https://www.health.harvard.edu/heart-health/the-sweet-danger-of-sugar #:~:text=%22The%20effects%20of%20added%20sugar,%2C%22%20says%20 Dr.%20Hu.

65. Marilyn Halter, *Shopping for Identity: The Marketing of Ethnicity* (New York: Schocken, 2000).

66. "Black & Positively Golden," McDonald's, https://www.mcdonalds.com/us/en -us/black-and-positively-golden.html.

67. "Go as Far as You Choose to with McDonald's HACER National Scholarship," McDonald's, https://www.mcdonalds.com/us/en-us/community/hacer.html.

68. "Asian Pacific American Community," McDonald's, https://www.mcdonalds .com/us/en-us/asian-pacific-americans/en.html.

69. "Share the Pride, McDonald's," https://www.mcdonalds.com/us/en-us /community/lgbtq-plus.html.

70. Monica Anderson and Jingjing Jiang, "Teens, Social Media and Technology," Pew Research, May 31, 2018, https://www.pewresearch.org/internet/2018/05 /31/teens-social-media-technology-2018/.

71. Frances Fleming-Milici et al., *Fast Food Facts: Food Advertising to Children and*

*Teens Score* (Hartford: University of Connecticut Rudd Center for Food Policy & Obesity, 2021), https://media.ruddcenter.uconn.edu/PDFs/SocialMedia2021 .pdf.

72. Anahad O'Connor, Caitlin Gilbert, and Sasha Chavkin, "The Food Industry Pays 'Influencer' Dietitians to Shape Your Eating Habits," *Washington Post*, September 13, 2023, https://www.washingtonpost.com/wellness/2023/09/13 /dietitian-instagram-tiktok-paid-food-industry/.

73. "Target Marketing Tactics," Digital Ads, https://digitalads.org/target-marketing -tactics/.

74. "Targeted Marketing," UConn Rudd Center for Food Policy and Health, https:// uconnruddcenter.org/research/food-marketing/targetedmarketing/#.

75. Georgina Cairns et al., "Systematic Reviews of the Evidence on the Nature, Extent and Effects of Food Marketing to Children. A Retrospective Summary," *Appetite* 62 (March 2013): 209; Rachel Smith et al., "Food Marketing Influences Children's Attitudes, Preferences and Consumption: A Systematic Critical Review," *Nutrients* 11, no. 4 (April 2019): 875.

76. "Descubrimiento Digital: The Online Lives of Latinx Consumers," Nielsen, August 2018, https://www.nielsen.com/insights/2018/descubrimiento-digital -the-online-lives-of-latinx-consumers/.

77. Sonya A. Grier, et al., "The Racialized Marketing of Unhealthy Foods and Beverages: Perspectives and Potential Remedies," *Journal of Law, Medicine & Ethics* 50, no. 1 (spring 2022) 52–29.

78. "The Whitewashing of Reggaeton and Why J. Balvin's Apology Falls Flat," *Takeaway* (podcast), December 29, 2021, https://www.wnycstudios.org/podcasts /takeaway/segments/whitewashing-reggaeton-andwhy-j-balvins-apology-falls -flat.

79. Doritos partnered with musician Lil Nas X, who is Black and queer, and white actor Sam Elliot for a Cool Ranch Dance challenge. #CoolRanchDance got over 5.6 billion TikTok views. In 2022, hip-hop artist Megan Thee Stallion released "Flamin' Hottie," a song celebrating Cheetos and Doritos products. Rockstar Energy made the song "Cobrar" with Latina rap artist Snow Tha Product. Cinnamon Toast Crunch partnered with reggaeton singer Manuel Turizo. PepsiCo's Tostitos worked with actor Danny Trejo and musician Sofía Reyes on a "Fiesta Remix" to promote Cinco de Mayo, a holiday of little significance in Mexico co-opted by the U.S. to sell tacos and margaritas. M&M candies dance a traditional Mexican quebradita and Red Bull hosts Spanish-language rap competitions.

80. Dianna Christie, "Sprite Ginger Debuts with Streetwear Line, Wide-Ranging Marketing Push," Marketing Dive, February 13, 2020, https://www.marketingdive .com/news/sprite-ginger-debuts-with-streetwear-line-wide-ranging-marketing -push/572251/.

81. Jeff Chester, Kathryn C. Montgomery, and Katharina Kopp, *Big Food, Big*

*Tech, and the Global Childhood Obesity Pandemic* (Washington, DC: Center for Digital Democracy, 2021), https://democraticmedia.org/assets/resources/full_report.pdf.

82. Federal Trade Commission, *A Review of Food Marketing to Children and Adolescents: Follow-Up Report* (Washington, DC: Federal Trade Commission, 2012), 91, https://www.ftc.gov/sites/default/files/documents/reports/review-food-marketing-children-and-adolescents-follow-report/121221foodmar ketingreport.pdf.

83. Companies also use woke washing to appeal to LGBTQ+ communities and to consumers concerned with issues such as mental health and the environment. For example, the UK's ubiquitous Marks & Spencer launched an LGBT sandwich in May 2019. Owen Jones, "Woke-Washing: How Brands Are Cashing In on the Culture Wars," *Guardian*, May 23, 2019, https://www.theguardian .com/media/2019/may/23/woke-washing-brands-cashing-in-on-culture -wars-owen-jones. "Burger King launched its #FeelYourWay campaign to mark Mental Awareness month, partly trolling its chief competitor, McDonald's Happy Meals, by selling products such as a 'Blue Meal' or a 'Pissed Meal' (because you don't always have to be happy to eat there). . . . Social media users were quick to point out that Burger King employees were unlikely to afford mental health care on their poverty wages—and there is an established correlation between financial insecurity and mental distress."

84. Rick Clough, "Aunt Jemima to Get New Name as PepsiCo Concedes 'Racial Stereotype,'" *Bloomberg*, June 17, 2020, https://www.bloomberg.com/news/articles /2020-06-17/pepsico-to-retire-aunt-jemima-as-racial-stereotype-doesn-t-fly #xj4y7vzkg; "PepsiCo's Net Revenue from 2007–2022," Statista, https://www .statista.com/statistics/233378/net-revenue-of-pepsico-worldwide.

85. Francesca Sobande, "Woke-Washing: 'Intersectional' Femvertising and Branding 'Woke' Bravery," *European Journal of Marketing* 54, no. 11 (December 2019): 2723.

86. Elijah C. Watson, "When Being Woke Goes Wrong: Pepsi, Black Lives Matter & Conscious Branding," Okayplayer, 2017, https://www.okayplayer.com /originals/pepsi-black-lives-matter-conscious-branding.html; Daniel Victor, "Pepsi Pulls Ad Accused of Trivializing Black Lives Matter," *New York Times*, April 5, 2017, https://www.nytimes.com/2017/04/05/business/kendall-jenner -pepsi-ad.html.

87. *Saturday Night Live*, "Pepsi Commercial-SNL," YouTube, April 8, 2017, https:// www.youtube.com/watch?v=Pn8pwoNWseM.

88. Christina Sharpe explains that "Zakiyyah Iman Jackson gets it precisely right when she tells me that 'Black excellence' is the answer to a racist question." Sharpe, *Ordinary Notes*, 92.

89. Jack Neff, "Black Consumers Are Group Most Swayed by Brand Values and Diversity Practices, Study Finds," Ad Age, January 18, 2021, https://adage.com

/article/cmo-strategy/black-consumers-are-group-most-swayed-brand-values
-and-diversity-practices-study-finds/2306566.

90. Ad Age staff, "A Regularly Updated Blog Tracking Brands' Responses to Racial Injustice," Ad Age, January 13, 2021, https://adage.com/article/cmo-strategy /regularly-updated-blog-tracking-brands-responses-racial-injustice/2260291.

91. Tarpley Hitt, "These Companies Have the Most Hypocritical Black Lives Matter Messaging," *Daily Beast*, June 5, 2020, https://www.thedailybeast.com/the -companies-with-the-most-hypocritical-black-lives-matter-messaging-from -fox-to-facebook.

92. Verónica Reyes, "Eskimo and Kiss of Black: Other Name Changes that Nestlé Applied in the World in Addition to 'Bold,'" biobiochile.cl, July 22, 2021, https://www.biobiochile.cl/noticias/economia/actualidad-economica/2021 /07/22/esquimal-y-beso-de-negra-otros-cambios-de-nombre-que-aplico -nestle-en-el-mundo-ademas-de-negrita.shtml.

93. Alyssa Auvinen, Mary Simock, and Alyssa Moran, "Integrating Produce Prescriptions into the Health Care System: Perspectives from Key Stakeholders," *International Journal of Environmental Research and Public Health* 19, no. 17 (2022), https://www.ncbi.nlm.nih.gov/pmc/articles/PMC9518562/. Produce prescriptions accompanied by vouchers is one innovative way to make positive dietary interventions.

94. Nadra Nittle, "People of Color Have the Highest Obesity Rates in the U.S. Food Marketing Is Part of the Problem," Vox, September 28, 2018, https:// www.vox.com/the-goods/2018/9/28/17910518/black-hispanic-obesity-rates -food-marketing-mcdonalds-commercials-sprite-fast-food-junk-food.

95. Ayebea Darko et al., "Nourishing Equity: Meeting Black Consumers' Needs in Food," McKinsey Institute for Black Economic Mobility, June 1, 2022, https:// www.mckinsey.com/bem/our-insights/nourishing-equity-meeting-black -consumers-needs-in-food.

96. "Student Leaders Urge Peers to 'Stick It' to Fast Food," Canadian Press, October 26, 2012, https://www.cp24.com/news/student-leaders-urge-peers-to-stick-it -to-fast-food-1.1011471.

## 7. WHAT'S LAW GOT TO DO WITH IT?

1. U.S. Const. amend. XIII, §1.

2. U.S. Const. amend. XIII, §2.

3. The Civil Rights Cases, 109 U.S. 3, 10 (1883).

4. George M. Stroud, *A Sketch of the Laws Relating to Slavery in the Several States in the United States of America* (Philadelphia: Kimber & Sharpless, 1856).

5. Andrea Freeman, *Skimmed: Breastfeeding, Race, and Injustice* (Redwood City, CA: Stanford University Press, 2019); Emily West and R. J. Knight, "Mothers' Milk: Slavery, Wet-Nursing, and Black and White Women in the Antebellum

South," *Journal of Southern History* 83, no. 1 (2017): 37, 43, citing Wilma A. Dunaway, *The African-American Family in Slavery and Emancipation* (Paris: Maison Des Sciences De L'homme; Cambridge, 2003), 134–41.

6. 10 Ala. 682, 688–89 (1846).

7. Cong. Globe, 38th Cong., 1st Sess. 1439–40 (1864); see also Alexander Tsesis, "Interpreting the Thirteenth Amendment," *University of Pennsylvania Journal of Constitutional Law* 11, no. 3 (March 2009): 1337, 1339.

8. Priscilla Ocen, "Punishing Pregnancy: Race, Incarceration, and the Shackling of Pregnant Prisoners," *California Law Review* 100, no. 5 (October 2012): 1239, 1296n351, quoting Cong. Globe, 39th Cong. 1st Sess. 1152 (1866).

9. Tsesis, "Interpreting the Thirteenth," 1339–1340, quoting Cong. Globe, 39th Cong., 1st Sess. 1152 (1866).

10. Meyer v. Nebraska, 262 U.S. 390, 400 (1923), recognizing a parent's fundamental right to control their children's education; Pierce v. Society of Sisters, 268 U.S. 510, 534 (1925), same.

11. Onora O'Neill, "The Dark Side of Human Rights," *International Affairs* 81, no. 2 (March 2005): 427, 428–29.

12. "Sudden Unexpected Infant Death and Sudden Infant Death Syndrome," Centers for Disease Control and Prevention, https://www.cdc.gov/sids/data.htm.

13. Ka Yan Cheung et al., "Health and Nutrition Claims for Infant Formula," *BMJ* 380 (2023), https://doi.org/10.1136/bmj-2022-071075.

14. 392 U.S. 409 (1968).

15. Jones v. Alfred H. Mayer Co., 392 U.S. 409, 430 (1968), quoting Cong. Globe, 39th Cong., 1st Sess., 43.

16. *Jones*, 392 U.S. at 429. "The report concluded that, even if anti-Negro legislation were 'repealed in all the States lately in rebellion,' equal treatment for the Negro would not yet be secured."

17. 403 U.S. 217 (1971).

18. "SNAP – Fiscal Year 2023 Cost-of-Living Adjustments" (official memorandum, Washington, DC: USDA, Food and Nutrition Service, August 9, 2022), https://fns-prod.azureedge.us/sites/default/files/resource-files/snap-fy-2023-cola-adjustments.pdf#page=4.

19. Lauren Hall and Catlin Nchako, *A Closer Look at Who Benefits from SNAP: State-by-State Fact Sheets* (Washington, DC: Center on Budget and Policy Priorities, 2023), https://www.cbpp.org/research/food-assistance/a-closer-look-at-who-benefits-from-snap-state-by-state-fact-sheets#Alabama.

20. Kathryn Cronquist and Brett Eiffes, *Characteristics of Supplemental Nutrition Assistance Program Households: Fiscal Year 2020* (Washington, DC: USDA, Food and Nutrition Service, Office of Policy Support, 2022, https://fns-prod.azureedge.us/sites/default/files/resource-files/Characteristics2020.pdf.

21. Dylan Matthews, "Study: Telling White People They'll Be Outnumbered Makes

Them Hate Welfare More," *Vox,* June 7, 2018, https://www.vox.com/2018/6/7/17426968/white-racism-welfare-cuts-snap-food-stamps.

22. "SNAP Work Requirements," USDA, Food and Nutrition Service, last updated September 1, 2023, https://www.fns.usda.gov/snap/work-requirements.

23. 7 C.F.R. § 273.7 (2019).

24. See LaDonna Pavetti, *Work Requirements Don't Cut Poverty, Evidence Shows* (Washington, DC: Center on Budget and Policy Priorities, 2016), 2, https://www.cbpp.org/research/poverty-and-inequality/work-requirements-dont-cut-poverty-evidence-shows.

25. Angela Hanks, Danyelle Solomon, and Christian E. Weller, *Systematic Inequality: How America's Structural Racism Helped Create the Black-White Wealth Gap* (Washington, DC: Center for American Progress, 2018), 4, https://www.americanprogress.org/issues/race/reports/2018/02/21/447051/systematic-inequality/.

26. *SNAP Helps Millions of African Americans* (Washington, DC: Center on Budget and Policy Priorities, 2018), 3, https://www.cbpp.org/research/food-assistance/snap-helps-millions-of-african-americans; Greg Trotter, "Limiting SNAP Benefits Would Make Food Insecurity Worse, Not Better," *Chicago Tribune,* March 8, 2019, https://www.chicagotribune.com/opinion/commentary/ct-perspec-snap-food-insecurity-trump-work-requirement-0311-20190308-story.html.

27. Daniel Littlefield, "The Varieties of Slave Labor," Freedom's Story, Teacher-Serve, National Humanities Center, accessed November 10, 2019, http://nationalhumanitiescenter.org/tserve/freedom/1609-1865/essays/slavelabor.htm.

28. Bekah Mandell, "Cultivating Race: How the Science and Technology of Agriculture Preserves Race in the Global Economy," *Albany Law Review* 72, no. 4 (2009): 939, 942–45. Mandell further argues that the "racialized feeder/fed dichotomy" established during chattel slavery is reproduced in the present through the global food distribution system.

29. Theodore D. Weld, *American Slavery as It Is: The Testimony of a Thousand Witnesses* (New York: American Anti-Slavery Society, 1839), 28–35.

30. Nina Martyris, "Frederick Douglass on How Slave Owners Used Food as a Weapon of Control," NPR, February 10, 2017, https://www.npr.org/sections/thesalt/2017/02/10/514385071/frederick-douglass-on-how-slave-owners-used-food-as-a-weapon-of-control.

31. Nicholas Boston, "The Slave Experience: Living Conditions," Slavery and the Making of America, Thirteen PBS, 2004, 1–2, https://www.thirteen.org/wnet/slavery/experience/living/history.html.

32. Martyris, "Frederick Douglass on How Slave Owners Used Food as a Weapon of Control."

33. Weld, *American Slavery as It Is,* 28–29.

34. Steve Kingston, *Frederick Douglass: Abolitionist, Liberator, Statesman* (National Negro Congress, Brooklyn and Manhattan Councils, 1941), 6.

35. Martyris, "Frederick Douglass on How Slave Owners Used Food as a Weapon of Control."

36. Pamela D. Bridgewater, "Un/Re/Dis Covering Slave Breeding in Thirteenth Amendment Jurisprudence," *Washington and Lee Journal of Civil Rights and Social Justice* 7, no. 1 (2001): 11, 17.

37. Ann Jones, "After I Lived in Norway, America Felt Backward. Here's Why," *Nation*, January 28, 2016, https://www.thenation.com/article/after-i-lived-in -norway-america-felt-backward-heres-why/.

38. Kaaryn S. Gustafson, *Cheating Welfare : Public Assistance and the Criminalization of Poverty* (New York: New York University Press, 2012), 46–47.

39. Brynne Keith-Jennings and Raheem Chaudhry, *Most Working-Age SNAP Participants Work, But Often in Unstable Jobs*, (Washington, DC: Center on Budget and Policy Priorities, 2018), https://www.cbpp.org/sites/default/files/ atoms/files/3-15-18fa.pdf; https://perma.cc/SD3B-KXEK.

40. The house passed a minimum wage bill in 2019: Raise the Wage Act, H.R. 582, 116th Cong. (2019).

41. Nandita Bose, "Half of Walmart's Workforce Are Part-Time Workers: Labor Group," Reuters, May 25, 2018, https://www.reuters.com/article/us-walmart -workers/half-of-walmarts-workforce-are-part-time-workers-labor-group -idUSKCN1IQ295; Hiroko Tabuchi, "Walmart to End Health Coverage for 30,000 Part-Time Workers," *New York Times*, October 7, 2014, https://www.nytimes .com/2014/10/08/business/30000-lose-health-care-coverage-at-walmart.htm.

42. Congressional Research Service, *Work Requirements, Time Limits, and Work Incentives in TANF, SNAP, and Housing Assistance*, by Gene Falk, Maggie McCarty, and Randy Alison Ausseberg, R45317 (February 12, 2014), 27, https://digital. library.unt.edu/ark:/67531/metadc811679/m2/1/highresd/R43400_2014Feb12. pdf. Other factors may include factory closures or decreases in imports due to trade wars.

43. Clyde Wilson, "John C. Calhoun and Slavery as a 'Positive Good': What He Said," Abbeville Institute, June 26, 2014, https://www.abbevilleinstitute.org /clyde-wilson-library/john-c-calhoun-and-slavery-as-a-positive-good-what -he-said/.

44. Nadra Kareem Nittle, "The Black Codes and Why They Still Matter Today," ThoughtCo, October 20, 2019, updated on December 21, 2020, https://www .thoughtco.com/the-black-codes-4125744.

45. Daniel Moynihan, *The Negro Family: The Case for National Action* (Washington, DC: Office of Policy Planning and Research, U.S. Department of Labor, 1965), 5–9.

46. Charles A. Murray, *Losing Ground: American Social Policy, 1950–1980* (New York: Basic Books, 1984), 81–82.

47. Paul Spicker, *Stigma and Social Welfare* (1994; self-pub., 2011), 25, 45, https://www.spicker.uk/books/Paul%20Spicker%20-%20Stigma%20and%20 Social%20Welfare.pdf.

48. A state can qualify for a waiver under the following conditions: "(1) an unemployment rate over 10 percent for the latest 12-month (or 3-month) period; (2) a historical seasonal unemployment rate over 10 percent; (3) a Labor Surplus Area designation from DOL [Department of Labor]; (4) a 24-month average unemployment rate 20 percent above national average; (5) a low and declining employment-population ratio; (6) a lack of jobs in declining occupations or industries; (7) described in an academic study or publication as an area with a lack of jobs; or (8) qualifies for extended unemployment benefits." "Administrative Uses of Local Area Unemployment Statistics," U.S. Department of Labor, Bureau of Labor Statistics, Local Area Unemployment Statistics Program (2017), https://www.bls.gov/lau/lauadminuses.pdf.

49. Timothy F. Harris, "Do SNAP Work Requirements Work?" (UpJohn Insitutue Working Paper; 19–297, Kalamazoo, MI: W.E. Upjohn Institute for Employment Research, December 2018), 9, https://doi.org/10.17848/wp19-297.

50. Lauren Bauer, Jana Parsons, and Jay Shambaugh, *How Do Work Requirement Waivers Help SNAP Respond to a Recession* (Washington, DC: Brookings Institution, April 10, 2019), https://www.brookings.edu/research/how-do-work -requirement-waivers-help-snap-respond-to-a-recession/.

51. Harris, "Do SNAP Work Requirements Work?," citing Niraj Chokshi, "Need Food? Maine's Governor Wants You to Work for It," *Washington Post*, July 24, 2014, https://www.washingtonpost.com/blogs/govbeat/wp/2014/07/24/need -food-maines-governor-wants-you-to-work-for-it/?noredirect=on.

52. Deborah Kogan, Anne Paprocki, and Hannah Diaz, *Supplemental Nutrition Assistance Program (SNAP) Employment and Training (E&T) Best Practices Study: Final Report* (Washington, DC: U.S. Department of Agriculture, Food and Nutrition Service, Office of Policy Support, November 2016), II-2, II-3, https: //fns-prod.azureedge.net/sites/default/files/ops/SNAPEandTBestPractices .pdf.

53. Stacy Dean, Ed Bolen, and Brynne Keith-Jennings, *Making SNAP Work Requirements Harsher Will Not Improve Outcomes for Low-Income People*, (Washington, DC: Center on Budget and Policy Priorities, March 1, 2018), https://www.cbpp.org/research/food-assistance/making-snap-work -requirements-harsher-will-not-improve-outcomes-for-low.

54. Pavetti, *Work Requirements*, 1–2.

55. Sentencing Project, *Report of The Sentencing Project of the United Nations Special Rapporteur on Contemporary Forms of Racism, Racial Discrimination, Xenophobia, and Related Intolerance* (Washington, DC: The Sentencing Project, March 2018), 1, 5, https://www.sentencingproject.org/wp-content /uploads/2018/04/UN-Report-on-Racial-Disparities.pdf.

56. Katherine J. Rosich, *Race, Ethnicity, and the Criminal Justice System* (Washington, DC: American Sociological Association, 2007), 8; Marilyn Elias, "The School-to-Prison Pipeline," *Teaching Tolerance* 52, no. 43 (Spring 2013): 43, https://www.tolerance.org/magazine/spring-2013/the-school-to-prison-pipeline.

57. Harris, "Do SNAP Work Requirements Work?," 11–12.

58. Dean, *Making SNAP Work Requirements Harsher*, 1.

59. H. Claire Brown, "When the Government Mandates Work Requirements for Food Stamps, Who Actually Profits?," New Food Economy, April 10, 2019, https://newfoodeconomy.org/work-requirements-snap-mandatory-employment-training-program-profits/.

60. Kenneth Hanson, *The Food Assistance National Input-Output Multiplier (FANIOM) Model and Stimulus Effects of SNAP*, Economic Research Report no. 103 (Washington, DC: USDA, Economic Research Service, October 2010), 29, https://www.ers.usda.gov/publications/pub-details/?pubid=44749.

61. Eric Holt-Giménez and Breeze Harper, "Food—Systems—Racism: From Mistreatment to Transformation," in *Dismantling Racism in the Food System* (Oakland, CA: Food First Institute for Food and Development Policy, 2016), 4, https://foodfirst.org/wp-content/uploads/2016/03/DR1Final.pdf.

62. *SNAP Helps Millions of African Americans*, 3.

63. The Slaughter-House Cases, 83 U.S. 36, 69 (1872).

64. The Civil Rights Cases, 109 U.S. 3, 22–28 (U.S. 1883).

65. *Plessy* 163 U.S. 537, 542–43, 562–63 (1896); The Civil Rights Cases, 109 U.S. at 24.

66. The Civil Rights Cases, 109 U.S. 3, 22–284.

67. *Plessy* 163 U.S. 537, 550–51 (1896); *id.* at 552 (Harlan, J., dissenting).

68. Pamela S. Karlan, "Contracting the Thirteenth Amendment: Hodges v. United States," *Boston University Law Review* 85 (2005): 783, 786, citing Transcript of Record at 4, Hodges v. United States, 203 U.S. 1 (1906) (No. 14 of October 1905 term).

69. Hodges v. United States, 203 U.S. 1, 17 (1906), at 14. The indictment was based on Sections 1977 and 5508 of the Revised Statutes of 1874. Section 1977 is now 42 U.S.C. § 1981 and Section 5508 is now 18 U.S.C. § 241.

70. *Hodges*, at 17.

71. Corrigan v. Buckley, 271 U.S. 323, 327–28, 330–31 (1926).

72. Pollock v. Williams, 322 U.S. 4, 24 (1944).

73. Eric Foner, *Reconstruction: America's Unfinished Revolution, 1863–1877* (New York: Harper & Row, 1988), 199–200, identifying the Black Codes prohibiting Black people from pursuing any occupation other than farmer or servant.

74. United States v. Kozminski, 487 U.S. 931 (1988). For further analysis of this case, see, generally, Kenneth T. Koonce Jr., "United States v. Kozminski: On the Threshold of Involuntary Servitude," *Pepperdine Law Review* 16, no. 3 (1989):

689; Catherine M. Page, "United States v. Kozminski: Involuntary Servitude—A Standard at Last," *University of Toledo Law Review* 20 (summer 1989): 1023.

75. *Kozminski*, 487 U.S. at 934. The first, § 241, "prohibits conspiracy to interfere with an individual's Thirteenth Amendment right to be free from 'involuntary servitude.'"; see 18 U.S.C. § 241 (2019). The second, § 1584, "makes it a crime knowingly and willfully to hold another person 'to involuntary servitude.'" *Kozminski*, 487 U.S. at 934; accord 18 U.S.C. § 1584 (2019).

76. *Kozminski*, 487 U.S. at 943, citing Pollock v. Williams, 322 U.S. 4 (1944); Taylor v. Georgia, 315 U.S. 25 (1942); United States v. Reynolds, 235 U.S. 133, 146, 150 (1914); Bailey v. Alabama, 219 U.S. 219, 244 (1911); Clyatt v. United States, 197 U.S. 207, 215, 218 (1905). Lauren Kares rues the Court's vague definition of involuntary servitude: "[N]early 130 years of judicial construction have failed to provide a uniform definition of involuntary servitude and thus have failed to afford the Thirteenth Amendment a clear role in the shaping of civil rights law." Lauren Kares, "The Unlucky Thirteenth: A Constitutional Amendment in Search of a Doctrine," *Cornell Law Review* 80, no. 2 (1995): 372, 375.

77. Brogan v. San Mateo County, 901 F.2d 762, 764–65 (9th Cir. 1990).

78. Yick Wo v. Hopkins, 118 U.S. at 373–74.

79. Gomillion v. Lightfoot, 364 U.S. at 341.

80. 481 U.S. at 286. "[N]otwithstanding these efforts, murder defendants in Georgia with white victims are more than four times as likely to receive the death sentence as defendants with black victims." This reflects Justice Brennan's calculations—the number may be higher.

81. USDA programs do not just discriminate by race. They also offer unequal protection to poor people. Although today's Supreme Court is not inclined to heighten scrutiny of laws and policies that discriminate against the poor, see Harris v. McRae, 448 U.S. 297, 323 (1980), it hasn't always been that way. In 1966, *Harper v. Virginia Board of Elections* found a poll tax that made Virginians pay for the privilege of voting unconstitutional because it violated equal protection, see Harper v. Va. Bd. Of Elections, 383 U.S. 663, 668 (1966). In a 2018 case, the Fifth Circuit decided that keeping poor defendants in custody because they can't pay bail also violates equal protection, O'Donnell v. Harris Cty., 892 F.3d 147, 157 (5th Cir. 2018).

82. Bethany R. Berger, "Reconciling Equal Protection and Federal Indian Law," *California Law Review* 98, no. 4 (August 2010):1165, 1168.

83. Amna A. Akbar, "An Abolitionist Horizon for (Police) Reform," *California Law Review* 108, no. 6 (August 2020): 1787.

84. Rachel Kushner, "Is Prison Necessary? Ruth Wilson Gilmore Might Change Your Mind," *New York Times Magazine*, April 17, 2019, https://www.nytimes.com/2019/04/17/magazine/prison-abolition-ruth-wilson-gilmore.html.

85. Christina Sharpe, *Ordinary Notes* (New York: Farrar, Straus and Giroux, 2023), 262.

# INDEX

## ABOUT THE AUTHOR

Andrea Freeman, a pioneer in the field of food politics, is a professor at Southwestern Law School, a Fulbright scholar, and the author of *Skimmed: Breastfeeding, Race, and Injustice*. Freeman's work has appeared in the *Washington Post, Salon*, the *Atlanta Journal-Constitution*, and *Black Agenda Report* and on *The Takeaway* and *Here & Now*, among others. She lives in Los Angeles.